MW01194044

Unending Auspiciousness

THE SUTRA OF THE RECOLLECTION OF
THE NOBLE THREE JEWELS
WITH COMMENTARIES BY JU MIPHAM,
TARANATHA, AND THE AUTHOR

BY TONY DUFF
PADMA KARPO TRANSLATION COMMITTEE

Copyright © 2010 Tony Duff. All rights reserved. No portion of this book may be reproduced in any form or by any means, electronic or mechanical, including photography, recording, or by any information storage or retrieval system or technologies now known or later developed, without permission in writing from the publisher.

Janson typeface with diacritical marks and
Tibetan Chogyal typeface
Designed and created by Tony Duff
Tibetan Computer Company
http://www.tibet.dk/tcc

First edition, October 10th, 2010
ISBN: 978-9937-8386-1-0

Produced, Printed, and Published by
Padma Karpo Translation Committee
P.O. Box 4957
Kathmandu
NEPAL

Committee members for this book: principal translator and writer, Lama Tony Duff; contributing translator Andreas Kretschmar; editors, Lama Richard Roth and Tom Anderson; Cover design, Christopher Duff.

Web-site and e-mail contact through:
http://www.tibet.dk/pktc
or search Padma Karpo Translation Committee on the web.

CONTENTS

❀   ❀   ❀

TEXTS

❀   ❀   ❀

INTRODUCTION

This book presents the *Sutra of the Recollection of the Noble Three Jewels* with extensive explanations. The *Sutra*, as it is referred to throughout this book, is not a discourse of the Buddha but a compilation based on his very early teachings called "the recollections". The recollections and the *Sutra* resulting from them are lists of epithets made for easy memorization. The epithets embody profound and vast points of understanding that need extensive explanation, so commentaries have been written for that purpose.

The book has been arranged so that an increasingly deep understanding of the *Sutra* and the many points of interest surrounding it will develop as the reader progresses through it.

The introduction consists of three chapters. The first chapter starts by tracing the development of the *Sutra* from its origins in the recollections and ends with an introduction to three commentaries to it that form the bulk of this book. Study of the *Sutra* demands a detailed examination of words and their meanings. The commentaries engage in this examination and delve into various translation issues that come with it. The second chapter considers these issues of words and their translations. It reveals the problems that Tibetan translators had when doing their work and raises important issues for those translating Tibetan texts into other languages. The third chapter examines the general meaning of the *Sutra* and explains how it has been and could be used by Buddhist practitioners. The body of the book begins with the texts of the recollections in Pali, Sanskrit, Tibetan, and English, continues with the *Sutra* in Tibetan and English, and culminates in three major commentaries to the *Sutra* presented in order of increasing difficulty.

Overall, the *Sutra* was composed in order to develop faith. There are many people who will want to approach it that way and not want to turn it into an exercise in intellectual development. However, in order to understand its words, commentaries are needed and the commentaries of the Tibetan tradition of Buddhism emphasize precise intellectual understanding, called prajna in Sanskrit. One of the aims in writing this book was to compose it in a way that would give everyone access to the *Sutra*. Therefore, the book has provision for those who emphasize faith as much as it does for those who emphasize study. In fact, there has to be some joining of the two; the Buddha himself pointed this out when he taught five qualities that are needed together in his followers for them to follow the path to enlightenment: faith, perseverance, mindfulness, concentration, and prajna[1]. This book, through its overall approach, shows that faith and intellectual development can be brought together, which is very much the teaching of the Buddha.

A Point of Style

Diacritical marks are needed to render Sanskrit words properly into English; for example, the term sangha is properly written as saṅgha. Readers who prefer a less intellectual approach tend to be put off by the use of diacriticals whereas scholarly types require

---

[1] Tib. rnam byang gi dbang po lnga. These are "the five faculties of complete purity" where "complete purity" is a name for nirvana and stands in contrast to "total affliction", which is a name for samsara.

them. As a result, books usually either do not use them at all or use them throughout. In its attempt to provide for a wide range of readers, this book takes the unusual approach of writing the less scholarly sections, such as the introductory chapters, generally without diacritical marks, and the more scholarly ones, such as the commentaries, with these marks.

The Recollections

A Buddhist is a person who has decided that the Buddha offers the best protection against the problems of life, and who, having made that decision, has turned towards the Buddha as a source of refuge or protection from them. A Buddhist is like a refugee who has left behind the normal approach to life and entered the refugee settlement set up by the Buddha and his followers. A Buddhist takes refuge not only in the Buddha but also in the Buddha's teaching and in the particular group of the Buddha's followers who have gained a certain, significant level of accomplishment that allows them to give selfless assistance to others. The latter two refuges are called the dharma and the sangha respectively.

This threefold refuge sits at the heart of Buddhist life. In it, the Buddha is seen as the teacher of the solution to the problems of life, his teaching is seen as the actual solution, and the group of advanced followers is seen as the one group of people who could provide non-deceptive guidance while the solution is being applied. Thus, a Buddhist takes refuge in three things: the Buddha as the teacher; the dharma as the path; and the sangha as the helper on the path.

Because taking refuge in the Three Jewels is so fundamental to the Buddhist journey, the Buddha taught the details of refuge in his earliest teachings. He taught the key point of how his followers should view themselves in relation to this threefold refuge. First, they should see themselves as people who are ill with a sickness that is causing their problems. Following that, they should view themselves as patients who turn to the Buddha as a doctor who has the skill and knowledge needed to dispense the appropriate medicine, the Buddha's teaching as the medicine itself, and his group of spiritually accomplished disciples as a nurse who has the capacity needed to assist the patients on their journey back to health.

The Buddha also taught the key point of the various qualities of the three refuges and how they should be named because of those qualities. He pointed out that, given their good qualities[2], the three refuges have the features of being special, rare, and precious, which are features of jewels. Thus he said that the three refuges are to be known as "the Three Jewels".

The Buddha then made the point that the Three Jewels are at a level beyond that of the ordinary world and named them accordingly. The first two Jewels are reality itself and the third is directly associated with reality. Therefore, the Three Jewels have a much higher connection with what is real than do ordinary beings or things of the world. That in turn means that these refuges are ultimately reliable. Because they are at the level of reality, they can be a final solution to the problems of life where the things and beings of the ordinary world cannot be. Because of this quality of

---

[2] Skt. guṇa, Tib. yon tan. The term "good qualities", which translates the words just shown, is one of the most used terms in this book. The original terms mean "good qualities" mainly in reference to good qualities of a being. The English word "quality" is neutral and does not mean good or bad even though American colloquial English, sometime in the early 1980's changed the meaning through cultural habits of laziness of speech. In other words, when "qualities" is used in reference to the Three Jewels, it has to be understood to mean good qualities in particular. Therefore, this book mostly uses the wording good qualities instead simply of qualities.

being superior to the ordinary world, the Buddha referred to the Three Jewels as the noble Three Jewels.

The word "noble" here translates the Indian word "ārya". The Indian word means something not at the common level but at a position both higher and better than that. For example, the word was and still is used to indicate the social class of nobility as opposed to the commoners. When Buddha used the word noble, he used it specifically to show something which is beyond the world spiritually speaking, something which belongs to a higher level of spiritual development or reality than is found amongst the ordinary people and things of the world. And when the Buddha used the word noble to describe the Three Jewels, he was saying this: the Buddha has totally transcended the ordinary world; the Buddha's dharma is reality itself or teaching that corresponds to that reality, so it too is beyond the ordinary world; and the Buddha's sangha is comprised of those who, through practise of that teaching, have transcended the ordinary world. Thus, the Three Jewels which are the primary refuge for all Buddhists are not ordinary refuges; they are beyond the world and completely aligned with what is real. In that way, they get their full name "the noble Three Jewels of refuge".

Anyone who has found a refuge will also need to sustain and deepen his relationship with his refuge. The Buddha taught the key point of faith for the purpose, though this is not a special teaching of Buddhism, it being well known that this is how the human mind works. A person who has taken refuge needs to maintain his faith in his refuge and will want to develop and deepen it as well. The best way to do that is to see the good qualities that belong to the refuge. A potent way to do that is to deliberately bring the good qualities of the refuge to mind and to contemplate them, and this is the technique that the Buddha taught his followers for sustaining and deepening their relationship with their refuge, the noble

Three Jewels. It is called "recollection of the good qualities of the Three Jewels".

These terms "refuge", "faith", and "recollection of the good qualities of the refuge" are the terms used in Buddhism, though the principles are universally applicable. They are fundamental to travelling any spiritual path and are found in one form or another in every religion. The Buddha taught these principles within the context of explaining the three refuges, their specific qualities, and their capabilities. He explained the meaning of faith and emphasized its value in various ways; for example, he taught faith as one of five states of mind that are essential for a person wanting to follow the path to enlightenment—the five faculties of complete purity mentioned earlier—and set it as the first of the five to indicate its fundamental importance. Then he explained six recollections of the good qualities of the Three Jewels that his followers were to do again and again in order to develop their faith and deepen their refuge; the six became known as "The Six Recollections".

Of the six recollections, the first three are recollections of the Three Jewels called "The Recollection of the Buddha", "The Recollection of the Dharma", and "The Recollection of the Sangha". The Buddha gave these recollections as lists of the good qualities of the Jewels in a pithy form that made them easy to memorize and recite. The listing for the Buddha consists of nine good qualities, the listing for the dharma of six good qualities, and the listing for the sangha of nine good qualities. The Buddha laid out these twenty-four good qualities when he taught the six recollections and often referred to them in his discourses after that. Later, they became a standard way of referring to the good qualities of the Three Jewels in Buddhist teaching in general.

The six recollections were taught in the first phase of Buddha's teaching, the teaching of the Lesser Vehicle[3]. After the Buddha passed away, the teachings of the Lesser Vehicle split into eighteen different lines of teaching. This had been predicted by the Buddha and he had stated that there would be no fault, that all of them would authentically carry the teaching of the Buddha. Today, those eighteen lines of the Lesser Vehicle have condensed into what is called the Theravada, whose lineages appeared primarily in Sri Langka, Burma, and Thailand and have now gone to many countries around the world. The teaching of the six recollections is carried on by the Theravada and remains a fundamental part of the teaching and practice of that tradition.[4]

The three recollections of Buddha, dharma, and sangha with their listing of the twenty-four good qualities as they were originally taught and are passed on by the Theravada, today can be seen in the first volume of Peter Skilling's work[5]. In it, he compares the

---

[3] The entirety of the Buddha's teaching can be summed up into the teachings of the Lesser, Great, and Vajra Vehicles.

[4] The Theravada of modern-day South-East Asia is one of the schools of the Lesser Vehicle. The name "Lesser Vehicle" was not intended to be a derogatory statement but an accurate one. It indicates that the scope of a person following the Lesser Vehicle is much smaller than that of a person following the Great Vehicle. The name tends to be disliked amongst Lesser Vehicle followers in Western cultures where there is the strong idea that everyone is equal. Nevertheless the Buddha pointed out that, even though everyone might be equal in having the seed of true, complete enlightenment within their mindstream, everyone is not equal in their karmic capabilities. He also said that the karmic lot of some people restricts them to the Lesser Vehicle but that later, after they have gained attainment in that vehicle, they will be able to go through the trainings of the higher vehicles.

[5] "Mahāsūtras: Great Discourses of the Buddha. Volume I, Texts", by

(continued...)

Pali, Sanskrit, and Tibetan sources for the original recollections. His listings are reproduced here on page 63. The second and third volumes of his work also give a good feel for the Theravada approach to these recollections[6]. To learn more about the Theravada approach to the Three or Six Recollections, you would consult the commentary on them that has been accepted and used in the Theravada tradition for many centuries. The commentary can be found in the famous text by Buddhaghosha called the Visuddhimagga[7]. Note that the Pali forms of the recollections were translated into Tibetan and included in the great Tibetan written collection of the Buddha's words called *The Translated Buddha Word*.

The Six Recollections are important in the teachings of the Great Vehicle, too, with the Great Vehicle taking them as is from the Lesser Vehicle. The first three Recollections as they were translated from Pali into in Sanskrit and later into Tibetan[8] are given after the Pali forms on page 63. In the fifth century C.E., the great Indian masters Asanga and his brother Vasubhandu wrote commentaries in Sanskrit on these three recollections as they are found in the Pali canon. Asanga wrote three short commentaries, one for each of the three recollections of buddha, dharma, and sangha, and Vasubhandu wrote a long commentary to the first recollection called *An Extensive Commentary to the Recollection of the*

---

[5](...continued)
Peter Skilling, Oxford : The Pāli Text Society, 1994.

[6] "Mahāsūtras: Great Discourses of the Buddha. Volume II, Parts I & II", by Peter Skilling, Oxford : The Pāli Text Society, 1997.

[7] "The Path Of Purification, (Visuddhimagga) by Bhadantācariya Buddhaghosa", translated from the Pali by Bhikkhu Ñāṇamoli, Buddhist Publication Society, Kandy, Sri Lanka.

[8] See for instance the Peking edition of the *Translated Word (Tib. Kangyur)* numbers 945 to 947.

Buddha. These four commentaries were later translated into Tibetan and included and in the great Tibetan collection of texts written to support the Buddha's teaching called *The Translated Treatises*[9].

The Recollections are Extended

Great Vehicle followers did use the original forms of the Six Recollections in their teaching as shown by the commentaries by Asanga and his brother. However, Great Vehicle followers also took the Pali forms of the first three recollections a step further by extending the lists of good qualities of each of the Three Jewels. They also changed the wording in some places to make the recollections encompass the Great Vehicle. For example, the original recollection of the buddha consists of a single sentence with nine epithets of the Buddha where the extended Great Vehicle recollection has that but adds a second list of over thirty more good qualities to it. And, the original recollection of the sangha says, "the sangha of shravakas" whereas the extended Great Vehicle recollection changes that to either "the sangha of the Great Vehicle" or "the sangha of noble ones", to make it inclusive of the sanghas of all Buddhist vehicles.

It is generally accepted within the Tibetan tradition that the extended recollections of the Great Vehicle were in use in India. It seems from Tāranātha, who went from Tibet to India and studied there for a lengthy time, that there were various versions of the extended recollections, with minor differences but all essentially the same. The three extended recollections were still being written down as separate texts. One version of the three extended

---

[9] The four can be found in the Derge edition of *The Translated Treatises Tib. Tangyur)*.

recollections was later translated into Tibetan and included in the
Derge edition of *The Translated Treatises*. I have included this
version of the extended recollections in this book because it shows
the first major development of the original recollections.

A Sutra of the Recollections Appears

The three recollections underwent a further development when
the extended recollections were combined into one text for convenient use. The compilation of the three was called *The Sutra of
the Recollection of the Three Jewels*. It is important to understand
that it is a compilation based on the Buddha's early teachings, not
a discourse given by the Buddha and for this reason was not
included in the Tibetan *Translated Buddha Word*. The general
opinion of Tibetan experts is that it is a development that happened in Tibet. I have not been able to find any evidence of it
being done in India and the fact that it is not included in the
Tibetan *Translated Treatises* suggests strongly that it was a Tibetan
development as Tibetans themselves say.

Readers might be surprised at this revelation of what the *Sutra*
actually is. A Buddhist sutra is usually a teaching given by the
Buddha that was heard by an audience and later recorded in writing. However, it is clear that this *Sutra* is not a recorded teaching
of the Buddha. This might lead some to argument over whether
it really is a sutra or not but that would miss the point. This final
development of the three recollections that has now been called
the *Sutra* is a list made using the words that the Buddha spoke at
one time or another when explaining the good qualities of the
Three Jewels. Thus, while it is not a discourse of the Buddha as
such, it is a record of his teaching and for that reason was given the
name "sutra".

There is not a single, accepted version of the *Sutra* but several versions of it. I have compared them and found that they are essentially the same. The edition used for the translation of the *Sutra* in this book is the one usually used nowadays. It represents a final development of the *Sutra* made for readability as much as anything else. It has been in existence for at least two hundred years. This edition can be obtained in many places and was obtained for this book from Dudjom Jigdral Yeshe Dorje's collection of liturgies[10] found in his *Collected Works*. This edition of the *Sutra* can, for instance, be compared with the editions used in the two Tibetan commentaries presented in this book and variations will be seen. All of these variations have been listed and discussed in my own commentary for easy access.

If you compare the original recollections, the extended recollections, and the various editions of the *Sutra* included in this book, you will see differences though you will also see that the *Sutra* represents the original recollections as the Buddha taught them and is very close to the extended recollections developed from them.

These differences between editions of the *Sutra* and the recollections preceding it do not have to be taken to mean that the *Sutra* is unreliable. Any variation of meaning that results can be understood within the dharmic sphere of understanding. An academic might not be comfortable with that but for a practitioner these differences can enrich a study of the *Sutra* through leading to a greater understanding of the amazing qualities of the Three Jewels.

Of course, it might come as a disappointment to some that the *Sutra* here is not a discourse of the Buddha's words but represents a development of his teaching that has occurred over time.

---

[10] Tib. bdud 'joms spyod chos.

However, every good quality mentioned in the *Sutra* does come from the teaching of the Buddha and each one contributes something important to the recollection of the Three Jewels. Thus, the content of the *Sutra* is simply an extended form of the original recollections taught by the Buddha and works equally well if not better. In either case, one brings the content to mind, mulls it over, and in the end faith arises from doing so.

There is another, particularly important point to notice. The good qualities that were chosen by Great Vehicle followers for addition to the original recollections were chosen for consistency with the original, Lesser Vehicle teaching. Thus the *Sutra* follows the style of the original, stays firmly within the bounds of the Lesser Vehicle level of teaching, and does not add anything at all that is unique to the Great Vehicle. Thus, even though the *Sutra* was produced within the Great Vehicle, it can still be taken as a Lesser Vehicle teaching. It still reflects the same basic principles that the Buddha taught for all of his disciples so that they could develop faith and hence take refuge in the Three Jewels. The best explanation I have heard for this came from the vidyadhara Chogyam Trungpa Rinpoche. He presented the concept that the *Sutra*, even though it was a Great Vehicle extension, should be understood through the "one vehicle" concept of Buddhism. It takes the view that there might be all sorts of people at different levels following the path to buddhahood but that all are on one vehicle, the path to buddhahood, which has an enormous body of teaching that is common to and works for everyone. This is, I believe, the right way to take the *Sutra*. It harks back to those days when the Buddha himself was expounding the good qualities of the Three Jewels in a way that was common to all followers. Therefore the *Sutra* and this book about it should be palatable, useful, and enjoyable to all Buddhists, regardless of which type of Buddhism they follow.

The Sutra Understood Through Commentaries

The *Sutra* is an easy-to-memorize list of many short epithets that bring to mind the good qualities of the noble Three Jewels. All of the epithets date from the time of the Buddha and are either well-known names that were given to him because of his greatness or descriptions that he or his followers used when talking about the good qualities of the noble Three Jewels. The phrasing of these epithets is very pithy and requires explanation.

A survey showed that a number of commentaries have been written by learned Tibetans with the ones by the great Jonang teacher Tāranātha and the great Nyingma teacher Ju Mipham Namgyal being very popular nowadays. These two commentaries were selected for this book.

These two commentaries do not engage in philosophical argument. They focus solely on explaining the *Sutra's* epithets so that the epithets can be understood and then used more effectively. However, translations of these Tibetan commentaries by themselves will not be enough for Western students to understand the *Sutra* fully. Both of them, Mipham's commentary in particular, use technical vocabulary that makes their meaning hard to understand unless one is well versed in the details of Buddhist philosophy. Moreover, the commentaries were written for a culture whose way of thought and expression is very different from that of Western culture with the result that they work for producing faith in a Tibetan mind but not always in a Western one. For these reasons, I composed my own commentary in English that is easy to follow yet still includes all the meaning of the *Sutra*.

About the Three Commentaries

My own commentary has the feature of being readable because of being written directly in English. It draws together points from many sources that clarify difficult points in the Tibetan commentaries. It also draws together and explains all the points of difference between the editions of the *Sutra* used in all three commentaries. It has been placed ahead of the two Tibetan commentaries because reading it will solve many points of difficulty in the Tibetan commentaries.

This commentary is informed by two extensive explanations of the *Sutra* heard in person from masters who were foremost teachers of their generation. One was heard from the vidyadhara Chogyam Trungpa Rinpoche in English over the course of a month at his Vajradhatu seminary. It was heard in the remarkable style that he developed for teaching dharma to Westerners. The other was heard from Khenchen Padma Tshewang in Tibetan in the exceptionally learned, though highly traditional, style of a khenpo teaching in a Tibetan monastic setting. Khenchen Padma Tshewang who has now passed on, was an honorary chief khenpo of the famous Shri Singha monastic college at Dzogchen Monastery in Eastern Tibet. Both the vidyadhara Chogyam Trungpa Rinpoche and Khenchen Padma Tshewang used Ju Mipham's commentary as a basis for their explanations.

Next comes Tāranātha's commentary. Tāranātha [1575–1634] was regarded as an extraordinary scholar. He was one of the very last Tibetans to go down to India in order to master Indian languages and learn Buddhism in its motherland. He was exceptionally learned. Every century in Tibet one or two people would appear who just seemed to know everything and were given the title "All-Knowing" because of it. Tāranātha was given that title as were masters like Longchenpa, Padma Karpo, and a few others of extraordinary breadth of knowledge. Tāranātha wrote an extraordinary number of treatises on a wide variety of subjects, his collected works being amongst the largest of any author in Tibetan history. His treatises are highly valued because of his first-hand knowledge of Indian language and Indian Buddhist thought and many of them are still popular today. His commentary on the *Sutra* benefits markedly from that knowledge. It is a shorter commentary as reflected in its title *A Little Explanation of the Meaning of "The Sutra of the Recollection of the Three Jewels"*. The text for the translation was obtained from the Dzamthing edition of Tāranātha's *Collected Works*; it is regarded as the best edition because of the careful correction work that was done on the content prior to cutting the blocks.

Finally, there is Mipham's commentary. Ju Mipham Namgyal [1846–1912] was a Nyingma teacher who lived during one of the great periods of renaissance in Eastern Tibet. He was a Buddhist master of such great knowledge and intelligence that he was considered to be Manjushri, the bodhisatva[11] of knowledge and intelligence, in person. It is reported that Mipham could read five or six volumes of Buddhist scriptures a day and remember every word due to his power of perfect recall. He had many other special qualities, too. Like Tāranātha, his collected works are amongst the largest of any author in Tibetan history and many are popular today. In fact, he has grown in fame in recent times with many of his works being used as the key texts for studies in his Nyingma tradition. Again like Tāranātha, his works have become widely used not only in his own tradition but in other traditions too, something that only occurred in Tibet with the very greatest of scholar-practitioners. Compared to Tāranātha's commentary, Mipham's commentary is more technical and more extensive.

---

[11] This is the correct spelling of bodhisatva according to the Tibetan tradition and has been that way since the 8th century C.E. when Tibetan translators started their great work, advised by many Indian scholars.

It seems, from the history known about Mipham's commentary, that he had not intended to write the commentary but was commanded to do so by his guru, Khyentse Wangpo. He says in the colophon that it caused him considerable suffering to receive this command. However, he is famous for having gone to his room and turned out the commentary in two days. In fact, oral tradition says that it only took one day; it seems that he spent two half-days on it as he mentions in the colophon. The text runs out to about thirty-five densely-written Tibetan folios. The text for the translation of Mipham's commentary was obtained from a wood block print of his *Collected Works*.

The texts of the two Tibetan commentaries were too large to include. However, fully searchable electronic editions have been made available through the Padma Karpo Translation Committee web-site.

Tāranātha certainly knew that there were problems with writing a commentary to this text. He says in conclusion to his commentary,

> This current *Sutra of the Recollection of the Jewels* is a Great Vehicle sutra. For the recollections of the Three Jewels that is part of the Lesser Vehicle there is one rough explanation by Noble One Asanga that exists; I find myself wondering whether it is extracted from within a larger commentary. Then, so many differences are seen in the wordings of the sutras that there is the question of how the two come to be so different, still, in the two later recollections, the ones that are consistent do suggest a commonality.

This is important to know; even four centuries ago there were editions of the *Sutra* with differences in wording. Mipham in his colophon also makes comments that suggest he knew the difficulties he was facing with the *Sutra*. He says that he was forced to write this commentary very hurriedly and that he had serious misgivings, to the point of being ill, about it. Although Tibetans nowadays explain his words to mean that he was being humble, I believe that he was reporting that he was pressed to write something much faster than he thought he should because he knew that there would be significant difficulties with writing about this particular *Sutra*. It is also noteworthy that he seems to have read Tāranātha's commentary, written nearly three centuries before, and used it as a basis for his own commentary. It certainly would have helped him to write such a long commentary in such a short time.

It would be very difficult to explain the *Sutra* without going into technical details of Buddhist philosophy. Accordingly, the commentaries of both Tāranātha and Mipham contain a substantial amount of technical explanation, much of which is difficult to understand unless one is already well-versed in Buddhist philosophy. Tāranātha's commentary is shorter so can seem less formidable in this regard, and some find it more useful than Mipham's commentary as a basis for developing faith. Mipham's commentary is very famous so people feel drawn towards it, though, on reading it, many non-Tibetans find that wading through its technical expositions defeats, at least to some extent, the development of faith. This whole situation is unfortunate because the *Sutra*, in its original form as the recollections, was meant to be a simple and straightforward way of developing faith. As someone who enjoys the study of Buddhism, I found both of these Tibetan commentaries to be very useful for understanding the *Sutra*. However, it was very noticeable that in translation they might not meet the requirements of those, especially non-Tibetans, who are trying to engage the Buddhist tradition in a very practical way. This was one of several factors that drove me to write my own commentary directly in English. I am sure that the result is easier for English speakers to read and more conducive to the development of faith than the Tibetan commentaries in translation. However, I am also aware that something else again is needed which will be less of a commentary on the *Sutra* and more of a practical manual on how to contemplate the recollections so that they become a basis for the development of faith.

Translation Style in Relation to the Tibetan Commentaries

The translations of the commentaries and the texts cited in them are very accurate. They not only reflect the content of the original but also reflect each author's idiom and style of composition. Therefore, you can be sure that, if you read something in the Tibetan commentaries or texts cited by them where the English seems unclear, then it is that way in the Tibetan, too. It is not a translator's job to re-word an author so that the author's presentation is clearer than in the original, rather, it is to show his presentation just as he has given it. One of the marks of the best possible translation is that a reader is able to get a feel for each author and his way of talking as it is in the original. Thus, if you find something in the commentaries and the texts cited by them that is hard to fathom or seems unclear, you can be sure that it is that way in the original. These are the places where one seeks assistance in order to establish the meaning. One of the features of my own commentary is that it will help to unravel many of these difficult spots.

TRANSLATION ISSUES RAISED BY THE SUTRA

Translations of Tibetan Buddhist texts into other languages often require comments from the translator about issues that came up during the translation from Tibetan. This is particularly true with the *Sutra* and its commentaries.

Before going on, it is important to say that this chapter is about words, their meanings, and how they are translated. Readers who are more interested in the central meaning of the *Sutra*, which is the development of faith through its practice, could pass over this chapter and move on to the next, though they should first consider the following two points. Firstly, the faith of Buddhists is an informed faith and one of the many avenues to informed faith in the Three Jewels is to learn their qualities through precisely understanding the words used to describe their qualities. This chapter does that, so, whether one is interested in translation issues or not, this chapter will help to develop one's understanding of the Three Jewels and to cultivate one's faith in them. Secondly, the commentaries explain the process that was followed when certain terms were translated from Sanskrit into Tibetan. These explanations were written out in brief for Tibetans who have already understood the various issues involved and they do not address the issues as they apply to other languages. This chapter is useful for all readers because it fills out these explanations so that they are clear and one gains more knowledge of the Three Jewels by reading them. In addition, the chapter is useful for translators because it discusses these issues as they apply to the work of translating into languages other than Tibetan.

In general, the *Sutra* is a list of many important Buddhist terms that shows how the terms were translated into Tibetan. A study of it will be a very informative for anyone involved with the translation of Tibetan Buddhist works into other languages. Such a study will help translators to increase their vocabulary of Sanskrit and Tibetan terminology.

In particular, all three of the commentaries to the *Sutra* that are contained in this book raise a variety of translation issues. For example, they reveal places where the Tibetan translation does not readily convey the meaning of the original Pali or Sanskrit wording, which is useful in a number of ways. The commentaries also point out differences of translation between editions of the *Sutra* then comment on them, which is a valuable learning opportunity for translators.

It is especially valuable that the two Tibetan commentaries document the approach that the early Tibetan translators took while translating a number of key terms from Sanskrit into Tibetan. When the commentaries do this, they lay out the official Tibetan translation rationales for the terms. This gives a clear view of the process that went on when the early Tibetan translators developed the vocabulary needed to translate from the Indian language into the Tibetan one, something that provides important knowledge for translators in general, though two points stand out. First, the presentations form an excellent basis for investigating how these terms should be translated into other languages, with those investigations in turn providing us with a model for how to translate Buddhist terms into other languages. Second, the presentations highlight something that is often not well known and understood, that the process of translating from the Indian language into the Tibetan one had considerable difficulties and was not always perfect.

Translation Difficulties for All

It is well known in translation circles altogether—not just in Buddhist ones—that translation from one language into another inevitably results in some loss of meaning. It is equally well known that translation from something that is already a translation is much less desirable than translation from the original source and can have significant problems with it. Both of these points apply to the translation of Indian Buddhist works into Tibetan and Tibetan Buddhist works into English. It might be surprising to hear that Tibetans had their own share of problems when translating from Sanskrit into Tibetan though it is a point that is known and discussed these days amongst Western translators who have a large body of experience, especially the few who have lived with Tibetans for many years.

I have had Tibetan Buddhist translators tell me that the translations of Indian Buddhist works into Tibetan were perfect and that the Tibetan texts that resulted are a perfect basis for translating works into other languages. A little probing usually reveals that they are just spouting Tibetan lore that their Tibetan teachers have told them and have not given proper consideration to it. Let us have a brief look at the story of Tibetan translations of Buddhist works.

The story begins with Thumi (also known as Thonmi) Sambhota who is often referred to as the inventor of Tibetan language, and who is worshipped by Tibetans for that, his contribution to the founding of Tibetan culture. In fact, Thumi did not invent

Tibetan language, though his work had an effect of similar pro-
portions. He created a lettering set and a grammar for the existing, spoken Tibetan language, turning it into a fully defined
language that could be used as the basis for the more sophisticated
culture, and a Buddhist one in particular, envisaged by the king,
Srongtsen Gampo. A cursory examination of the history of the
events has led some to say that Thumi Sambhota built a new
Tibetan language based on Sanskrit, but that also is not true. He
went to India and studied Indian languages extensively, then
returned to Tibet where he created a form for the already-existing,
spoken Tibetan language. In doing so, he retained the Tibetan
spoken language but gave it a form that allowed Indian Buddhist
texts, written in Sanskrit and its variations, to be translated into
Tibetan language to a remarkable degree of accuracy[12]. Contrary
to popular belief, he did not make the Tibetan language into a
carbon copy of Sanskrit and, as a result, many problems were
encountered during the task of translating Indian Buddhist texts
into Tibetan language.

About two hundred years after Thumi Sambhota created the basis
for the translation of Indian Buddhist texts into Tibetan language,
there was a period of about one hundred years during which the
bulk of the work of translation was done and the re-done in order
to finalize it. The lore that has grown up amongst Tibetans in
regard to that great work of translation is that the translations
were perfect. When Tibetans present the matter to Westerners,
they tend to pass on that lore as absolute fact instead of giving
more careful consideration to what actually happened. Their
stance makes for faith in the scripture that resulted and faith is key
to the journey to enlightenment so their faith is not something to
undermine without reason. However, blind faith has to give way

---

[12] A very complete presentation of this history can be found in *Standard
Tibetan Grammar Volume I: The Thirty Verses of Minister Thumi* by
Tony Duff, published by Padma Karpo Translation Committee.

to informed faith and with that in mind, translators need to be attuned to what actually happened during the great translations of Indian Buddhist texts into Tibetan language.

What happened during the great translations can be summed up like this. Although the meaning of the original Indian texts was generally very well represented in the Tibetan translations, and sometimes perfectly so, the translation work did have its problems and was, when you look at the details, not perfect. The problems were documented by order of the king at the time for the sake of people like ourselves who, in the future, might need to know about these things. They were documented in a text called *The Second Tome on Grammatical Composition* and the text was preserved in the Various section of the Tibetan *Translated Treatises* (its title meaning that is was a second treatise on language coming after Thumi's original set of treatises that gave form to Tibetan language). The important point is that, although there were many problems with language during the great translation effort, these problems did not turn into an obstacle for the transmission of Buddhism into Tibetan culture. To understand why not, we have to remember that the Buddha's teaching is transmitted in two ways: by realization and by word, with the word later becoming scripture. The problems with translation concerned scripture not realization. It is universally agreed that the transmission of realization into Tibet was perfect. This realization informed the Tibetan Buddhist culture with the result that the translations of scripture, regardless of problems encountered during their translation, could be correctly understood. In that sense, the translations from Indian Buddhist texts into Tibetan language were not perfect but became perfect.

Having clarified that, we could look at specific words that the early Tibetan translators dealt with to get a feeling for some of the problems they faced. Because of the parallels that Thumi Sambhota created between the Sanskrit and Tibetan languages,

Sanskrit words sometimes would go perfectly into Tibetan. For example, the commonly used word "paramārtha" in Sanskrit goes perfectly into its Tibetan equivalent དམ་པའི་དོན་ "dam pa'i don", with even the etymological parts of the Sanskrit term being fully present[13]. It is a perfect translation in every way. (Incidentally, it can be made to go nicely into English in a similar way by choosing the appropriate roots and combining them: "superfact".)

There were many times when a Sanskrit word could not be broken into its etymological parts and rebuilt into a perfectly-matching Tibetan equivalent. On those occasions, the Tibetan translators had to borrow existing terms or invent new ones to do the translation. Sometimes, they borrowed an existing Tibetan word and assigned it as the official equivalent of the Sanskrit one, giving the word a new range of meaning in the process. There are many words like that in the Tibetan Buddhist vocabulary and many examples of them in the *Sutra*. Sometimes, they invented a new word, and assigned it as the official equivalent of the Sanskrit, an example of which is found in the *Sutra* with the translation of the Sanskrit "buddha" into Tibetan with སངས་རྒྱས་ "sangs rgyas". There were even cases where they created a new word which they assigned as the equivalent of a Sanskrit term but whose meaning did not exactly match the original, examples of which are found in the *Sutra* with the translations of the Sanskrit words arhat and bhagavat into Tibetan with དགྲ་བཅོམ་པ་ "dgra bcom pa" and བཅོམ་ལྡན་འདས་ "bcom ldan 'das" respectively. There were yet other cases where they felt that a Tibetan word that had been accepted as the official equivalent for a given Sanskrit word failed to capture the meaning in particular contexts. Therefore, they either chose another word, so that there were now two (and sometimes many more) equivalents for the one Sanskrit word, or made up a new word again. An example of needing to make up a new Tibetan word to match a

---

[13] See superfactual in the glossary.

particular usage of a Sanskrit word can be found in the *Sutra* with the translation of the Sanskrit word ratna when it is being used to refer to the Three Jewels; the newly constructed Tibetan word was དཀོན་མཆོག་ "dkon mchog".

Now how does all of the above affect those who are now going a step further and translating Tibetan Buddhist works into languages such as English, and so on? As mentioned earlier, it is generally accepted that using a translation as a basis for a translation is not desirable. It is much better to turn to the original language and use that as a basis. However, in the case of translating Tibetan Buddhist works, there is the major problem that the texts of the source language, Sanskrit, have, for the most part, ceased to exist. Therefore we have to rely on the Tibetan works. However, because, as the Tibetans themselves have explained, the Tibetan translations are not perfect, we cannot just go ahead and translate from the Tibetan into our language without investigating the Tibetan system of translation.

In the case where Tibetan words are etymological replicas of the Sanskrit, as with the term paramārtha mentioned above, it will not matter whether the Sanskrit or Tibetan is used as the basis for the translation into another language. However, in most other cases, using the Tibetan term as a basis for translation into another language can bring problems. This is the point where a translation of a translation does not always work and the translator has to turn to the original or source language, if possible, and work from there. As the translator considers the terminology and how to translate it, he will want to know what the Tibetan translators did in relation to these terms. That is possible in some cases because the rationale for the translation of Sanskrit words into the Tibetan language was documented in a number of cases by the early Tibetan translators.

The Rationales of Tibetan Translation

Without looking further than the title of the *Sutra*, we can find a term that has given both Tibetan and English translators trouble. It is the case, mentioned just above, of the Sanskrit term "ratna" when used to refer to the Three Jewels of refuge. This term was problematic for the Tibetans. An equivalent for its most general meaning already existed in the Tibetan language—the word རིན་ཆེན་ "rin chen" meaning "valuable, rich". However, ratna has other meanings, including the one intended in the case of the Three Jewels, of something jewel-like. The existing equivalent did not convey that meaning clearly enough, so the translators invented a new term to meet the needs of this particular usage, then wrote a rationale for the translation.

This rationale and the many others like it set out the reasoning that went with a translation for people of future generations. The rationales have been faithfully preserved and presented within the tradition for three purposes: to explain the meaning of the source terms, to provide the reasoning behind the choice of translated terms, and thereby to ratify the translation. With that, the work of the translators was complete and their rationales needed only to be faithfully handed down by successive generations of Tibetan Buddhists—which they were.

It is very important to realize that the rationales behind the translations of Sanskrit into Tibetan words are connected with and particular to the functioning of Tibetan language. Thus, although it has been widely assumed that these rationales can and do apply in the translation of these terms into Western languages, it could be a mistaken assumption. To find out whether this is so, we will examine several of the terms at the beginning of the *Sutra* that have a Tibetan translation rationale and see whether that rationale is applicable to translations made into other languages or not. All of the examples we will use were referenced above when the examples of various situations faced by the Tibetan translators were being laid out. Through this we will find out that the rationales for Tibetan translation are not universally applicable even though they are very informative.

The Meaning and Translation of "ratna"

The title of the *Sutra* in Sanskrit is "ārya ratna traya anusmṛti sūtra". In it, "ratna traya" or "Three Jewels" refers to the buddha, dharma, and saṅgha as the three refuges of Buddhism.

The Sanskrit "ratna" is used in several ways. In general, it means "value, valuable, having the quality of richness" and was frequently used with that meaning in Indian Buddhist texts. However, it is also used to refer to precious things, for instance jewels. When the Buddha called the three refuges the three ratnas, he meant that they were a set of three things with the qualities of jewels. He explained that these three jewels of refuge are very rare for beings to connect with, that they are very precious given their good qualities, that they are very valuable given that they are the basis for becoming enlightened, and so on.

The Buddha's teachings on the meaning of the Three Jewels are important to the topic of taking refuge. One way to get a feel for them is to look at the listings made in Indian Buddhist literature in which the qualities of the Three Jewels are explained to be equivalent to six qualities of jewels. 1) The Three Jewels are "byung bar dkon pa <> rare in occurrence" because they are only discovered when beings have accumulated sufficient merit to meet with them, which is similar to jewels being very rare and difficult to find. 2) The Three Jewels are "dri ma med pa <> stainless" because they are naturally free of stain, similar to jewels being free of stain by nature. 3) The Three Jewels are "mthu dang ldan pa <> powerful" because they have the capacity to benefit oneself and others, similar to jewels having the capacity to accomplish one's wishes.

4) The Three Jewels are " 'jig rten gyi rgyan <> ornaments for the world" because they beautify the beings of the world by producing virtuous thoughts in them, similar to jewels beautifying the persons who wear them. 5) The Three Jewels are "mchog tu gyur pa <> supreme" because there is nothing better than them in this world, similar to jewels being regarded as supreme things of this world. 6) The Three Jewels are " 'gyur ba med pa <> unchanging" because they are by nature without change, similar to jewels being everlasting and without change.

Tibetan language has a term for translating ratna when its general meaning is intended: རིན་ཆེན་ "rin chen" literally meaning "valuable". However, this Tibetan term does not show the meaning of precious things such as jewels that is also conveyed by ratna, so the early Tibetan translators set it aside as insufficient for translating ratna when used to refer to the Three Jewels of refuge. The translators could not find an existing Tibetan term that was fitting so they were forced to invent one for the purpose. They looked at the summary listing of six qualities of the Three Jewels that was available in Sanskrit literature and can be seen immediately above and decided that two of those six terms encapsulated the jewel-like meaning of ratna: དཀོན་ "dkon <> rare" and མཆོག "mchog <> supreme". The two words were combined into དཀོན་མཆོག "dkon mchog" which was set as the official Tibetan equivalent for ratna when used to refer to the Three Jewels. Following that, the translators wrote down the rationale for their translation for the information of future generations.

Now, how should we translate this usage of ratna into English? Should we presume that the Tibetan rationale is a rationale that is true for all languages? Or, should we understand that it was for the Tibetan context and might very well be suitable only for that? Should we see that the Tibetan is a translation already and acknowledge the principle that translators in general understand, that a translation is not generally suitable as a basis for translation? Or, should we literally translate the Tibetan into English?

If we literally translate the term ratna into English on the basis of the invented Tibetan term, we get something like "rare and supreme ones". This has been done by a number of English translators but is very flawed as we can easily see. Firstly—and as the Tibetans themselves freely admit—"dkon mchog" is not a perfect translation but a word invented to point in the right direction. Secondly, it does not have all of the meanings that the Buddha taught for this use of ratna but only two of them, so it only approximates the meaning. Therefore, if we use the Tibetan as a basis for a literal English translation, the translation will inherit those faults; we will lose meaning and arrive at a less-than-precise translation of the original term. On top of that, attempts so far have resulted in unwieldy phrases in English, entirely unsuited to the term's position as one of the main terms of the Buddhist vocabulary; note that neither the Sanskrit nor Tibetan terms have this fault, each being short and eminently suited to their task.

If, instead of using the Tibetan translation and its rationale as a basis for an English translation, we use the original language, Sanskrit, we find that the term ratna in this specific usage corresponds exactly to the English word "jewel". We tread the same paths of thought that the Tibetans did but, unlike them, we find that we already have a word in the target language that fulfills our requirements. Thus, there is no need to use the Tibetan term as a basis for the translation and by not doing so we avoid all the faults mentioned above.

This highlights two very important points. First, it is an excellent example of why using a translation of a translation rather than a direct translation from a source language is undesirable. Second, it shows that it can be a mistake to follow the rationale that the Tibetan translators gave for their translations. It is very important to realize that their rationales were not intended as the one, correct rationale for translations into all languages, but as a correct one for their own, Tibetan language.

In sum, we should not slavishly use the translations made for the Tibetan language as a basis for our own translations. Instead, we should try to find a word in our own language that fits the source language, Sanskrit, where possible. If one cannot be found, we might consider doing what the Tibetans did, which is to make our own word. Certainly, the English language, with its wide range of roots, is eminently suited to that task. The Tibetan rationales for translation should be studied in conjunction with this because they will inform the work. Once we have selected or created our word, we must—as I have done here—write a rationale for that. Later still, when it has been understood that this rationale is correct, that rationale should become the standard explanation of the word for the language in question, parallelling what happened in Tibetan culture.

The Meaning and Translation of "buddha"

Next, there is the word "buddha" at the beginning of the body of the *Sutra*. There is a very clear explanation of the meaning of the word buddha in the Sanskrit language. Its root is "budh" which conveys the sense of illumination with knowledge, an absence of darkness within the sphere of knowing. Moreover, the primary synonym for "buddha" in Sanskrit is the word "avagamana" which translates as "full comprehension" or "full realization"[14]. From a Sanskrit perspective, the main sense conveyed by the word buddha is knowledge, and knowledge that has had all obscuring factors

---

[14] The official Tibetan equivalent for avagamana is "rtogs pa". The Tibetan term is usually translated into English with "realization" though it contains more meaning than that. It means "full comprehension" or "full knowledge". See realization in the glossary.

removed from it. Please note that it does not have the sense of "waking" or "awakening" conveyed with it, about which more is said below. The above, by the way, is the result of study and much discussion with many scholars, especially the learned Brahmans of Varanasi who hold the lineage of Sanskrit in India nowadays. Furthermore, the explanations of Tāranātha and Mipham clearly support this understanding that the main meaning in "buddha" is knowledge, illumination. A buddha, according to the meaning of the word itself, is an enlightened one, not an awakened one!

Again the Tibetan translators did not use a literal translation but invented a new word in order to translate this word buddha. Their new word was སངས་རྒྱས་ "sangs rgyas". There is a very clear explanation of how the term was derived in my own commentary, which is reproduced in brief below, and Mipham also gives the rationale for it.

To make their word, the Tibetan translators relied on a famous description of the Buddha that existed in Sanskrit poetry. The poetry likened the Buddha to a lotus, picking out two particular features of a lotus that were applicable. A lotus starts in and grows up from a filthy swamp. When it has elevated itself some distance above and thus cleared itself of all the filth, it blossoms into a beautiful flower with many good qualities. The poetry makes it clear that the two, pertinent features are "being cleaned out" and "blossoming into something full of good qualities". The Tibetans chose the two words from their language that matched these features—སངས་ "sangs" and རྒྱས་ "rgyas" respectively, combined them, and arrived at the new word སངས་རྒྱས་ "sangs rgyas".

It is particularly important to understand that the primary meaning of སངས་ "sangs" is "to be cleared out". For example, I have heard some Tibetan experts explain it as "to have pollution cleared out, as happens when the windows of a stuffy room are opened". This is the meaning intended in the original poetry; for a buddha, the obscurations of mind that would prevent total knowledge have been cleared. There is a secondary meaning in Tibetan only in which "sangs" is equated with the verb སངས་ "sad pa <> to wake up". Some Tibetans, not knowing of the Sanskrit poetry and its meaning, have assumed that this secondary meaning for སངས་ "sangs" is the correct one then mistakenly explain "buddha" to mean "awakened and blossomed". The mistake is compounded when Western translators take that as proof that "buddha" means "Awakened One", then set that as the correct translation. This has happened and people have become very attached to what their teacher has said and reluctant to hear that it might be mistaken. For this reason, we non-Tibetans have to start with the Sanskrit language and its own definitions; from that we understand that the word buddha conveys the idea of knowledge that has been cleared of contamination, not awakening.

It is important to note that one *could* say that the Buddha is an awakened person; it is an apt metaphor! However, it is *not* the metaphor that was in use when the Tibetans derived their word "sangs rgyas" and therefore could not be used to inform the translation into other languages of the word buddha.

In short, and as Mipham observes in his commentary, the Tibetan word སངས་རྒྱས་ "sangs rgyas" describes a buddha but is not a straightforward translation of the original term. Moreover, it bears the danger of a mistaken understanding that can lead to a mistaken translation, as just noted. Thus, the Tibetan word is not a suitable basis for an English translation. Again, there is a word in English already that serves the purpose exactly.

Another point of translation that surfaces here is the fact that the English language and other European languages are much closer to Sanskrit linguistically and have stronger ties to it culturally than to the Tibetan language. Thus, it often happens that Buddhist words can be translated into English without having to rely on the Tibetan, which is already a translation.

There is yet another and no less important point that surfaces here. In Sanskrit, the two words buddha and bodhi have the same root "budh". The connection between the two words is immediately obvious in the course of using the language, and that immediately promotes the acquisition of meaning. The Tibetans lost this great advantage when they did not translate the root "budh" with one Tibetan term and then create variants on it. The Tibetan translators produced different words to represent the derivatives of budh, none of which have an obvious connection. Contrast this with English: finding that there is an excellent match —enlighten—for "budh" in English, we can easily build translations of cognate terms whose connections are readily apparent. For example, buddha and bodhi become "enlightened one" and "enlightenment" respectively. This is a small but very important point in translation of Buddhist language.

The Meaning and Translation of "bhagavat"

The next word in the *Sutra* is "bhagavat". This ancient Indian term was and still is used as a term of high respect for someone who is considered to be very holy and this is how the term should be understood. It did not ever, in the Indian system, refer exclusively to the Buddha.

The Indian term bhagavat, which is also used in the form bhagavan without any change of meaning or etymology, is comprised of the two roots "bhaga" meaning "defeat" and "vat" meaning "in possession of". In Indian culture, it is explained to refer to a person who has or *possesses* the good quality of having overcome or *defeated* negativities that hold beings back from being holy. Negative aspects of being were generally personified in ancient India as "the four maras", whose name means the four types of negative forces that kill the possibilities of goodness[15]. Thus, bhagavan ends up meaning a person who has the good quality of having defeated the four maras.

Now the Hindu system, when speaking of its great god Śhiva— also called Iśhvara because he is the "Almighty God" of the system —and all of the other great gods of its pantheon such as Indra, Brahmā, and Viṣhṇu, and also the other holy beings of its system such as Kṛiṣhṇa, states that in the positive sense a bhagavat possesses the qualities of being "fortunate" in general or "good in six ways[16]". Buddhism uses this same explanation of the etymology of bhagavat, though when it explains sixfold goodness for a buddha, it explains that it is a result of practising the six paramitas, which differs from the explanation given in the Hindu system for Śhiva and the others of the Hindu pantheon.

Turning now to the Tibetan language, it is important to understand that all of the terminology involved translates perfectly: bhaga is བཅོམ་ "bcom", vat is ལྡན་ "ldan", and bhagavat is the two combined to give བཅོམ་ལྡན་ "bcom ldan". The fortune involved is སྐལ་བ་ "skal ba" and the sixfold goodness is ལེགས་པ་དྲུག་ "legs pa drug". Thus, the Tibetan translators could have simply and perfectly translated bhagavat with བཅོམ་ལྡན་ "bcom ldan". However, they did not.

The Tibetan translators state in the rationale for their translation of bhagavat that to translate it literally as བཅོམ་ལྡན་ "bcom ldan" would not be sufficient because it would then refer to any kind of

---

[15] For maras, see the glossary.

[16] Tib. legs pa drug. A bhagavat has the six goodnesses of: 1) "dbang phyug" dominion over others; 2) "gzugs bzang" an excellent body; 3) "dpal" glory; 4) "grags" fame; 5) "ye shes" wisdom; and 6) "brtson 'grus"perseverance.

holy being—including those of non-Buddhist religions, such as were listed above—and not just to the Buddha. They looked at how to augment the meaning of "bcom ldan" so that it would refer only to a buddha type of bhagavat and saw that, if the word འདས་ " 'das <> transcended" were simply added to indicate transcendence over the two types of obscuration[17], it would create a listing of three qualities in one word—defeat of the four maras, possession of the six goodnesses, and transcendence over the two obscurations—that could refer only to a buddha. Their new term, བཅོམ་ལྡན་འདས་ "bcom ldan 'das", was no longer an exact translation of the original Sanskrit word bhagavat; it was now a description of a *buddha* type of bhagavat in particular.

It is generally accepted that all the holy beings of Indian religions —Shiva, and so on—have conquered the four māras and thereby come to possess the six good qualities but, according to Buddhism at least, only a buddha has transcended both of the two obscurations. Using the process explained just above, this understanding has been embodied in the Tibetan translation of bhagavat. Commentaries on the *Sutra* then connect "bhagavat" to "buddha" as follows. One of the prime definitions of a buddha is abandonment and realization; a buddha is one who has abandoned all that needs to be abandoned and realized all that there is to be realized. In relation to that, although persons who have defeated the four maras have abandoned a great deal of what needs to be abandoned and ones who have come to possess goodness have realized much of what there is to be realized, they do not achieve full abandonment and realization until they transcend both of the two obscurations. Thus, the various gods and holy beings do have abandonment and realization, just as their respective religions claim. However, they do not have the perfection of full abandonment and

---

[17] The two obscurations are the coarser obscuration to being all-knowing of having afflictions and a subtler one which prevents total knowledge even when the coarser ones have been removed.

realization which is the hallmark of a buddha. In this way, an explanation of bhagavat leads to an explanation of the meaning of buddha.

It is plain from the foregoing that the Tibetan translation of bhagavat is *not* a translation of the original word but an invention made to fit the translators' wish that the term refer only to a *buddha* bhagavat. This to me is a very surprising situation. It is regarded within Tibetan Buddhist circles in general that the willful addition of meaning is a major fault for a translator. Yet here is a case where the venerable Tibetan translators deliberately added meaning to a word so that it would reflect their particular teacher as the holy of holies! They claimed that they needed the addition in order to specify more clearly to whom bhagavat refers. However, anyone who has lived for a period in India will know that one can always tell which bhagavat is being referred to by context. In other words, no meaning would have been lost by translating the original Sanskrit word literally and without further addition. We have already established that the Tibetan rationales for translation should not be taken as universally applicable. The case here shows, moreover, that we must be extremely careful when using these rationales.

Given that we have no word that matches bhagavat in English and given that a literal translation of the Tibetan term is simply unusable in its unwieldiness, bhagavat seems best brought into English without translating it.

The Meaning and Translation of "arhat"

Then there is the Sanskrit term "arhat". The term is explained according to Tibetan understanding to be derived from the Sanskrit word "arhan" meaning "to be worthy of praise" or "venerable". This fits with the Buddha's explanation that an arhat is a person who has extricated himself from samsara and has therefore become noble, spiritually speaking, compared to those who are still in samsara. This new, higher position that makes an arhat worthy of praise or veneration.

Unexpectedly then, the Tibetan translators have translated arhat with དགྲ་བཅོམ་པ་ "dgra bcom pa" meaning "one who has defeated the enemy". The rationale given is that, "An arhat in the Buddhist tradition is someone who has *defeated* (བཅོམ་ bcom) the principal *enemy* (དགྲ་ dgra) of sentient beings, the afflictions[18]". Professor Jeffrey Hopkins has nicely translated the Tibetan into English with "foe destroyer".

Interestingly, Professor Hahn and other very learned European Sanskritists regard the position taken in Tibetan scholarship that the root of arhat is "arhan" as mistake that has developed in Tibetan circles. They point out that there is the Sanskrit combination of words "arī han" which means exactly "defeated the enemy". They maintain that "arī han" is the root of arhat and that, therefore, the Tibetan term is a perfect translation! This difference of opinion over whether the root of arhat is arhan or arī han and, therefore, whether the meaning of arhat is "worthy of praise" or "foe destroyer" has not been resolved. It certainly is deserving of further study. The best way to resolve it would be to look into the discourses of the Buddha and see if the Buddha or his disciples said something that would determine it without question.

The Meaning and Translation of "sūtra"

Mipham explains in his commentary that the word "sūtra" conveys the sense of something that is the root or heart of some matter. In fact, the Sanskrit word means "that which was told for others to hear". Tibetans translated it with their word མདོ་ "mdo" literally meaning "a point of confluence" which, in this context, comes to

---

[18] For affliction, see the glossary.

mean "the heart of the matter". In this case, the Tibetans used a word whose meaning does not correspond to the literal meaning of the original term. If we were to translate the Tibetan into English we would stray far from the actual meaning. However this problem is solved because the Sanskrit word has already become standard usage in English.

The Meaning and Translation of "sugata"

The Sanskrit "sugata" is translated into Tibetan with བདེ་གཤེགས་ "bde gshegs". This is as perfect a translation as can be made given that བདེ་ "bde" is the exact equivalent of "su" and གཤེགས་ "gshegs" the exact equivalent of "gata". This is an example of a Sanskrit word that goes perfectly into Tibetan but not into English.

The Sanskrit "su" and its Tibetan equivalent བདེ་ "bde" are used to refer to good situations of all types, situations in which there is no problem. The terms indicate the entire range of the good side of things—happy, easy, pleasant, nice, comfortable, blissful, and so on. We have no means to convey this in English so, although sugata is usually translated with something like "the one gone to bliss", this does not capture the meaning of "su". The term sugata actually means "the one gone to an easy, excellent, pleasant, fine, wonderful state with nothing bad about it"—the word "bliss" alone conveys the wrong meaning.

There is a second difficulty which is that the one word both in Sanskrit and Tibetan has two meanings because "gata" or གཤེགས་ "gshegs" means both "gone" and "went". The word sugata equally means one who has gone to the goodness of enlightenment and one who went on a path which was pleasant and good to take. The Buddhist path is defined as being easy, pleasant, comfortable to travel, and so on and its fruition is defined as a place of ease, a place that is pleasant, comfortable, and so on; the one particle "su" refers to both path and fruition possibilities. Therefore, sugata does not quite mean "gone to bliss" as it is usually translated because it equally means "went blissfully".

Indian Buddhism goes further and explains the meaning of this word sugata with a set of synonyms, each of which sheds further light on the meaning of a buddha. Sugata meaning "gone bliss-fully to bliss" also means: ལེགས་པར་གཤེགས་པ་ "legs par gshegs pa <> gone well to goodness" or མཛེས་པར་གཤེགས་པ་ "mdzes par gshegs pa <> gone beautifully to beauty", སླར་མི་ལྡོག་པར་གཤེགས་པ་ "slar mi ldog par gshegs pa <> gone irreversibly to irreversibility", རབ་ཏུ་གཤེགས་པ་ "rab tu gshegs pa <> gone utterly to utterness", and མ་ལུས་པར་གཤེགས་པ་ "ma lus par gshegs pa <> gone not missing anything to nothing missed" or རྫོགས་པར་གཤེགས་པ་ "rdzogs par gshegs pa <> gone completely to completeness". These various terms are explained at length in the commentaries of Tāranātha and Mipham, and those commentaries should be consulted in conjunction with the explanation here.

The Meaning and Translation of "upanāyika"

One of the epithets in the original recollection of dharma taught by the Buddha is "upanāyika". Its translation is a very interesting exercise for two reasons. Firstly, it is a specific term from ancient Hindu culture which is not frequently used and which will barely be known to people in other cultures. It would be very easy to miss its meaning because of it. Secondly, the Tibetan translators could not agree on a single term for its translation. It is an example that shows the difficulties of translation and which also proves that the process of translating from the Indian language into the Tibetan one was not perfect.

The term "upanāyika" refers to the specific situation in which a young Hindu man is taken to his family's Hindu guru in order to prepare him spiritually. The guru takes the young man, draws him right up to himself, then empowers him into the Hindu understanding of liberation, which the guru represents. The meaning contained in that has been applied to the dharma in the Buddhist recollections of the Three Jewels. The dharma, as the final state of realization is represented through its conventional teaching. That takes hold of us, draws us in from the far-removed state of samsara, bringing us closer and closer, then finally causes us to merge with the final state of realization.

Having uncovered the meaning of the Sanskrit term, we find that it can be literally and correctly translated into English with "brings one in" and that is how its occurrence in the *Sutra* has been translated in this book.

The Tibetans had more difficulty with it. The Tibetan experts whom I consulted agree that the official Tibetan translation is ཉེ་བར་ གཏོད་པ་ "nye bar gtod pa". However, this term is so rarely used that it is almost unknown in the Tibetan dharma language, a problem which is compounded by the fact that the actual meaning is not obvious from the words in the Tibetan phrase. The Tibetan words convey that something aims and sends you *away* in a certain direction. However, that is the wrong way around. Therefore, some Tibetan translators rejected the official equivalent for this term and instead used the phrase ཉེ་བར་འདྲེན་པ་ "nye bar 'dren pa" to translate it. It literally means "to lead in close", which is the required sense.

Tāranātha also notes that one Tibetan translator translated it with "having insight". He would have done so in deference to the fact that the finally point of this process is that one is brought into the dharma of realization, which is insight into superfactual truth. Tāranātha rightly says, "If that were so, it would have to be 'uparyayika', so his explanation does not quite fit".

This is another case where translating from the Tibetan into English will not go well, where we have to look at the original term, in

Sanskrit, and translate from that into English, as has been done here.

Differences of Translation and Explanation of the *Sutra*

The previous section focussed on the rationales of Tibetan translation that appear in the course of examining the *Sutra* and how they can be used to inform the work of translation into other languages. There are also, as mentioned at the beginning of this chapter, other aspects to this *Sutra* and its commentaries that are useful for translators. One of them is that there are different editions of the *Sutra* because of different ways of translating the words in it. In fact, as pointed out in the first chapter, there are sufficient differences in the wordings of various editions of the *Sutra* that there cannot be one, all-encompassing translation of the *Sutra* into English. This is an important point not only for translators but for anyone studying the *Sutra* in depth. Because the differences are so valuable to study, I have covered them fully in my own commentary. There are also differences in the way that the commentaries explain the epithets of the *Sutra*. Again, these differences are valuable for translators to study and again, for that reason, I have covered them fully in my own commentary.

THE MEANING AND USE OF THE SUTRA

The *Sutra* Leads Back to Reality

The *Sutra* is a tool for developing faith in the Three Jewels. It was given to us by the Buddha because faith in the Three Jewels is the foundation of taking refuge in them and that in turn is the root of the path to enlightenment.

Taking refuge in the Three Jewels has great power and the Buddha explained many benefits of doing so, such as being free of enemies, receiving constant protection, and so on. Most importantly though, taking refuge is the single door to all practices and realizations of the Buddhist path. That is so because taking refuge is actually a process of committing one's being to reality and after that connecting to it. In other words, taking refuge is the one doorway that everyone has to go through in order to enter the path back to the fundamental reality that the Three Jewels represent. A teacher in Tibet called the Hermit of Mandong, wrote a very nice, poetic introduction to his teaching on refuge that makes this point:

> The incomparable teacher, through his love for
>   migrators,
> Taught an ocean of dharmas in the profound and vast
>   styles

But the only entrance for all of them is taking refuge.
Any of them could be correctly practised but, unless
　　refuge has been taken.
None can be entered, so refuge is the most important
　　one of all.
Therefore I will explain briefly and just as the holy ones
　　have done,
This great entrance to the excellent house of the con-
　　queror's precious teaching,
The communal wealth of the faithful ones, men and
　　women ...[19]

Refuge is crucial to the path but refuge requires faith. For some, that faith might be directed towards the outer form of the historical Buddha, his teaching of the dharma, and the monastic sangha. For others, there might be the profound faith that comes in relation to the fundamental reality that the outer Buddha, dharma, and sangha represent, and which is the real goal. However, if there is no faith, there will be no real interest in those things and a person will not connect with them or take refuge in them; the path to enlightenment will remain inaccessible.

The recollections in the *Sutra* serve to draw forth faith. That is not just dogma. If the recollections are used and contemplated, it happens. Therefore, the recollections make the teaching of the Buddha, all of the practices that go with it, and all the realizations which come from them, available to us. Thus, the recollections are important for everyone who has heard about the extraordinary practices and depths of reality that are available on and through the Buddhist path, whether the person is formally Buddhist or not.

---

[19] *Teachings of the Mountain Hermit of Mandong, Taking Refuge and Arousing Bodhicitta Explained According to Atisha's Lineage* by Tony Duff, published by Padma Karpo Translation Committee, 2009, ISBN 938-9937-9031-8-9.

The truth of this is reflected in the widespread and constant use of the recollections in all of their forms amongst all kinds of followers of the Buddhist path.

There are many sutras in the Buddhist canon and most are recited only by monks or on certain occasions. However, the original three recollections and their extension, the *Sutra*, with their focus on development of faith and what that leads to, are so fundamental to being Buddhist that they are recited by lay people and monastics alike as a part of their daily practice. For example, the six recollections have long been incorporated into the collection of sutras and prayers that lay people in the Sri Langkan Theravada tradition use for their daily recitations and the *Sutra* was and still is widely used in Tibetan Buddhism in the daily recitations of lay people and monastics alike.

The *Sutra* Leads to Auspiciousness

The prime value of using the *Sutra* would seem to be the development of faith in relation to taking refuge because it opens the door to the whole Buddhist path. However, the *Sutra* is not classified within the Buddhist tradition as a sutra concerned with faith and refuge but as a sutra concerned with auspiciousness[20]. The classification is based on statements from the Buddha such as this one:

> When the good qualities of the Three Jewels are expounded, the banner of dharma is hoisted, the banner of the māras is upturned, the assaults of the asuras are averted, the higher beings are victorious, and all positive forces are strengthened.

---

[20] Tib. bkra shis pa'i mdo.

How does the faith that is developed through the use of the *Sutra* connect with auspiciousness? Buddhists normally think of the Three Jewels as the historical Buddha, his dharma teaching in scripture, and his sangha of Noble Ones. Looked at more deeply, these Three Jewels are expressions of the ultimate; they are none other than fundamental reality showing its face in various ways. In fact, the Buddha is a person who has become reality; the dharma is that reality expressed in various ways; and the sangha of Noble Ones is the group of people who have connected sufficiently with that reality that they can guide others towards it. Generally speaking, this is why the Three Jewels can function as the ultimate refuge that the Buddha stated them to be and followers of the Buddhist path need them to be. Specifically, in terms of auspiciousness, the reality that the Three Jewels represent is good from beginning to end and because we are, choicelessly, part of that reality, it is possible for its goodness to be immediately available to us in our direct experience. In other words, using the *Sutra* arouses faith, which leads to taking refuge, which leads to connection with the historical Buddha, dharma, and sangha, and that itself is a connection with fundamental reality, which is by nature good. Thus the *Sutra* leads, ultimately, to auspiciousness.

Overall, the recollections in the *Sutra* make it is possible to connect, through faith, with fundamental reality in two ways. When the recollections function in the conventional way, they create causes that lead a person on to becoming sangha and later still to becoming a buddha and the dharma personified. When they function in a very unconventional way, they connect a person on the spot to the realities of buddha, dharma, and sangha.

Western practitioners sometimes have trouble making the connection to the Three Jewels and to the magical possibilities that exist because of the Three Jewels connection to fundamental reality. It happens because of a disconnection to faith. It is well known that Western cultures have lost their connection to faith—this issue and the themes that go with it have been discussed extensively within Western cultures and I will not develop that topic extensively here. Still, we, as Westerners, do not live in faith-based cultures. We live in intellect-based ones. This has drawbacks that have been well-documented, such as a loss of ability to connect with anything except what our logic tells us must be there. Ghosts, fairies, and all sorts of other beings become inaccessible and drop out of the culture. The magical possibilities of life are denied and drop away, too. It can be very hard for Westerners to connect with anything but the realities of their hard-headed, logical cultures and they end up being trapped within a rather mechanical and dry existence, even when they are trying to practise a spiritual discipline. Faith is like a key that can open the door so that possibilities other than what are known or allowed by intellect can come in.

The fundamental reality that the Three Jewels represent is good by nature. It is the basic goodness inherent in all beings and which all beings are driven to return to, even if they sometimes go about it the wrong way. Connection to fundamental reality brings out the basic goodness in beings and in doing so brings on the auspiciousness connected with that basic goodness. The recollections, including the *Sutra*, have the power to rouse faith that will, as mentioned above, connect us to fundamental reality both gradually and on the spot. That reality embodies auspiciousness, so the recollections can and do bring forth auspiciousness in various ways. That is why the *Sutra* is classed as a sutra of auspiciousness.

The *Sutra* Leads to Unending Auspiciousness

The fundamental reality that the Three Jewels represent is timeless and all-pervasive. Correspondingly, the auspiciousness connected with it is unending in that it never wanes or stops and encompasses every kind of goodness possible. Therefore, the *Sutra*

has the capacity to connect us not merely with auspiciousness but
with unending auspiciousness. This section highlights a number
of ways in which the *Sutra* is connected with unending auspiciousness.

The *Sutra* is considered to be one of several liturgies that are
useful to recite before undertaking large projects because of the
auspiciousness connected with it.

Taking refuge in the Three Jewels is the one door that has to be
entered in order to do any Buddhist practice and hence to gain any
realization. Taking refuge in the Three Jewels depends on knowing the good qualities of the Buddha, the dharma, and sangha.
This *Sutra* lists their good qualities, so it creates all of the auspiciousness of the entrance to and practise of the Buddhist path.

In general, many Buddhists recite the *Sutra* daily because it is such
an excellent reminder of the Three Jewels. By doing so, they
never forget the Three Jewels, they deepen their refuge in them,
and they develop auspiciousness in their lives and practice. In
regard to this, the Buddha taught[21]:

> For the one who recalls the moon[22] of the Muni,
> Whether he is walking, sitting, standing, or lying,
> The teacher will remain constantly in front of him and
> He will attain the vast nirvana.

It is considered in the Buddhist tradition—and Mipham makes a
strong point of it in his commentary—that just the name of the
Buddha is a great source of power. The *Sutra* contains many epithets of the Buddha, each one extolling one or another of the good

---

[21] From the *Samādhirājāsūtra*, chapter 30.

[22] The brilliant and affliction-cooling personage of ...

qualities of the Buddha. There is a lot of magic associated with reciting these epithets and many kinds of blessing can descend from doing so. For example, a direct connection to buddha-mind can happen just because one's attention is being turned to that. Using the *Sutra* is a little like finding the telephone number for someone then calling him and connecting with him; after the connection has been established, you actually engage the person's energy. Similarly, a person who thinks strongly of the Buddha can connect with buddha-mind and that in itself can bring many changes, on the spot; for example, afflictions can simply vanish and unexpected good states of mind can suddenly shine forth.

The Buddha said that for a person to hear the name Buddha Shakyamuni once is sufficient to prevent the person's birth in a lower realm in the next life and cause birth in a god realm instead. He said that the person would be born in that god realm into a fine family, with good body, and with natural devotion to the Three Jewels, allowing the person to continue easily on the path of dharma. Of course, for someone who practises dharma in this life, the effects are even stronger and more immediate. For this kind of person, simply hearing the name of the Buddha will evoke a strong faith and many other good states of mind with it on the spot, bringing auspiciousness with it. More than that, when a practitioner makes a concentrated effort to recollect the good qualities of the Three Jewels, as can be done using this *Sutra*, the effects can be very powerful.

A person who holds the Three Jewels in high esteem will be accompanied by an uplifted mind. Holding the Three Jewels in mind and in high esteem naturally eliminates depressed, unpleasant, and undesirable states of mind and naturally leads to a bright and cheerful state. For this reason, Buddhists make the Three Jewels their main focus of mind. For a Buddhist, the Three Jewels are respected and honoured at all times because their blessing, which can arrive immediately, purifies the mind, brings its good qualities to the fore, and ultimately leads it to dharmakaya.

Recollecting the good qualities of the Three Jewels is the key that opens the treasury of all the good qualities of the Buddhist path. In relation to this, it is said that the person who has the Three Jewels for his refuge is a person of great wealth and riches and that his mind will never be impoverished.

There is a special feature associated with teaching the *Sutra*. Normally, one has to offer food and drink to the dharma protectors then command them to do their work. However, it is said that simply teaching this *Sutra*, because doing so expounds the good qualities of the Three Jewels, gladdens the protectors and causes them to do their activities.

The *Sutra* connects people from time to time and in various ways to the unending auspiciousness of fundamental reality. When, because of developing faith, taking refuge, and practising the path, they have reached buddhahood, it has caused them to be permanently re-united with the state itself of unending auspiciousness.

Because unending auspiciousness encapsulates the meaning of the *Sutra* so completely, this book and Mipham's commentary were named after it.

The *Sutra* as a Preface to Other Activities

Because the use of the *Sutra* leads to unending auspiciousness, it is commonly used as a preface to other activities. For example, it is common to chant it prior to undertaking large projects. And, Tibetan masters such as Dza Patrul have incorporated it into liturgies for taking refuge and for taking the bodhisatva vows, as part of the preparation for those vow ceremonies. Moreover, it is recited prior to taking meals in Buddhist monasteries, as discussed below.

Buddha saw that eating was a hot spot for the appearance of affliction in the minds of his followers, so he instituted a code of practice to turn monastic meals into times of practice. Over the centuries, it developed into various forms in various countries. In Tibetan monasteries it included the recitation of a liturgy that began with the *Sutra*.

One such Tibetan liturgy for monastic eating was translated into English in 1980 by the Nalanda Translation Committee. It was used with the monastic eating practice that the vidyadhara Chogyam Trungpa Rinpoche introduced at that time into his Vajradhatu, now renamed Shambhala, community. The liturgy itself is short and does not have a name but begins with the *Sutra*, so there is now a widespread belief that *The Sutra of the Recollection of the Noble Three Jewels* is the whole meal liturgy when it is not. Moreover, the monastic eating practice was the Japanese one called "Oryoki" so the Tibetan meal liturgy has also become widely known as "The Oryoki Chant" and many people confuse *The Sutra of the Recollection of the Noble Three Jewels* with the Oryoki Chant. To clarify then, this book is about the actual *Sutra* itself and not about the Tibetan meal liturgy whose name has been mistakenly given the name of the *Sutra* and which has also been called the Oryoki Chant. A detailed explanation of the Tibetan meal liturgy is available in the book called *Oryoki and the Oryoki Chant* [23].

---

[23] *Oryoki and the Oryoki Chant* by Tony Duff, published by Padma Karpo Translation Committee, 2008, ISBN 978-9937-9031-0-3, 2010.

Using the *Sutra*: the Discipline of Learning

The *Sutra* can be read silently or recited aloud. Just reading the words should evoke a sense of wonder at the extraordinary good qualities of the Three Jewels and provoke faith in them. Anyone who has taken refuge in the Three Jewels will, no doubt, have stirrings of appreciation on reading the *Sutra*. Of course, for this to happen, one has to understand the words of the *Sutra*, so a study of it is indicated. Moreover, as the *Sutra* itself repeatedly says, the good qualities of buddha, dharma, and sangha are "immeasurable" and also "inconceivable", so repeated study of it also is indicated.

How are the words of the *Sutra* that describe the good qualities of the Three Jewels being used? Are they just general words being thrown around to describe their good qualities in the way that the normal world throws superlatives around without thinking? Or do they have very precise meanings that always convey a great deal of meaning? The answer is found in the *Sutra* itself when it says that one of the good qualities of the dharma is that "its words are meaningful". In Buddhism in general, all words are meaningful and in the *Sutra* and commentaries to it every word is meaningful.

Because every word in the *Sutra* and the commentaries is meaningful, the vocabulary for their translations has been very carefully chosen and consistently applied in this book to ensure that all of the meaning contained in the original Tibetan texts is accessible in the translations. For example, you will come across the words "immeasurable" and "inconceivable". When you do, do not approach them thinking that they are just superlatives being causally, and possibly interchangeably, used to convey the general sense of extensive, vast, and so on. Immeasurable is the literal translation of a term that specifically means that the thing being described cannot be measured by a dualistic mind. Inconceivable is the literal translation of another term that does not simply mean that something is hard to conceive of but specifically means that the thing is outside the range of conceptual understanding. Thus, when you read, "His knowledgeability is inconceivable", you must be very precise and know that these words have been carefully chose to mean that Buddha has wisdom, not just the ordinary dualistic mind of sentient beings, and that the various qualities of his wisdom, such as his abilities with knowledge, cannot be conceived of by our non-wisdom mind.

It can be very frustrating for some people to be confronted by this need for precision and some will tend give up on it. Rather than being upset by the need for precision or the effort required to develop a correct understanding, it is important to rouse ourselves and develop a discipline of learning. Then we can turn our lack of knowledge to our advantage; for example, we could ponder the words here, thinking, "What is inconceivable wisdom? What exactly does it mean that wisdom is inconceivable? What is dualistic mind?", and so on.

The recollection of dharma says of the dharma that "its wording is excellent". With that in mind, we might think, "Is inconceivable being used in the normal, loose way of talking, or is it being used very precisely and consistently? Is it perhaps part of a transmission of meaning that was not spoken loosely but spoken out of great insight and requires a different kind of attention than we normally give to words? Perhaps I have to give up on my normal concepts of speech and look closely into what is actually being said here?"

It does take effort to stay with the precision of dharma and to develop that quality of precision within ourselves! If we can manage to do it, we can gain access to an extraordinary body of conceptual knowledge. Moreover, this discipline, because it is being developed in relation to an expression of fundamental reality, can lead to a sudden flash of non-dualistic knowledge. The words of dharma, with all their precision and excellence, are only intended as a cause that will remove the coverings of dualistic mind. Again, we can find this understanding in the *Sutra* when, in the recollection of dharma, it lays out the four purities.

There will be times when we exert ourselves and contemplate these epithets of the Buddha, but the understanding that comes will not be clear. For that, we need to find someone who or something that can help to clarify these matters. This book offers the assistance of three commentaries, all of which can be used to clarify the meaning of the words and then contemplate them further. This process leads to an ever-deepening understanding of the Buddha.

Every word of dharma is meaningful. Even a single word of the *Sutra* or its commentaries can lead you on to further levels of understanding and realization. As it says in the *Sutra*, one of the good qualities of the dharma is that it "brings you in". That could simply be a nice-sounding phrase—but it is not; the dharma actually does what the *Sutra* says. The words of dharma have the power to take you by the shoulders, steer you in towards the truth, and finally connect you directly with the truth of fundamental reality—all of which is meant by this epithet. As a matter of interest, the words of this particular epithet are not understood by anyone, Tibetan or otherwise, without study. When the meaning of the epithet has been understood, the words come alive because of how true they are. Many of the other good qualities of the dharma mentioned in the *Sutra* can easily be seen like this to be very alive, one hundred percent up-to-date, and working on the spot, even as you read them.

Correct Logic

There is a great requirement in Buddhism not just for logical process but for correct logical process. For example, Mipham's presentation of how to develop faith and take refuge repeatedly says that correct logical process is needed for it. This highlights a major problem faced by Westerners in relation to studying dharma, which is that they have been taught how to think during many years of mandatory schooling and told that they are capable of thinking correctly because of it. However, what Westerners are taught is the habit of thinking in a logical kind of way, and not necessarily how to think correctly using logic. Because of this, it is common to see in Westerners the certainty that they are correct when in fact, although they have been using logical process, they have not been using *correct* logical process.

In this regard, Mipham says in his commentary,

> This mode of going to buddhahood begins with the fact that mind's nature is luminosity but has adventitious stains on it. Therefore, the path to be travelled has a specific antidote for removing the stains, which is prajna that realizes lack of self. The path also has methods to go with that prajna. There is a force that comes from familiarization using the methods and, if the familiarization is taken through to the finish, the methods have the ability to produce a complete abandonment and realization. For this type of path, trust based in establishment through Reasoning of the Force of the Thing is important and more about that can be known from the Indian texts of Dharmakīrti, and so on.

Here is a paraphrase:

> You had pure knowing of mind—luminosity—once upon a time but lost it when surface stains started popping up on it. That created the problem of your becoming ignorant compared to how you were before. That is your present condition and the condition of everyone else who has lost direct contact with his luminosity. The Buddha understood this situation, so

he came up with a path to lead others out of it, a path
with two aspects. On the one hand the path has
knowledge, called prajna, that discerns the original, un-
stupefied state of bare luminosity. That is the actual
antidote to the problem because the fundamental problem is not loss of good qualities such as compassion, and
so on, but loss of knowledge. However, there are many
people who cannot simply use knowledge to get back to
the purity of the luminosity. They need assistance with
it, so a support for the development of the knowledge
also was taught. The support consisted of a variety of
techniques, called methods, which help a person to get
to the desired state of knowledge. To follow this path of
two aspects, a person needs faith and, specifically, the
type of faith called trusting faith. That trust has to be
developed not just through reasoning but through *correct*
reasoning of a specific type called Reasoning of the
Force of the Thing[24]. Correct reasoning was taught, for
instance, in seven texts on valid ways of knowing
composed by the Indian Buddhist master logician
Dharmakīrti.

Westerners do not necessarily need to study Dharmakīrti's texts
and become expert in the details of Indian ways of logic, but they
do need to acknowledge the requirement for *correct* logical process.

Correct logical process requires prajna, one of the three principal
trainings of Buddhism. Prajna is a specific function of mind that
can and does make a correct decision over two alternatives. Note
that the definition is not "can make a decision" but "can make a
correct decision". It requires quite a lot of training to be able to
exercise prajna on the spot because it not only needs the general

---

[24] For Reasoning of the Force of the Thing, see the glossary.

training of using intellect logically but needs the specific training of ensuring that the logic has correct assumptions, correct reasons, and correct joining of the reasons to the matter under consideration. The study of dharma requires, but as the same time is a means for, the development of correct discernment, that is, prajna.

One person replied to the foregoing, "There is no heart in this; it is all brain". The above is not saying that dharma is a path of prajna or intellect or brain alone; it says clearly that it also is a path of method, which includes love for oneself and others, compassion, and so on. However, our basic problem is loss of knowledge, so we must attend to the development of knowledge, and that in turn means that we have to develop prajna. At this point, someone else replied, "No, it is not necessary! Buddha is beyond intellect!" Here again, the *Sutra* helps us by pointing out in the recollection of Buddha that "his prajna cannot be overpowered". This tells us that a Buddha does have an intellect but it also tells us that it is an aspect of wisdom, not of dualistic mind, so cannot be beaten by the intellect of ordinary beings. Hearing this, anyone with the belief that a buddha does not have intellect can both learn of his mistake and be prodded on to a more precise level of understanding. Moreover, the *Sutra* says that a buddha is a "possessor of insight and its feet"; this also makes it clear that the Buddha has prajna because, as Tāranātha's commentary explains, the insight mentioned in this epithet is part of the larger function of mind called prajna. This epithet tells us something further: the "insight" of this epithet is equated with prajna and the "its feet" is equated with method. It shows that prajna is pre-eminent in the Buddhist journey, that prajna shows the way and then the other qualities of mind serve and support it. In this way, the *Sutra* informs us of the qualities of the Three Jewels but it also provides us with an excellent way to develop prajna and, with it, correct logical process.

Study Hints

The way to approach the vocabulary of the *Sutra* is to see that any given word has a certain meaning and will be used over and again with exactly that meaning. This is different from English where it is considered to be good form when composing to switch between different words for the same thing. Tibetan Buddhist compositions are not like that. They use words carefully and very precisely all of the time in order to convey their information as precisely as possible.

The way to approach the meaning of the *Sutra* is to contemplate the meaning of the words carefully and to develop precision about the meaning. It will entail reading the *Sutra* and then each of its commentaries carefully, comparing meanings as you go and then giving careful thought to what you have discovered. This might simply lead you to the realization that you do not understand a point or topic. Instead of feeling helpless and possibly even indignant that the meaning has not just been handed to you, you might say to yourself, "Well, clearly I need to know more about this, who can I ask for further information?"

The commentaries should be read in their entirety because they are written in such a way that an understanding of something that was not clear in one place can be gained from something explained in another. Tibetan scholars have an axiom for how to read commentaries and the like. It says, "A treatise should be read seven times. The first time, one gets a rough idea only. The second time, some of the gaps are filled in. The third time, there should be a general and overall comprehension. In the remaining readings, more and more meaning will seem to pop out from the page, as the deeper meanings reveal themselves and the magic of dharma makes unexpected connections". Many of my learned friends have said this to me and I have discovered the truth of it on many occasions, including with this text.

Using the *Sutra*: The Real Meaning is the Magic

The Tibetan commentaries to the *Sutra* might seem stiff, dry, or very formalized at times but that is their way of conveying the message that there is enlightenment and that its qualities, which are amazing and unlike anything that is part of our normal world, can be contacted. For instance, Mipham loosens up at the end of his commentary on the qualities of the Buddha and writes a long piece in which he tries to give a sense of what a buddha actually is. His writing contains a growing sense of awe at something just behind human comprehension and capability and inspires the same awe in the reader.

The awesome reality of enlightenment is the basis for our human reality, though its qualities are very different. We humans live within that amazing and good reality but dull it down and solidify it into an existence which is very unsatisfactory. Nonetheless, we are still part of that reality and it can and does bleed through into our existence. When it does, it can seem like magic because it has qualities that are so different from those of our type of existence. It is magic, real magic! It is the magic of a reality which is unrestricted, all-pervasive, unendingly auspicious, a treasury of all the amazing qualities of the enlightened beings, making itself known to us.

Fortunately for us, the very nature of enlightenment is that it has no purpose except to bring beings like ourselves back to the same, amazing state that is filled with good qualities. It is said that fundamental reality is constantly available to work for sentient beings but that the beings must orient themselves towards that reality in order for it to be able to connect with them. Reading and understanding the *Sutra* is one of many ways to do that. The *Sutra* takes the particular approach of orienting a person towards the fundamental reality by expressing its inconceivable, inestimable, amazing, unending, potent qualities as seen through the Three Jewels. That helps us to open to the possibility of its seemingly magical qualities and activities bleeding through into our existence in order to help us. Thus, reading what for some will be stiff commentarial texts written in traditional Buddhist fashion could punch a little hole in the fabric of our otherwise solidified reality and some of the magic could bleed through. We might even get a flash—or more—of direct experience of the realm of enlightenment, the very juicy meaning behind what can at times be very dry words.

This could happen to anyone, whether the person is formally a Buddhist or not, simply because the words of the *Sutra* are expressions of a truth that really exists. For those who have taken refuge formally, it touches on the deeper meaning of refuge and its connection to the magic of reality. The commentaries do not draw this out so the essence of it is mentioned here.

For most Buddhists, refuge is something done by reciting a formula and sort of agreeing with oneself that one has now taken refuge in the Three Jewels. Doing so is very useful in many ways but remains a conventional, dualistic way of taking refuge. There is another way to take refuge; it is called, and it is, the ultimate way to take refuge. When a Buddhist practitioner has progressed to the point of having some understanding of the Three Jewels as fundamental reality itself, taking refuge could be a doorway to actually entering that reality to some degree or another. Taking refuge in that case has an immense level of power associate with it because it has become the immediate actualization, to some extent at least, of buddhahood and all that that entails. This kind of refuge cannot be done with the mouth or with the ordinary thinking mind. In fact, it cannot even be done! It can only happen when a connection to fundamental reality results in a fundamental opening up to it. This could happen to anyone at all but, because most people have solidified their existence very strongly, a person usually has to follow the path and open himself up a little before the reality of enlightenment can be accessed directly.

In relation to this, there is a teaching which says that "taking refuge is the whole path" meaning that the one method practice of refuge is the whole practice for gaining enlightenment. According to the Kadampa tradition, this teaching is saying that refuge is the doorway to the Buddhist path and all of its realization. According to the highest tantras, this same teaching is saying that if a person truly knows how to take refuge at the ultimate level, then there is nothing more to be done. In the latter case, taking refuge in the Three Jewels is the final teaching of all for the simple reason that the true Three Jewels are reality itself. The feeling that goes with this latter kind of refuge does not exclude the prajna of understanding words and distinctions that is brought to the fore when studying the *Sutra*, as was explained earlier in this chapter, but there is a strong shift towards the magic of enlightenment.

The ultimate teaching on refuge is very useful even for those who are not capable of practising at the ultimate level because it emphasizes the profound understanding that the real refuge for a Buddhist is not the historical Buddha, nor the teachings of dharma, nor the other followers who together are the noble sangha, but is fundamental reality. A clear understanding of that, even at the intellectual level, can cause a deep re-orientation in a person's mind towards fundamental reality and that, in turn, cracks open the door to being able to join directly with the magic of that profound reality.

With that understanding, you yourself can open up to all the buddhas and their capabilities and also to the whole domain of truth, which is dharma. By opening up that way, your life as a whole can become much more magical. You can get more in touch with your world, not just in the general sense that comes from the conventional meditation practice of sitting and taming the mind, but through the ultimate approach of joining in with the magic.

You can access the magic! According to the approach of the *Sutra*, you start by understanding conventionally or intellectually what buddha, dharma, and sangha are. Through that, you might develop faith in the possibilities of the three. Then you might develop a real orientation, a decision to go that way. Then you might develop an absolute determination about it. At some point, there might be a breakthrough in which you just open up and find that buddha and dharma are there, gloriously true and real despite their unreality. Then life starts to have a magic that is very satisfying, one that is so much more juicy than the dry, materialistic ways that have spread across the world and so much more real. After that, if someone else asked you about it and how to contact the magical possibilities of life, you would find that you had to answer by talking about the Noble Three Jewels because they themselves are not only representatives of reality but are the reality itself, appearing as a beacon.

Tony Duff
October 10th, 2010,
Swayambhunath,
Nepal

THE ORIGINAL RECOLLECTIONS OF BUDDHA, DHARMA, AND SANGHA TAUGHT BY THE BUDDHA: PALI, SANSKRIT, AND ENGLISH TEXTS[25]

Pali

buddhānusatti

itipi so bhagavā arahaṃ sammāsambuddho vijjācaraṇasampanno sugato lokavidū anuttaro purisadammasārathi satthā devamanussānaṃ buddho bhagavā ti

dhammānusatti

svākkhāto bhagavatā dhammo sandiṭṭhiko akāliko ehipassiko opaneyyiko paccattaṃ veditabbo viññūhi ti

saṅghānusatti

supaṭipanno bhagavato sāvakasaṅgho/ ujupaṭipanno bhagavato sāvakasaṅgho/ ñāyappaṭipanno bhagavato sāvakasaṅgho, sāmīcippaṭipanno bhagavato sāvakasaṅgho/ gadidaṃ cattāri purisayugāni aṭṭa purisapuggalā/ esa bhagavato sāvakasaṅgho āhuneyyo/ pāhuneyyo/ dakkhiṇeyyo añjalikaraṇīyo/ anuttaraṃ puññakkhettaṃ lokasā ti

---

[25] Excerpted from *Mahāsūtras: Great Discourses of the Buddha. Volume I, Texts*, by Peter Skilling, Oxford : The Pāli Text Society, 1994.

63

Sanskrit

buddhānusmṛti

iti hi sa bhagavāṃ tathāgato 'rhāṃ samyaksaṃbuddho vidyā-
caraṇasaṃpanna sugato lokavid anuttaraḥ puruṣa-damya-sārathi
śāstā devamanuṣyāṇāṃ buddho bhagavāṃ

dharmānusmṛti

svākhyāto bhagavatā dharmaḥ sāṃdṛṣṭiko nirjvara ākālika
anupanāyika ehipaśyikaṃ pratyātmavedyo vijñaiḥ

saṅghānusmṛti

supratipanno bhagavataḥ śrāvakasaṅghaḥ nyāyapratipannaḥ
ṛjudṛṣṭi pratipannaḥ sāmīcīpratipannaḥ dharmānudharmaprati-
pannaḥ anudharmacārī/ āhavaīyaḥ prāhavanīyḥ añjalikaraṇīyaḥ
sāmīcīkaraṇīyaḥ anuttaraṃ puñyakṣetraṃ dakṣaṇīyo likasya

English

Thus indeed it is: the bhagavat, tathāgata, arhat,
samyaksaṃbuddha, possessor of insight and its feet, sugata,
knower of the world, unsurpassed driver who tames beings, and
teacher of gods and men is the buddha bhagavat.

The bhagavat teaches dharma just so. It is authentic sight, is
free from sickness, its time has no interruption, it brings one in,
it is a "come and see here!" sort of thing, it is known to the wise
through personal self-knowing.

The bhagavat's śhrāvaka saṅgha have entered into good, have entered into insight, have entered into straightness, have entered into harmony, are the four pairs of beings, are the eight types of person, are worthy of all generosity, are worthy of total generosity, are worthy of joined palms, are worthy of prostration, are an unsurpassed field of merit, are the place of good qualities within the world.

THE GREAT VEHICLE EXTENDED
RECOLLECTIONS OF THE THREE JEWELS:
TIBETAN TEXTS[26]

ༀ། །རྒྱ་གར་སྐད་དུ། ཨཱརྱ་བུད་དྷ་ཨ་ནུ་སྨྲྀ་ཏི། བོད་སྐད་དུ། འཕགས་
པ་སངས་རྒྱས་རྗེས་སུ་དྲན་པ། སངས་རྒྱས་དང་། བྱང་ཆུབ་སེམས་དཔའ་ཐམས་
ཅད་ལ་ཕྱག་འཚལ་ལོ། །འདི་ལྟར་སངས་རྒྱས་བཅོམ་ལྡན་འདས་དེ་བཞིན་གཤེགས་
པ་དགྲ་བཅོམ་པ་ཡང་དག་པར་རྫོགས་པའི་སངས་རྒྱས། རིག་པ་དང་ཞབས་སུ་ལྡན་པ།
བདེ་བར་གཤེགས་པ། འཇིག་རྟེན་མཁྱེན་པ། སྐྱེས་བུ་འདུལ་བའི་ཁ་ལོ་སྒྱུར་བ།
བླ་ན་མེད་པ། ལྷ་དང་མི་རྣམས་ཀྱི་སྟོན་པ། སངས་རྒྱས་བཅོམ་ལྡན་འདས་སོ།
དེ་བཞིན་གཤེགས་པ་དེ་དག་ནི་བསོད་ནམས་དག་གི་རྒྱུ་མཐུན་པ། དགེ་བའི་རྩ་བ
རྣམས་ཆུད་མི་ཟ་བ། བཟོད་པས་བརྒྱན་པ། བསོད་ནམས་ཀྱི་གཏེར་རྣམས་ཀྱི་གཞི།
དཔེ་བྱད་བཟང་པོ་རྣམས་ཀྱིས་སྤྲས་པ། མཚན་གྱི་མེ་ཏོག་རྒྱས་པ། སྤྱོད་ཡུལ་རན
པར་འཐུན་པ། མཐོང་ན་མི་འཐུན་པ་མེད་པ། དད་པས་མོས་པ་རྣམས་ལ་མངོན་པར
དགའ་བ། ཤེས་རབ་ཟིལ་གྱིས་མི་གནོན་པ། སྟོབས་རྣམས་ལ་བརྫི་བ་མེད་པ།
སེམས་ཅན་ཐམས་ཅད་ཀྱི་སྟོན་པ། བྱང་ཆུབ་སེམས་དཔའ་རྣམས་ཀྱི་ཡབ།
འཕགས་པའི་གང་ཟག་རྣམས་ཀྱི་རྒྱལ་པོ། མྱ་ངན་ལས་འདས་པའི་གྲོང་ཁྱེར་དུ་འགྲོ་བ
རྣམས་ཀྱི་དེད་དཔོན། ཡེ་ཤེས་དཔག་ཏུ་མེད་པ། སྤོབས་པ་བསམ་གྱིས་མི་ཁྱབ་པ།

---

[26] From the Derge edition of the Tibetan *Translated Treatises*.

གསུང་རྣམ་པར་དག་པ། དབྱངས་སྙན་པ། སྐུ་བྱུང་བལྟ་བས་ཚིག་མི་ཤེས་པ། སྐུ་མཆོངས་པ་མེད་པ། འོད་དཔག་གིས་མ་གོས་པ། གཟུགས་དག་གིས་ཏེ་བར་མ་གོས་པ། གཟུགས་མེད་པ་དག་དང་མ་འདྲེས་པ། སྒྲ་བསྒྲལ་ལས་རྣམ་པར་གྲོལ་བ། ཕུང་པོ་དག་ལས་རབ་ཏུ་རྣམ་པར་གྲོལ་བ། ཁམས་རྣམས་དང་མི་ལྡན་པ། སྐྱེ་མཆེད་རྣམས་བསྒྲམས་པ། མདུད་པ་རྣམས་ཤིན་ཏུ་བཅད་པ། ཡོངས་སུ་གདུང་བ་དག་ལས་རྣམ་པར་གྲོལ་བ། སྲེད་པ་ལས་ཤིན་ཏུ་གྲོལ་བ། ཆུ་བོ་ལས་བརྒལ་བ། ཡེ་ཤེས་ཡོངས་སུ་རྫོགས་པ། འདས་པ་དང་། མ་བྱོན་པ་དང་། ད་ལྟར་བྱུང་བའི་སངས་རྒྱས་བཅོམ་ལྡན་འདས་རྣམས་ཀྱི་ཡེ་ཤེས་ལ་གནས་པ། སྐུ་ངན་ལས་འདས་པ་ལ་མི་གནས་པ། ཡང་དག་པ་ཉིད་ཀྱི་མཐའ་ལ་གནས་པ། སེམས་ཅན་ཐམས་ཅད་ལ་གཟིགས་པའི་ས་ལ་བཞུགས་པ་སྟེ། འདི་དག་ནི་དེ་བཞིན་གཤེགས་པའི་ཡེ་ཤེས་ཡང་དག་པའི་ཆེ་བའི་ཡོན་ཏན་ཡིན་ནོ། །འཕགས་པ་སངས་རྒྱས་རྗེས་སུ་དྲན་པ་རྫོགས་སོ།། ༄༅། །རྒྱགར་སྐད་དུ། རྣམ་ཨ་ནུ་སྨྲྀ་ཏི། བོད་སྐད་དུ། ཆོས་རྗེས་སུ་དྲན་པ། སངས་རྒྱས་དང་། བྱང་ཆུབ་སེམས་དཔའ་ཐམས་ཅད་ལ་ཕྱག་འཚལ་ལོ། །དམ་པའི་ཆོས་ནི་ལེགས་པར་གསུངས་པ། མཚང་པར་སྟོན་པ། ཐེག་མར་དགེ་བ། བར་དུ་དགེ་བ། ཐ་མར་དགེ་བ། དོན་བཟང་པོ། ཚིག་འབྲུ་བཟང་པོ། མ་འདྲེས་པ། ཡོངས་སུ་རྫོགས་པ། ཡོངས་སུ་དག་པ། ཡོངས་སུ་བྱང་བ། སངས་རྒྱས་བཅོམ་ལྡན་འདས་ཀྱིས་ཆོས་འདུལ་བ་ལེགས་པར་གསུངས་པ། ཡང་དག་པར་མཐོང་བ། ནད་མེད་པ། དུས་ཆད་པ་མེད་པ། ཉེ་བར་གཏོད་པ། འདི་མཐོང་བ་ལ་དོན་ཡོད་པ། མཁས་པ་རྣམས་ཀྱིས་རང་གིས་རིག་པར་བྱ་བ། ཆོས་འདུལ་བ་ལ་ལེགས་པར་བསྟན་པ། ངེས་པར་འབྱུང་བ། རྫོགས་པའི་བྱང་ཆུབ་ཏུ་འགྲོ་བར་བྱེད་པ། མི་འཐུན་པ་མེད་ཅིང་འདུས་པ་དང་ལྡན་པ། རྟེན་པ་དང་ལྡན་པའོ། རྒྱུན་ལས་ཆད་པའོ། །ཆོས་རྗེས་སུ་དྲན་པ་རྫོགས་སོ།། ༄༅། །རྒྱགར་སྐད་དུ། སང་གྷ་ཨ་ནུ་སྨྲྀ་ཏི། བོད་སྐད་དུ། དགེ་འདུན

རྗེས་སུ་དྲན་པ། སངས་རྒྱས་དང་། བྱང་ཆུབ་སེམས་དཔའ་ཐམས་ཅད་ལ་ཕྱག་འཚལ་ལོ། །འཕགས་པའི་དགེ་འདུན་ནི། ལེགས་པར་ཞུགས་པ། རིགས་པ་ ཞུགས་པ། འཐུན་པར་ཞུགས་པ། དྲང་པོ་ཞུགས་པ། ཕྱག་འཚལ་བའི་འོས་སུ་ གྱུར་པ། ཐལ་མོ་སྦྱར་བའི་འོས་སུ་གྱུར་པ། ཡོན་ཡོངས་སུ་བྱུང་བ་ཆེན་པོ། ཡོན་ ཡོངས་སུ་སྦྱོང་བ། སྦྱིན་པའི་འོས་སུ་གྱུར་པ། ཀུན་གྱི་སྦྱིན་པའི་འོས་སུ་གྱུར་ པའོ། །དགེ་འདུན་རྗེས་སུ་དྲན་པ་རྫོགས་སོ། །

THE SUTRA OF THE RECOLLECTION OF
THE NOBLE THREE JEWELS:
TIBETAN TEXT[27]

༄༄། །འཕགས་པ་དཀོན་མཆོག་གསུམ་རྗེས་སུ་དྲན་པའི་མདོ་ནི། །ཐམས་ཅད་མཁྱེན་པ་
ལ་ཕྱག་འཚལ་ལོ། །འདི་ལྟར་སངས་རྒྱས་བཅོམ་ལྡན་འདས་དེ་བཞིན་གཤེགས་པ་
དགྲ་བཅོམ་པ་ཡང་དག་པར་རྫོགས་པའི་སངས་རྒྱས་རིག་པ་དང་ཞབས་སུ་ལྡན་པ།
བདེ་བར་གཤེགས་པ། འཇིག་རྟེན་མཁྱེན་པ། སྐྱེས་བུ་འདུལ་བའི་ཁ་ལོ་བསྒྱུར་བ།
བླ་ན་མེད་པ། ལྷ་དང་མི་རྣམས་ཀྱི་སྟོན་པ། སངས་རྒྱས་བཅོམ་ལྡན་འདས་ཏེ། དེ་
བཞིན་གཤེགས་པ་དེ་ནི་བསོད་ནམས་དག་གི་རྒྱུ་མཐུན་པ། དགེ་བའི་རྩ་བ་རྣམས་ཆུད་
མི་ཟ་བ། བཟོད་པ་དག་གིས་རབ་ཏུ་བརྒྱན་པ། བསོད་ནམས་ཀྱི་གཏེར་རྣམས་ཀྱི་
གཞི། དཔེ་བྱད་བཟང་པོ་རྣམས་ཀྱིས་སྤྲས་པ། མཚན་རྣམས་ཀྱི་མེ་ཏོག་རྒྱས་པ།
སྤྱོད་ཡུལ་རན་པར་མཐུན་པ། མཐོང་ན་མི་མཐུན་པ་མེད་པ། དད་པས་མོས་པ་
རྣམས་ལ་མངོན་པར་དགའ་བ། ཤེས་རབ་ཟིལ་གྱིས་མི་གནོན་པ། སྟོབས་རྣམས་ལ་
བརྫི་བ་མེད་པ། སེམས་ཅན་ཐམས་ཅད་ཀྱི་སྟོན་པ། བྱང་ཆུབ་སེམས་དཔའ་རྣམས་
ཀྱི་ཡབ། འཕགས་པའི་གང་ཟག་རྣམས་ཀྱི་རྒྱལ་པོ། མྱ་ངན་ལས་འདས་པའི་གྲོང་
ཁྱེར་དུ་འགྲོ་བ་རྣམས་ཀྱི་དེད་དཔོན། ཡེ་ཤེས་དཔག་ཏུ་མེད་པ། སྤོབས་པ་བསམ་
གྱིས་མི་ཁྱབ་པ། གསུང་རྣམ་པར་དག་པ། དབྱངས་སྙན་པ། སྐུ་བྱད་བལྟ་བས

---

[27] From Dudjom Jigdral Yeshe Dorje's *Collected Works*.

ཚིག་མི་ཤེས་པ། སྐུ་མཆུངས་པ་མེད་པ། འདོད་པ་དག་གིས་མ་གོས་པ། གཟུགས་དག་གིས་ཉེ་བར་མ་གོས་པ། གཟུགས་མེད་པ་དག་དང་མ་འདྲེས་པ། སྡུག་བསྔལ་ལས་རྣམ་པར་གྲོལ་བ། ཕུང་པོ་དག་ལས་རབ་ཏུ་རྣམ་པར་གྲོལ་བ། ཁམས་རྣམས་དང་མི་ལྡན་པ། སྐྱེ་མཆེད་རྣམས་བསྡམས་པ། མདུད་པ་རྣམས་ཤིན་ ཏུ་བཅད་པ། ཡོངས་སུ་གདུང་བ་དག་ལས་རྣམ་པར་གྲོལ་བ། སྲེད་པ་ལས་གྲོལ་བ། ཆུ་བོ་ལས་བརྒལ་བ། ཡེ་ཤེས་ཡོངས་སུ་རྫོགས་པ། འདས་པ་དང་། མ་བྱོན་པ་ དང་། ད་ལྟར་བྱུང་བའི་སངས་རྒྱས་བཅོམ་ལྡན་འདས་རྣམས་ཀྱི་ཡེ་ཤེས་ལ་གནས་པ། མྱ་ངན་ལས་འདས་པ་ལ་མི་གནས་པ། ཡང་དག་པ་ཉིད་ཀྱི་མཐའ་ལ་གནས་པ། སེམས་ཅན་ཐམས་ཅད་ལ་གཟིགས་པའི་ས་ལ་བཞུགས་པ་སྟེ། འདི་དག་ནི་སངས་ རྒྱས་བཅོམ་ལྡན་འདས་ཀྱི་སྐུ་ཆེ་བའི་ཡོན་ཏན་ཡང་དག་པ་རྣམས་སོ། །དཀའ་བའི་ཚོར་ ནི་ཐེག་མར་དགེ་བ། བར་དུ་དགེ་བ། མཐའ་མར་དགེ་བ། དོན་བཟང་པོ། ཚིག་འབྲུ་བཟང་པོ། མ་འདྲེས་པ། ཡོངས་སུ་རྫོགས་པ། ཡོངས་སུ་དག་པ། ཡོངས་གྱུང་བ། བཅོམ་ལྡན་འདས་ཀྱིས་ཚོས་ལེགས་པར་གསུངས་པ། ཡང་དག་ པར་མཐོང་བ། ནད་མེད་པ། དུས་ཆད་པ་མེད་པ། ཉེ་བར་གཏོད་པ། འདི་ མཐོང་བ་ལ་དོན་ཡོད་པ། མཁས་པ་རྣམས་ཀྱིས་སོ་སོར་རང་གིས་རིག་པར་བྱ་བ། བཅོམ་ལྡན་འདས་ཀྱིས་གསུངས་པའི་ཚོས་འདུལ་བ་ལ་ལེགས་པར་སྦྱོན་པ། དེས་པར་ འབྱུང་བ། ཐེག་པའི་བྱུང་རྒྱབ་ཏུ་འགྲོ་བར་བྱེད་པ། མི་མཐུན་པ་མེད་ཅིང་། འདུས་པ་དང་ལྡན་པ། བརྟེན་པ་ཡོད་པ་རྒྱབ་བཅད་པའོ། ཁྱིག་པ་ཆེན་པོའི་དགེ་ འདུན་ནི། ལེགས་པར་ཞུགས་པ། རིག་པ་ཞུགས་པ། དྲང་པོ་ཞུགས་པ། མཐུན་པར་ཞུགས་པ། ཐལ་མོ་སྦྱར་བའི་འོས་སུ་གྱུར་པ། ཕྱག་བྱ་བའི་འོས་སུ་གྱུར་ པ། བསོད་ནམས་ཀྱི་དཔལ་གྱི་ཞིང་། ཡོན་ཡོངས་སུ་སྦྱོང་བ་ཆེན་པོ། སྦྱིན་པའི་ གནས་སུ་གྱུར་པ། ཀུན་ཏུ་ཡང་སྦྱིན་པའི་གནས་སུ་གྱུར་པ་ཆེན་པོའོ། །འཕགས་པ་ དཀོན་མཆོག་གསུམ་རྗེས་སུ་དྲན་པའི་མདོ་རྫོགས་སོ།། ||

THE SUTRA OF THE RECOLLECTION OF THE NOBLE THREE JEWELS: ENGLISH TEXT

I prostrate to the All-Knowing One.

Thus it is: the buddha bhagavat tathāgata arhat samyaksambuddha, possessor of insight and its feet, sugata, knower of the world, unsurpassed driver who tames beings, and teacher of gods and men is the buddha bhagavat. This tathāgata corresponds to a cause of merits. His roots of virtue do not go to waste. He is fully ornamented with all patience. His basis is troves of merit. The excellent minor signs adorn him. The flowers of the major marks bloom on him. Perceiving his activity, it being just right, there is harmony. Seeing him, there is no disharmony. He brings overt joy to those who long through faith. His prajñā cannot be overpowered. His strengths cannot be challenged. He is a teacher to all sentient beings, a father to the bodhisatvas, a king to the noble persons, a captain to those who journey to the city of nirvana. His wisdom is unfathomable. His knowledgeability is inconceivable. His speech is complete purity. His melody is pleasing. One never has enough of viewing the image of his body. His body is unparalleled. He is not contaminated by the things of desire. He is very much not contaminated by the things of form. He is not mixed with the things of formlessness. He is completely liberated from the sufferings. He is utterly completely liberated from the skandhas. He does not possess dhātus. His āyatanas are restrained. He has totally cut the knots. He is completely liberated from the torments. He is liberated from craving. He has crossed over the river. His wisdom is totally complete. He abides in the wisdom of the buddha bhagavats who arise in the past, present, and future. He does not abide in nirvana. He abides in the limit of the authentic itself. He abides on the level of looking upon all sentient beings. These are the true qualities of the greatness of the body of the buddha bhagavat.

The holy dharma is good in the beginning, good in the middle, and good at the end. Its meaning is excellent, its wording is excellent. It is not adulterated, is totally complete, is total purity, is total purification. The bhagavat has taught dharma well. It is authentic sight. It is free from sickness. Its time has no interruption. It brings one in. This is meaningful to see. It is known to the experts through personal self-knowing. The dharma spoken by the bhagavat was well taught for taming. It is renunciation. It causes one to go to complete enlightenment. It is without disharmony and it has inclusion. It has reliability. It does end the journey.

The saṅgha of the great vehicle have entered into good, have entered into insight, have entered into straightness, have entered into harmony. They are worthy of joined palms, they are worthy of prostration. They are a field of the glory of merit. They are great ones thoroughly trained in gifts. They are a place for generosity. They are in all places even a great place for generosity.

A COMPLETE COMMENTARY TO
THE SUTRA OF THE RECOLLECTION OF THE NOBLE THREE JEWELS

by Tony Duff

I. THE TITLE

The title in the Sanskrit language is *āryaratnatraya anusmṛti-sūtra*[28]. The title in the English language is *The Sutra of the Recollection of the Noble Three Jewels*. The *ārya* of the Sanskrit title corresponds to "noble", the *ratnatraya* to "Three Jewels", the *anusmṛti* to "recollection", and the *sūtra* has been carried untranslated into English.

The Buddha used the Sanskrit term "ratna" as a metaphor for buddha, dharma, and saṅgha as the objects of refuge. Ratna has several meanings, the most general one being something of value. The specific meaning of ratna when it is used to refer to the buddha, dharma, and saṅgha as the objects of refuge translates easily and exactly into English with the word "jewel". The Buddha taught the meaning of this metaphor so that his followers could understand the preciousness of the Three Jewels and develop their faith and trust because of it. He taught that the Three Jewels have

---

[28] When the text of the *Sutra* is cited, it is set off from the commentary by showing it in bold italics.

the qualities of being rare and hard to find, great in value, and so on. These teachings were summed up into six ways of understanding the qualities of the Three Jewels in relation to the qualities of jewels in the Indian treatises which explain the Buddha's teachings.

A consideration of the etymology of terms like that is a valuable way to understand the qualities pointed to by the terms. For this reason, Tibetan commentaries go through the etymology of a number of terms in the recollections, especially of ones used to describe the Buddha. These can be hard to follow because they deal with the translation of Sanskrit terms into the Tibetan language, not the English language. Therefore, clarifications of the meanings of these terms and how they should be translated have been gathered into an earlier chapter on translation issues. A complete treatment of the meaning of "ratna" in relation to the Three Jewels, including the six ways of understanding their qualities can be found on page 27 of that chapter.

II. THE TRANSLATORS HOMAGE

I prostrate to the All-Knowing One is the translator's homage for this sutra. In Tibet, in the ninth century C.E., a great revision of all the translations of Buddhist works that had been made up to that time was undertaken, with the intention of producing a final, accepted set of translations. The king, Tri Ralpachen, in conference with the senior Tibetan translators, declared that a translator's homage would placed immediately after the title on all translated texts. The homage would be one of a few, pre-defined forms to indicate what the text was about. A text that was related to the Vinaya section of the Buddha's teachings was to have the wording, "I prostrate to the All-Knowing One", for the translator's homage. Thus, the homage here tells us that this is a sutra connected with the Vinaya section of the teachings of the Buddha and that sets the tone for the whole of what follows. Here "the

All-Knowing One" means "the Buddha, the one who has the kind of knowledge that sees all phenomena in both their depth, meaning their actuality, and in their extent, meaning their appearance".

III. THE MAIN PART

Following the homage, there is the actual text of the *Sutra*. It is in three sections, one each for the recollections of the Buddha, the dharma, and the saṅgha. Each of the three sections comes out to one English paragraph in the translation.

The main point of recollecting the noble Three Jewels is that it arouses the faith which is the basis for the trust needed to take refuge in the Three Jewels. In general, faith in Buddhism is said to be of three types and these should be explained here. Tāranātha has an excellent and relatively practical explanation of the states of mind of the three faiths and how they are to be developed whereas Mipham treats them and their development in a very technical way. Those who want a totally non-technical approach can simply recite and contemplate the recollections; doing so will result in stirrings of faith, which can later be understood in terms of the three types of faith and then refined.

The faith has to turn into trust. This is brought about by contemplating why the Three Jewels, and especially the Buddha, are a true and complete refuge. Some of the trains of thought involved are mentioned briefly by Mipham but more about them needs to be known for the contemplation to be effective. There are a number of texts in the Tibetan Buddhist tradition which explain these trains of thought, such as Tsongkhapa's *Great Stages of the Path to Enlightenment*, Gampopa's *Jewel Ornament of Liberation*, and many other texts in the Stages of the Path genre. The Hermit of Mandong, a Kagyu yogin who became famous amongst Tibetans for teaching the poor people of his district in the nineteenth century, gave a very practical teaching on refuge which is particularly good for understanding the contemplations that lead to trust in the Three Jewels[29].

Thus, a follower of the Buddha learns and recites the recollections of the Three Jewels in order to develop first the faith then the trust needed to take refuge in them. The recollection of the Buddha comes first.

1. The Recollection of the Good Qualities of the Buddha

This recollection is in two parts: a summation followed by a longer exposition. The summation is the original recollection of the Buddha, consisting of nine epithets in a single sentence. The longer exposition consists of the epithets added when the recollection was extended by Great Vehicle followers.

The summation, which occupies the first sentence of the *Sutra*, reads ***Thus it is: the buddha bhagavat tathāgata arhat ... is the buddha bhagavat***. This original recollection taught by the Buddha has been recited day in and out in every Buddhist culture from the time of the Buddha. It is well known and greatly loved by all of his followers.

Before going into an explanation of individual words, we should look at the overall structure to see how to read and understand it. It is in three parts. It starts in Tibetan with ***Thus it is:*** though the original wording of recollection is a little stronger than that—it says "Thus indeed it is: ". Either way, this first part has to be understood to mean exactly "This is how the Buddha is:— ". The

---

next part is a list of eight main features or good qualities of the Buddha: "... *bhagavat, tathāgata, arhat ...*". The third part is a conclusion which says: "*is the buddha bhagavat*" in order to indicate the person in whom those features will be found.

Note that the original recollection starts with "*bhagavat*". The extended recollection in the Derge *Translated Treatises* and the Tibetan *Sutra* changes this to "*buddha bhagavat*". This addition seems to be connected with the Tibetan translators not wanting to accept the straightforward meaning of bhagavat but wanting it refer only to a buddha bhagavat, the details of which are mentioned just below in this commentary and on page 33 of the chapter on translation issues. This causes some complicated and, I think, un-necessary explanations in the Tibetan commentaries on the *Sutra*. Altogether, I think it would be best in future to make a standard version of the *Sutra* in English (and other languages) using the original recollection. If we were to do that, this first section of the recollection of the buddha would become: *Thus indeed it is:— a bhagavat, tathāgata, arhat, truly complete buddha, one gone pleasantly to pleasantness, possessor of insight and its feet, unsurpassed driver who tames beings, and teacher of gods and men is the buddha bhagavat.*

Now we move on to the epithets which present the features of a buddha. In general, the Buddha had an enormous number of epithets given to him while he was alive. Individually they have much meaning, pointing out, as they do, what a buddha is.

As mentioned above, the edition of the *Sutra* used here starts with the word **buddha** which has been added to modify and clarify the meaning of the word bhagavat that follows it. Therefore, we begin not with this but with the actual first epithet **bhagavat** of the original recollections. The meaning of buddha is explained later in conjunction with the epithet "truly complete buddha".

The first actual epithet of the recollections is *bhagavat*. It could be explained here or it could be explained at the end of this first sentence of the recollections when it says "the buddha bhagavat". Taranatha explains it here, pointing out that this is the first actual epithet of the sequence, and this commentary does the same. Mipham explains it at the end and gives his reasons for doing so.

This is a very ancient Indian term. If we look directly at Sanskrit to obtain the etymology of the term, we find that it is a term of high respect for someone who is seen "vat" to *possess* a great degree of holiness because of "bhaga" having *defeated* negative aspects of being. The word was and still is used by many Indian spiritual traditions as a term of the highest respect for the holy beings of their system, and that is how the term should be understood here. Note that in normal use this word is also used in the form "bhaga-van" with no difference at all in meaning.

"Bhagavat" translates literally and perfectly into Tibetan with བཅོམ་ ལྡན་ "bcom ldan" where བཅོམ་ "bcom" is the equivalent of "bhaga" and ལྡན་ "ldan" is the equivalent of "vat". However, the early Tibetan translators rejected that as a translation because the term referred to a holy person in all religious groups, not just to a buddha. They wanted it to refer only to a buddha so they added an extra word འདས་ " 'das", to the end of བཅོམ་ལྡན་ "bcom ldan" to make བཅོམ་ལྡན་འདས་ "bcom ldan 'das" which they explained to mean "he who has conquered the four māras, he who has come to possess the six goodnesses, and he who has transcended the two obscurations". Holy beings in general are considered to have the first two qualities but Buddhists, at least, consider that transcendence of the two obscurations—the coarser obscuration to total knowledge of having afflictions and the subtler one preventing total knowledge even when the coarser ones have been removed—is a feature of a buddha alone.

It is noteworthy that Mipham chooses not to explain bhagavat until the end of this first sentence of the recollections, where the term comes in conjunction with the term buddha. By doing so, he attempts to show the value of the new meaning that Tibetan translators gave to bhagavat. However, the complication involved can be confusing for non-Tibetans. There is a complete explanation of the meaning of bhagavat and how it can be translated on page 33 of the chapter on translation issues.

Tathāgata from a Sanskrit perspective primarily means "one who has (gata) gone to (tathā) suchness" and refers to someone who has attained enlightenment due to having returned to his own suchness, his own inner reality. "Gata" also means "going" in which case tathāgata refers to the followers of the tathāgata who are being taken to enlightenment by him. Thus, this epithet is taken to mean that the Buddha is a perfection of explanation because the tathāgata, having become perfected himself, explains suchness perfectly to his disciples and causes them to return to it.

Arhat is regarded in Tibetan understanding to be derived from the Sanskrit word "arhan" meaning "to be worthy of praise" or "venerable". This fits with the Buddha's explanation that an arhat is a person who has extricated himself from samsara and has therefore become noble, spiritually speaking, compared to those who are still in samsara. It is this new, higher position that makes an arhat worthy of praise or veneration.

The Tibetans translated "arhat" with the word དགྲ་བཅོམ་པ་ "dgra bcom pa" meaning "one who has destroyed the enemy" or, as Professor Jeffrey Hopkins translated it into English, "foe destroyer". The Tibetans gave the rationale that an arhat in the Buddhist tradition is someone who has defeated the principal enemy of sentient beings, the afflictions, and therefore is a "foe destroyer". Some European Sanskritists claim that arhat is derived not from arhan but from "arī han" which means exactly "defeated the enemy" and which fits exactly with "foe destroyer". This needs to be researched further. The translation issues surrounding arhat are discussed on page 36 of the chapter on translation issues.

Some people become confused at this point because of thinking that "arhat" is a name used only for those who have attained the fruition of the Lesser Vehicle. They cannot see how the Buddha could be an arhat because of thinking that an arhat has a lesser level of realization than the Buddha. Arhat in this context does not mean that the Buddha is a Lesser Vehicle arhat with a lower level of attainment. Rather, it points out that the Buddha has an arhat's level of attainment as part of his attainment of truly complete buddhahood.

The Buddha was not merely an arhat of the Lesser Vehicle. He was much more than that. He was a *samyak saṃbuddha* meaning a "truly complete buddha". In the ancient tradition of Buddhism, beings who had fully realized the teachings of the Lesser Vehicle were called buddha; specifically, they were the shrāvakabuddhas and pratyekabuddhas who were the arhats of the Lesser Vehicle. Thus, they were also called arhat buddhas, which might seem strange if it has not been heard before, but it is part of the tradition; it is like saying in English "the enlightened type of person called an arhat". Then there were the bodhisatva buddhas, the ones who have been through the bodhisatva journey and attained the highest possible level of buddhahood. The bodhisatva buddhas were not merely arhats with their partial enlightenment but were "truly complete buddhas", ones who really were buddhas with the most complete type of enlightenment possible. Therefore, the Buddha himself coined this term "truly complete buddha" to indicate a person who has gone through the Great Vehicle journey and attained an enlightenment which is truly—that is to say *really and truly*—complete. Thus, the Buddha has the qualities of an arhat buddha but is, more than that, a truly complete buddha.

From the perspective of the Sanskrit language, "buddha" means "enlightened one". It has been translated into English as "awakened one" but this is a mistake that has come primarily from misunderstanding the Tibetan word for buddha. The root of the word buddha is "budh" which conveys the sense of a person who is illuminated with knowledge, an enlightened person. The primary synonym for "budh" in Sanskrit is "avagamana", which means to have full comprehension or to be fully realized. When these words are examined from the Sanskrit side, they give the sense of the Buddha being a person who, having cleared off all obscurations to knowing, has achieved a state of illumination. The emphasis is on unimpeded knowledge, a state of full comprehension. In short, a buddha is an enlightened one.

The Tibetans did not have a word that was a good match for buddha. They turned to Sanskrit literature and found a description of the Buddha in a very famous piece of poetry about the Buddha which they used as a basis for creating a new word.

The poetry presents the image of the Buddha being like a lotus. Lotuses start as a seed in the muck of a swamp, then grow up through the swampy water until they have risen several inches above it and are completely clear of the filth of the swamp, and finally blossom into a beautiful flower, replete with excellent qualities. The metaphor is really excellent. The Sanskrit poetry emphasizes two features which apply to the Buddha. The first is that a lotus has been through a process of cleaning itself, journeying through and finally past all the contamination of the swamp so that it is pristine. The second is that it then blossoms into a flower that abounds with good qualities of all kinds. This fits exactly with what a buddha has done: he has cleared all the obscuration that was contaminating and preventing his mind from total knowledge, and in doing so has turned into a thing of beauty replete with all of the amazing qualities of enlightenment.

Tibetan translators took the Tibetan words for each of these two features, སངས "sangs" and རྒྱས "rgyas" respectively, combined them, and came up with the new word སངསརྒྱས "sangs rgyas", which they then set as the Tibetan word for buddha.

It is particularly important to understand that the primary meaning of སངས "sangs" is "to be cleared out". Tibetan experts have explained it as "to have pollution cleared out, as happens when the windows of a stuffy room are opened". This is the meaning intended in the original poetry; for a buddha, the obscurations of mind that would prevent total knowledge have been cleared. There is a secondary meaning in Tibetan only in which "sangs" is equated with the verb སད་པ "sad pa <> to wake up". Some Tibetans, not knowing of the Sanskrit poetry and its meaning, have assumed that this secondary meaning for སངས "sangs" is the correct one then mistakenly explain "buddha" to mean "awakened and blossomed". The mistake is compounded when Western translators take that as proof that "buddha" means "Awakened One", then set that as the correct translation. This has happened and people have become very attached to what their teacher has said and reluctant to hear that it might be mistaken. For this reason, we non-Tibetans have to start with the Sanskrit language and its own definitions; from that we understand that the word buddha conveys the idea of knowledge that has been cleared of contamination, not awakening.

It is important to note that one *could* say that the Buddha is an awakened person; it is an apt metaphor! However, it is *not* the metaphor that was in use when the Tibetans derived their word "sangs rgyas" and therefore could not be used to inform the translation into other languages of the word buddha.

Thus, through examining the etymology of the word "buddha" and also through looking at the correct meaning of the Tibetan term for it, we find out the basic meaning of "buddha". Ancillary to that, we get a glimpse of various issues surrounding the translation of "buddha". All of this has been also been explained on page 30 of the chapter on translation issues.

Possessor of insight and its feet. The literal translation of the original Sanskrit phrase is "possessor of insight and what comes at foot" which further conveys the sense of "what carries the insight around" and comes out exactly in English to "possessor of insight and its feet". This phrase was occasionally used in ancient India for the worldly meaning of someone who has intelligence and good character with it, which has resulted in one English translation of this epithet as "learned and virtuous". However, the meaning in regard to the Buddha is "one who possesses insight and the various qualities that go with and serve it, like feet that carry it along". Mipham's commentary gives the excellent example of a person walking along a road—the eyes see the place to be travelled and the feet below it make the journey; similarly, insight sees the way and the other qualities that it has below it serve to carry it along.

This epithet can be understood in many ways and there are many commentaries within the Indian and Tibetan traditions that explain it. In this book, Tāranātha's commentary gives a very clear explanation of the main ways that it can be understood. Insight and the qualities that serve it are what is needed on the path to go to enlightenment; for this reason Indian commentaries explain that this epithet is stating the cause of the buddha that has been explained in the preceding epithets. However, the fruitional forms of insight and the qualities that serve it are present once one has attained enlightenment, and it is explained that they then function to benefit others.

The sugata. The Sanskrit word has two parts: "su" means any kind of happy, easy, pleasant situation and "gata" means "gone", the same as in "tathāgata". Just as in tathāgata, "gata" can be taken in two ways with the result here that the term equally means someone who went in a pleasant way and someone who has gone to a pleasant state. In other words, the full meaning of sugata is "someone who went pleasantly to pleasantness".

Thus, sugata points out the nature of the Buddhist path and its fruition, showing the kind of journey the Buddha has taken and the destination he has arrived at. The Buddhist path is pleasant because it is a straightforward path that leads without sidetracks or convoluted travel directly to its destination; because it passes through all the happy, pleasant, and even blissful states of mind on its way; and because it is presented in a way that allows someone to have an easy journey, free of suffering, to the goal. The fruition is a pleasant one in many ways—it has no unsatisfactoriness connected with it at all, it is final and requires no more effort, it is naturally beneficial to oneself and all others, and so on.

The Indian Buddhist tradition mentions several synonyms for sugata, all of which clarify the type of path and fruition to which the Buddha has gone. The commentaries of Tāranātha and Mipham explain them at length and should be consulted at this point. They are mentioned together with the meaning and translation of the word sugata on page 38 of the chapter on translation issues.

The great similarity between this term and tathāgata can be confusing. The term tathāgata has a more philosophical quality to it whereas sugata conveys the very practical sense of having travelled a path that is fundamentally workable and having reached an excellent fruition because of it.

The preceding epithets have explained the qualities that a buddha has achieved for his own purposes. In general, practitioners of the Great Vehicle work towards buddhahood with two aims in mind: they aim to solve their own problems by becoming a buddha and they aim to bring others to the same place. In this sense, buddha hood is the attainment of the complete purity of mind, called the dharmakāya, and the two complete purities of body, called saṃbhogakāya and nirmāṇakāya. Attainment of the first fulfills one's own aims or purposes because it brings personal, final release from all problems. Attainment of the second fulfills others' aims or purposes because it naturally responds to all other sentient beings with the assistance needed to relieve them finally of their problems. The remaining four epithets in this first sentence show four qualities that the Buddha possesses because of fulfilling others' purposes.

The Buddha is *the knower of the world*. "World" here primarily means the beings in all worlds and their individual situations—happy, sad, and so on—as seen by the knowing aspect of the Buddha's mind and "knower" here means the Buddha as a compassionate being. Thus, knower of the world is someone who has both aspects of knowledge and compassion unified. The Buddha knows all beings everywhere and their situations, and knows all of that always and in every moment, and because of the compassion which is integral to that knowledge, he does whatever needs to be done to benefit those worlds of beings.

A buddha benefits all beings in any way possible but primarily benefits them by steering them away from samsara towards enlightenment. Steering them to enlightenment entails getting them to pacify their own afflictions and remove the obscurations in their own minds, a process which is called "taming" them. For those reasons, he is called *the driver who tames beings*. More than that, no one else can match his capacity for steering and taming beings, because a buddha alone knows the minds of all beings and knows exactly which methods to use to tame them. Therefore, he is not merely any driver who tames beings but is *the unsurpassed driver who tames beings*.

Note that the word driver here is a generic term used to mean anyone in control of any vehicle, animal, or situation. It refers to the person anyone in the driver's seat, the person at the helm, the steersman. In ancient India it would have been used to refer to the drivers of chariots, and selephants, horses, and so on. If one then asks, "Well, what kind of driver is he?" The answer is that he is not a charioteer or elephant driver or driver of any other kind of vehicle. Rather, he steers beings out of the mire of samsara towards enlightenment, so he is specified as a *driver who tames beings*.

Note that *unsurpassed* appears in the Tibetan *Sutra* as a separate item that comes after "driver who is the tamer of beings". However, that is not an accurate translation of the original recollection in which it is an adjective describing "driver who tames beings". This is noted here because there is already one English translation that misreads the Tibetan and incorrectly shows "unsurpassed" as a separate epithet—"the unsurpassed one". Tāranātha and Mipham both understood this point, with both of them explicitly stating that "unsurpassed" has to be understood as an adjective modifying "driver who is the tamer of beings" despite the wording of the Tibetan which seems to make it into a separate item.

Well then, how did this unsurpassed driver who tames beings actually go about taming the beings? The next epithet says that he was *the teacher of gods and men*. The Buddha did not merely manifest as a buddha in the world of humans, but manifested his enlightenment throughout all the abodes of beings. Nonetheless, there were only some places where the beings had the capacity to actually receive the dharma directly from him or one of his followers and then to contemplate and cultivate it. Those places were certain heavens of the gods—some in the high levels of the desire realm and some in the lower levels of the form realm—and the human realms. Therefore, although his enlightenment manifested cosmically, it was specifically in the worlds of gods and humans that he tamed beings.

Note that the word teacher here does not mean any teacher but refers specifically to a person who founds and is the proclaimer within the world of a whole system of teaching. The Buddha aided many beings in many ways but, specifically, he was the founding teacher who showed the teachings of enlightenment to gods and humans, both. Thus he is the founding teacher of the Buddhist system who teaches and thereby tames gods and men.

That completes the listing of the qualities of the buddha of the original recollection. The conclusion is drawn with the words *is the buddha bhagavat.* In a more technical way of talking, the list of epithets has shown the good qualities themselves and this concluding phrase shows the person in whom the good qualities are based.

Note that Mipham makes a point in his commentary of including the explanation of the term "bhagavat" here rather than earlier when the term is first used. He does so because there is an explicit reference here to the buddha as the "buddha bhagavat" which, by its very presence, supports the decision of the Tibetan translators to translate bhagavat so that it specifies a buddha type of bhagavat in particular. This clever arrangement of his is intended to clarify and justify that decision of the Tibetan translators. This comes through very clearly in the Tibetan but is almost lost after it has been translated into another language; this is a case where translation inevitably loses some of the meaning.

With that, the summary of the Buddha's qualities—both those connected with the achievement of his own purposes and those connected with the achievement of others' purposes—is complete.

❀   ❀   ❀

The longer exposition of the Buddha's qualities begins. It has two parts. First it sets out how he manifested to fulfil the aims of others, then it sets out how he totally abandoned samsara and realized nirvana to fulfill his own aims.

The first two epithets go together and show the magnitude of the cause of the tathāgata and how it leads to him being steady and never-ending.

That tathāgata corresponds to a cause of merits. The wording here is not "the tathāgata" but "that tathāgata". The word "that" is deliberately used to indicate "that kind of tathāgata whose qualities have just been summarized". For the meaning, if you were to ask, "What sort of cause gave rise to our tathāgata, the Buddha?", the answer would be that he came from the accumulation of merit. He is the result of an immeasurable merit collection accumulated over cosmic ages.

"Corresponds to a cause" is a technical phrase. When there is an effect coming from a cause, this terminology is used to indicate that the effect is one that corresponds to a particular cause, for example, wheat corresponds to having the cause of wheat seed and not some other cause. We can ask, "To which cause does the tathāgata correspond?" The tathāgata, meaning the Buddha, comes from merit, in particular. Therefore, what the tathāgata is does indeed correspond to that.

His roots of virtue do not go to waste. In general, virtuous action produces roots of virtue. The word root in relation to virtue means a karmic seed that could grow; a virtuous root is one that will grow into a virtuous result.

While the Buddha was on the path, he did not waste his roots of virtue by using them for results within samsara nor did he waste them on merely becoming an arhat. Instead, he used his roots of virtue only for the attainment of truly complete enlightenment. Moreover, having attained buddhahood, his roots of merit are never used in a way that would be squander them. Instead, they are only ever used as the cause of unending goodness both for himself and all beings.

On becoming a buddha, the roots of virtue that he had accumulated became part of the pool of virtue of enlightenment, which is an unending situation. Thus, even though his roots of virtue as a buddha are used for the production of goodness, they are never exhausted by it and hence never go to waste. In other words, the Buddha achieved an accumulation of merit that unendingly produces good.

The next six phrases go together and show the nature of the body he has manifested for others' sake.

He is fully ornamented with all patience. The Buddha practised all of the different types of patience on his way to buddhahood and so perfected patience in all ways possible. Moreover, once he had become a buddha, he had achieved types of patience that were beyond ordinary patience; for example, he could sit unmoving in one place for countless aeons, if necessary. In that way, the Buddha is fully ornamented with all types of patience, both the types of patience known on the path to buddhahood and the ones that come with the fruition of buddhahood.

His basis is troves of merit. The word "trove" here means a source that is like a treasure that never ends. The Buddha, as a buddha, comes from an immeasurably large collection of merit. On one hand, he is a trove of merit because of what he accumulated during his practise of the path. On the other hand, he is a trove of merit because as a buddha he becomes a basis for others' development of their own troves of merit.

Signs of these extraordinary accumulations of merit appear on the Buddha's nirmāṇakāya body as the thirty-two major marks and eighty minor signs. Thus the *Sutra* says *the excellent minor signs adorn him* and *the flowers of the major marks bloom on him*. This is the correct wording—as Mipham points out in his commentary, the major marks bloom on him and the minor signs are like anthers of those freshly opened flowers that serve to enhance the appearance of the major marks.

All buddhas have these signs and marks present on their nirmāṇakāya bodies. For instance, they have the large protuberance on top of the head, dark head hair with each hair individually curled in a particular manner, very long earlobes, beautiful eyes, a curled hair between their eyebrows called the ūrṇā, and so on. You can see these signs on representations such as statues and paintings, and they are listed in a number of Great Vehicle sutras and in Maitreya's text *Ornament of Manifest Realisations*[30].

Perceiving his activity, it being just right, there is harmony. This epithet concerns the way that the Buddha acts in relation to others. He always acts in such a way that his behaviour is perfectly fitting or just right for the being perceiving it. Because his actions are always just right for that person, the person only has good or harmonious states of mind arise upon seeing his actions. Then, because that is so, no-one who sees him has negative or disharmonious states of mind arise; lack of faith, negativity, or the like never arise from seeing him so, *seeing him, there is no disharmony*.

The next three phrases show qualities which are a basis for his acting for the sake of others.

---

[30] Skt. Abhisamayālaṅkāra. A translation is contained in Edward Conze's *Sutra of the Perfection of Wisdom* and extensive listings and explanations are given in *The Illuminator Tibetan-English Dictionary*.

He brings overt joy to those who long through faith. His beyond-worldly beauty combined with his virtuous presence is such that anyone who goes before him will have a very pure faith arise in him. That pure faith leads to the development of such strong appreciation of him that the person becomes totally absorbed with him. That appreciation, which is a kind of longing, then leads to a very pure kind of joy which is so strong that it is overt, or visibly apparent. This sequence of events is summed up as: faith, leading to appreciation with longing, leading to overt joy.

His prajñā cannot be overpowered. The knowing quality of the Buddha's wisdom is totally unobscured because of which the Buddha has total knowledge of all things through time and space. As a result, he cannot be tricked, tripped up, or have anything hidden from him. There are many stories in the sutras about this, for example, the stories about his jealous cousin Devadatta who was constantly trying to outdo the Buddha but who could never win because the Buddha's knowledge was always on top of the situation. The Buddha is always on top of every situation because of his knowledge, which is the meaning of this epithet.

His strengths cannot be challenged. The Buddha's many good qualities of mind and body include abilities called "strengths". These strengths of the Buddha can never be matched. If someone were to challenge him to a contest of abilities, the person would not be able to defeat him, let alone match him because of these strengths, which is the meaning of this epithet. There are many stories in the sutras about his strengths and challenges to them that he successfully met.

The next four epithets go together, showing four ways in which the Buddha leads sentient beings.

Overall, *he is a teacher to all sentient beings.* Even if there were a human who could teach everyone in the human world successfully, that person could not teach hell beings and hungry ghosts, and so on, let alone gods in the form and formless realms. The Buddha does not have limitations like that on who he can teach or help, but has the capacity to be and is a teacher for all beings throughout time and space.

The next three epithets show three specific ways that he leads beings. In the Great Vehicle, his main job is to be father to the bodhisatvas so it says he is *a father to the bodhisatvas*. There is a whole vision to the Great Vehicle that is enacted with him as the father and them as the sons. Amongst other things, the Great Vehicle speaks of the sons who hold the family lineage of a buddha and who conduct themselves according to the ways of that family until they have prepared themselves for the final coronation; at that time, their father, their buddha, enthrones and empowers them into buddhahood.

He is *a king to the noble persons* meaning that he acts as a king who presides over and leads the arhats of the Lesser Vehicle. He goes together with them on their journey and acts out the culture of their Lesser Vehicle with them so that they can attain the fruition of that particular path. He is like a king presiding over them, the commoners compared to the bodhisatvas, who engages in the norms of their culture in order to help them along.

Then, the Buddha in general is like a captain who actually does the work of taking all like-minded beings from the dank dungeon of samsara to the grand city of nirvana, as it is often referred to in Buddhist scripture. Therefore, he is *a captain to those who journey to the city of nirvana*. The wording here is very specific. It does not merely mean that he is a driver or helmsman or guide who is steering a group of followers to the city of nirvana. It has the greater meaning that he is captaining his followers. He does all the work, as a captain does, of gathering them up and sailing them to their destination. He provides a gangway onto the ship to start with, then welcomes them as passengers and puts them onto the ship, then makes his rounds during the cruise in order to ensure that they are doing well, solves any problems they might have on the way, and finally brings them to and sets them down at their destination.

The next six phrases show how he uses his enlightened body, speech, and mind in the service of sentient beings.

His wisdom is unfathomable is connected to the activity of enlightened mind. Wisdom is the name for the particular type of mind that a buddha has. That wisdom cannot be fathomed—cannot be understood—by the rational, dualistic type of mind that ordinary beings have. Therefore, his wisdom is unfathomable. Note that this does not mean that the Buddha possesses an unfathomable amount of a wise kind of mind. It means that he has a wisdom kind of mind which is beyond the scope of rational mind.

His knowledgeability is inconceivable is said by some to be connected to the activity of his enlightened mind and by others to his enlightened speech. It concerns the use of his speech to present the dharma but that speech is based on his ability with knowledge. Therefore, this particular good quality could be defined in either way, though it starts with the qualities of his enlightened mind.

The quality of knowledgeability[31] refers to an ability to instantly recall to mind the knowledge needed, for example, when teaching someone, and a confidence of knowledge that comes with it. The Buddha's level of knowledgeability is inconceivable: his wisdom knows all things throughout all times so he can recall an inconceivable array of knowledge and with an ultimate level of confidence that he can do so. Moreover, the Buddha's presentation of

---

[31] Tib. spobs pa.

his knowledge is inconceivable: his abilities of speech are miraculous and beyond the reach of ordinary being's spoken abilities. For example, with one instance of speech he can answer the questions of countless numbers of beings, with each answer appearing to each listener in a language that the listener understands, and in a way that the listener can comprehend.

His speech is complete purity is connected with enlightened speech. The Buddha has removed all impurities from his being. Because of this, the special name "complete purity" is given to the various aspects of his being. In this case, it is applied to his speech. Thus, this epithet conveys the understanding that the Buddha's speech has passed beyond the sort of speech had by ordinary beings.

The speech of an ordinary being and a buddha are two, very different processes. The speech of ordinary beings comes from deluded mind which is impure whereas the speech of a buddha comes from wisdom which is complete purity. On the one hand, the speech of a buddha is a complete purity that has none of the faults that occur with the impure speech of ordinary beings. On the other, it has all of the amazing qualities that go with something produced from wisdom. For example, when a buddha speaks, it might seem to each person listening that it is the speech of a clear-minded and well-spoken but ordinary person. However, if the people involved were to discuss it later, they would find that each person had heard what he needed to hear, in his own language.

Moreover, the way that a Buddha's enlightened speech is intoned has many features. In the Great Vehicle, it is explained as having six root characteristics, each having ten specific aspects, making a total of sixty aspects of intonation all together. For this reason it is exceptionally pleasing to hear. Therefore, *his melody is pleasing*.

The next two epithets concern the way his enlightened body manifests for the sake of others. Not only is his voice pleasing to hear but, as described earlier, his form is pleasing to see. Everything about his body is perfect and his skin has a wonderful glow to it. No matter how much a person views it, the person will not be able to get enough of looking at it. Therefore, *one never has enough of viewing the image of his body*. Note that in normal English one would more likely say "one never has enough of viewing his form" or, even more colloquially, "Oh, I just can't get enough of seeing him". However, for the sake of properly representing the *Sutra*, this epithet has been translated literally. Following on from that epithet, another feature of his body is that in the experience of other beings, no-one else in the world has a bodily form like his, therefore, in their eyes *his body is unparalleled*.

That completes the section on the Buddha's good qualities in terms of fulfilling the aims of others. The remaining good qualities of the Buddha concern his abandonment of samsara and realization of the wisdom of nirvana as a matter of fulfilling his own aims.

He is not contaminated by the things of desire. He is very much not contaminated by the things of form. He is not mixed with the things of formlessness. These three epithets indicate that the Buddha has transcended a samsaric style of being so that, even when he manifests in samsara for the sake of beings, he remains unaffected by it.

Samsara as a whole consists of three planes of existence. The coarsest one, and hence the lowest and first mentioned, is the desire realm. It includes six major places of existence: the abodes of hell-beings, pretas, animals, humans, asuras, and gods of the desire-realm. A more subtle plane of existence, and hence the next one mentioned, is the form realm. It contains many abodes of god-like beings in four main strata. The most subtle plane of existence, and hence the last one mentioned, is the formless realm. It includes many abodes of beings who have a mental existence only and who live in four main strata; these beings are at the peak of samsaric existence.

Each plane of existence has specific delusions, and hence specific afflictions, associated with it. The Buddha lived, went to, and taught within the various places of the desire realm but his being was not contaminated by the things—meaning the afflictions—specific to the desire realm. Similarly, he fully experienced the various mental absorptions that constitute all of the various places of the form realm and was involved with them, but was not contaminated by the things of that realm. The various things of the form realm are more subtle than those of the desire realm so the *Sutra* does not say that he was not contaminated by them but says that he was very much, meaning not even faintly, contaminated by them. The wording for the formless realm is different again. He participated in the desire and form realms but did not participate at all in the formless realm. Therefore, the epithet for the formless realm says that he was not even mixed with it, meaning that he was completely uninvolved with it. All in all, his wisdom mind remains unaffected by any and every type of samsaric mind; it is beyond samsaric possibilities altogether.

The next four epithets show how the Buddha is beyond becoming.

Overall, *he is completely liberated from the sufferings*. Because the Buddha has transcended all samsaric existence, he has passed beyond all the unsatisfactoriness associated with that type of existence. When the Buddha talked about the nature of samsaric existence, he said that it was unsatisfactory. He used the term "duḥkha", which includes actual suffering but means much more than that. Duḥkha is one of a pair of terms, the other being "sukha", which is usually translated as, but does not only mean, bliss. The real meaning of duḥkha is "everything on the side of bad"—not good, uncomfortable, unpleasant, not nice, and so on. Thus, it means "unsatisfactory in every possible way". Note that its opposite, sukha, means "everything on the side of good"—not bad, comfortable, pleasant, nice, and so on. Therefore, that he is completely liberated from the sufferings actually means that he has completely liberated himself from the unsatisfactoriness of samsara, which includes all types of suffering and happiness, too.

The next several epithets show how he is completely liberated from samsaric suffering.

He is utterly completely-liberated from the skandhas. He does not possess dhātus. His āyatanas are restrained. "Completely-liberated" is a standard phrase in Buddhist philosophy with a specific meaning. Thus, it is possible that he could be partially completely-liberated, but he is not, he is utterly completely liberated.

Clear descriptions of the psycho-physical makeup and the perceptual process of beings living in samsara were an important part of the Buddha's early teaching. The skandhas, dhātus, āyatanas are the fundaments of those descriptions. The skandhas or aggregates are the basic building blocks that make up a samsaric being. That makeup houses a samsaric perceptual process that consists of three main things: dhātus or bases, āyatanas or igniters, and deluded consciousnesses that result from those two.

The first epithet in this group points out that the Buddha has completely and utterly gone beyond the psycho-physical makeup of a samsaric being. The second and third epithets point out that he does not have the perceptual process of a samsaric being: firstly, he does not have the dhātus, the bases, required for samsaric perceptions; and secondly, he does have the āyatanas, the igniters, needed to produce samsaric perceptions because, having completely abandoned dualistic mind, he has constrained the igniters into a wisdom context.

"Dhātu" is a Sanskrit word with many meanings. Here it refers to those parts of samsaric being which act as bases for the process of samsaric perception. The Buddha taught the dhātus in order to expose the bases of samsaric perceptions and hence the root causes of samsaric existence. There are eighteen dhātus in three sets of six: the objects of the eye, ear, nose, tongue, body, and mind sense faculties; the faculties that sense them; and the consciousnesses generated by the six faculties. (Note that the sense faculties are not the gross physical organs such as the eyeball but are the subtle things within those organs which empower them, enabling them to give rise to consciousness.) Thus, to say that the Buddha *does not possess dhātus* means that his buddha type of existence does not have any of the bases that would produce a samsaric type of being with a samsaric type of perception.

There are twelve āyatanas or igniters. They are the six sense objects and the six sense faculties. When they connect, samsaric consciousness is ignited and the burning house of samsara appears. The twelve are the same as the first twelve dhātus listed above but the Buddha put them into a group separately from the dhātus specifically to identify them as the things that ignite samsaric consciousness and are thereby a crucial part of the evolution of samsaric existence. The subject of āyatanas is very profound and was taught in the sutras and in the tantras as well. In the sutra approach, the āyatanas are explained as part of the problem; in the tantric approach they are explained as part of the solution. Simply eliminating them would result in a kind of non-existence that would be useless to others. Therefore, the possibility is taught of not eliminating them but restraining them from a samsaric style of being into a non-samsaric one. Thus, *his āyatanas are restrained* means that he is not like samsaric beings whose āyatanas run rampant within dualistic mind and result in suffering now and later, but that he has attained wisdom and constrained his āyatanas into that wisdom context and so is free of suffering.

In short, the Buddha has attained wisdom so has liberated himself from a samsaric style of being with its aggregates, bases, and igniters.

The next four epithets show how he has gone beyond the causes of suffering because of having removed the source of suffering.

He has totally cut the knots. He is completely liberated from the torments. He is liberated from craving. He has crossed over the river. The Buddha abides in wisdom. These four epithets show the abandonment aspect of his attainment of wisdom. The four epithets following them show the realization aspect. The first four go together in this way:

> Because he has cut what are the knots, he is liberated from craving. Because he has liberated himself from torment, he has crossed over the river.

The Buddha used the words knots and torment as general names for the afflictions. The Buddha taught that knots happen when samsaric consciousness meets with an object it desires and that torment happens when samsaric consciousness meets with an object it does not want.

Craving was highlighted by the Buddha as a principal cause of samsara. It is the key point in the twelve links of interdependent origination that propels being into further existence within samsara. As Lord Tsongkhapa says in the interdependent origination section of his *Great Stages of the Path to Enlightenment,*

> Craving selects, nourishes, and gives power to a particular karmic seed so that it is selected as the cause

of a future birth and given the power needed to produce that birth.

When the knots have been cut, craving in particular, which is the root of the whole of samsara, is removed. The tormenting afflictions are like a strong river whose current helplessly carries being away, preventing them from escaping from the river of samsara. When the torments are removed, beings cross over this river and reach enlightenment. The Buddha, having cut the knots and liberated himself from the torments, has become completely liberated from craving and completely liberated from the river of samsara.

The remaining epithets of the recollection of the buddha show the realization aspect of his attainment of wisdom.

Having left behind the dualistic mind of samsara as described above, the Buddha has returned to his original state, wisdom. Wisdom is classified in various ways—two, five, and so on—for the sake of explaining the Buddha's qualities to followers but, no matter how it is classified, the Buddha has all of the aspects enumerated and has all of them totally complete, which is what is meant by saying that *his wisdom is totally complete.*

Wisdom is a term used in Buddhism and other Indian religions, too, to indicate the most basic quality of knowing that there is. In that sense, the wisdom of all buddhas is the same thing. Therefore, the *Sutra* says *he abides in the wisdom of the buddha bhagavats who arise in the past, present, and future.* Note that this is not saying that all buddhas have one, universal consciousness. It is saying that the Buddha resides in that wisdom which is the same wisdom that all of the buddhas have attained and all of the buddhas-to-be are attaining or will attain.

What is the quality of that wisdom? It is described here in two ways. First, *he does not abide in nirvana* is a way of pointing out that his wisdom is at the highest level. He has transcended samsara and hence has wisdom rather than a dualistic mind. Moreover, he has also transcended the lesser wisdom of the arhats who abide in a nirvana to which they are attached. Thus, the Buddha has not only transcended the trap of samsara but has also passed beyond the trap of abiding in the Lesser Vehicle nirvana.

Second, if the Buddha does not abide in either of the two extremes of samsara and nirvana, then where does he abide? The *Sutra* says that *he abides in the limit of the authentic itself*. "Limit of the authentic" is a Sanskrit phrase. "Limit" is the same word as "extreme" just used in the last paragraph. He does not abide in the extremes of samsara or nirvana but does abide in the extreme, so to speak, of having entered ultimate reality, which is also known as "the authentic". Here you could understand "limit" as "final point". Ultimate reality is not an extreme in the sense of a place where you are stuck but is the limit, the final point, that is possible.

What does he do there? *He abides on the level of looking upon all sentient beings.* There are two points here. First, Buddha's knowing is non-dual wisdom, not the dualistic consciousness of sentient beings, and operates in a way that is fundamentally different from consciousness. Thus, the Buddha does not know all phenomena in the way that ordinary beings know many things, instead, he knows everything, all at once—and that is the quality which is being referred to here. It is precisely because the Buddha is completely free of skandhas, dhātus, and āyatanas and has left behind craving and torment that his buddha nature is thoroughly manifest. Dwelling in that state of wisdom, he knows all phenomena, including all sentient beings, effortlessly and spontaneously.

Second, the wisdom of a truly complete buddha is focussed not on one or a few or even many sentient beings but constantly has every single sentient being as its reference. This is the bodhichitta or enlightenment mind of a buddha, a mind which does not merely have an aspiration to benefit all beings but is actually cognizant of every being and actively engaged in doing whatever could be done for all of those beings in every given moment. Such is the power of a buddha.

That brings us to the conclusion of this recollection of the buddha, which says that *these are the true qualities of the greatness of the body of the buddha bhagavat*. Tāranātha's edition of the *Sutra* reads exactly the same, Mipham's edition of the *Sutra* reads the same except for saying "buddha bhagavats", and the extended recollection of the Buddha found in the Derge edition of the *Translated Treatises* has instead "These are the true qualities of the greatness of the tathāgata's wisdom" with essentially the same meaning.

This epithet is concluding by saying that the qualities mentioned really are the qualities of a buddha; it conveys the sense: "all of these claims are not mere posturing; it is really is like this".

The word "body" in the conclusion translates the Tibetan word "sku" which is the honorific form for body, translating the Sanskrit word "kāya". This use of "kāya" causes confusion for some people because it usually means the form body of a buddha. However, the Sanskrit word "kāya" actually means "an assemblage" with the sense of body coming after that. Here the meaning of assemblage comes down to meaning the being as a whole of the Buddha. Therefore, this could be translated as, "Truly, these are the true qualities of the greatness that is the being of the buddha bhagavat". Again, for the sake of representing what the *Sutra* actually says, a literal translation has been used.

2. The Recollection of the Good Qualities of the Dharma

This recollection has two parts: a summary and longer exposition.

The summary consists of what are called the three goodnesses, the two excellences, and the four ways of purity.

The holy dharma is good in the beginning, good in the middle, and good at the end sums up the good qualities of dharma. Some years after the Buddha started teaching the dharma, word of the teaching had spread across India and there was a demand for the teaching that the Buddha could not personally fulfill. By that time, there were a number of monks in his community who knew the teaching and had realized it. He sent them off with the injunction to spread the word of the Buddha and famously reminded them that the dharma was: "Good in the beginning, good in the middle, and good in the end". The Buddha's statement is true in general: the actual dharma has no blemish or obscuration anywhere; it is reality itself or teaching that accords with reality. Thus, it is always good. However, there are other ways to understand the meaning of good in the beginning, middle, and end.

Traditionally, good in the beginning, middle, and end are equated with hearing, contemplating, and cultivating. In a more practical way these three qualities mean that dharma is good all the way through the initial step of hearing it, the intermediary step of practising it, and the final step of realizing it. In other words, the Buddha's dharma is good from the day it is first heard all the way through to the time that it is fully realized. The vidyadhara Chogyam Trungpa commented on this in his own unique way, saying that, even though the dharma is always perfect, practitioners have a tendency to gloss over parts of it or their practice of it as being less meaningful, not meaningful, and so on. He explained that these words should remind practitioners that the practice of dharma is "on" all the time and that every bit of it is good and is meaningful. When a practitioner understands this point of dharma, it tends to bring a lot of brilliance into his life because his whole life is seen as non-stop goodness.

Now this dharma which is always good has two features of excellence. Firstly, the teaching of the Buddha's dharma deals only with what is real and how to get to that reality. In doing so, it leaves aside all teaching on subjects that are of little real meaning and concerns itself only with the very meaningful subject of removing the ignorance of sentient beings. Therefore *its meaning is* always and only ever *excellent*. Secondly, the wording of the teaching is always good; it has no bad expression, poor composition, unnecessary wording, or any of the other faults of poor composition. Two features of good composition are that the composition says just what needs to be said for, and in words that can be understood by, the person who receives it. These features are very evident in the teachings of dharma given by the Buddha; on reading his words, one gets the sense of just how well chosen and arranged they are. Thus, *its wording is excellent*.

Next, this dharma has four specific qualities known as "the four brahmacharyas". In Indian language, there are two, similar words: "Brahmā" meaning "Pure One" is the name of the god Brahmā, and "brahma" is the word meaning "pure" in general. "Charya" means way of behaviour so "brahmacharya" means "the pure way of behaviour". The Buddha's dharma can be seen to have four ways of being utterly pure so these were called "the four brahmacharyas" or "four ways of purity". The next four epithets are these four ways of purity.

The first way of purity is that *it is not adulterated*. Parts of the Buddha's teaching—for example the teaching on impermanence—

are similar to teachings found in other religions. However, unlike the teachings of other religions, the Buddha's teaching is given by someone who views reality and gives the teaching only out of love and compassion for the sake of bringing others to that reality. This means that the Buddha's teaching is uncommon compared to the others and is not adulterated with lesser or mistaken teachings. The literal wording of this epithet is that the Buddha's dharma "is not mixed up with anything", meaning that it is quite distinct from the other, more common types of teaching and does not have their lesser kind of teaching mixed in with it. In accord with the ultimate purity that it comes from, the Buddha's teaching of dharma has no impurity mixed in with it.

The second purity is that it *is totally complete*. The Buddha's dharma is like medicine for the disease of the afflictions. However, it is not a partial cure for just one affliction or another. It is a complete cure, one that deals with the entirety of afflictions that appear throughout the three realms of samsaric existence.

The third purity is that it *is total purity*. No dharma in the entire dharmadhātu—no phenomenon in the entire range of phenomena —has ever had any samsaric impurity within its nature because all phenomena have a nature of complete purity to begin with. The Buddha's teaching of dharma is shown for the purpose of bringing the complete purity that is the nature of all phenomena to the attention of sentient beings. Thus, this epithet means that the dharma taught conventionally is representative of the pre-existing purity that is the ground state of reality.

The fourth purity, that it *is total purification*, is connected to the third purity. Because the ground state of reality is total purity, the path of dharma can be applied to purify any sentient being and be successful. The Buddha explained that sentient beings are in "total affliction", which is equivalent to saying that they are in a situation of total impurity. He explained that, if they follow the path of the Buddha's dharma, the impurity of the afflictions will be removed. When the work of purification is complete, they will have left behind total affliction and arrived at what the Buddha called "total purification". Total purification here specifically refers to the result of having become purified after doing the work of purification. Thus, the dharma teaching has the power to take one to the total purity mentioned as this fourth good quality.

The summary section of the three goodnesses, two excellences, and four purities is complete. Now the longer exposition of the good qualities of the dharma begins. It has its own summary and exposition.

The summary is the sentence *the bhagavat has taught dharma well*. This epithet arose in ancient India and specifically referred to the fact that the dharma taught by the Buddha was taught properly whereas that taught by other religious leaders of his time was not. Therefore, it was said that the dharma taught by him was good dharma because of being well-taught with the implication that the dharma taught by other teachers was not. This epithet focusses on the issue of the how the dharma was explained. The Buddha explained dharma in a good way because the Buddha always taught in accord with reality and in accord with the needs and dispositions of the audience; other teachers did not and their dharma was regarded as inferior because of it.

The longer exposition begins here and continues to the end of the recollection of dharma. It shows dharma firstly from the perspective that it is free of faults and secondly from the perspective that it possesses good qualities.

First, there is a set of three epithets starting with "It is authentic sight". These show the ways in which the dharma taught by the bhagavat Buddha is good dharma.

The first of the three epithets has two different readings. The editions of the *Sutra* used for this book and by Mipham for his commentary say here that the dharma *is authentic sight*. This differs from the extended recollection of the dharma found in the Derge edition of the *Translated Treatises* and also from the *Sutra* used by Tāranātha for his commentary, both of which say that "it is authentic teaching". Despite the difference, the explanation is essentially the same.

The explanation of its being authentic sight is that Buddha himself, having unmistakenly seen the situation of phenomena, taught the meaning accordingly. Therefore, beings who rely on that dharma to tame themselves will be able, unmistakenly, to see reality. Thus, the Buddha's dharma is a case of correct vision in operation. In other words, the buddha has correct vision, so he teaches the dharma accordingly, and that means that sentient beings who rely on that teaching also have the ability to gain correct vision; it is a case of correct vision throughout. The explanation for "it is authentic teaching" is that the Buddha saw the authentic—reality —so whatever he taught always was correct.

It is free from sickness. Sickness is a manifestation of affliction. This dharma which removes afflictions and their latencies is never defiled with affliction.

Its time has no interruption. This is a way of talking that comes from ancient India which has been translated literally in order to retain the wording of the *Sutra*. It is the equivalent of saying, "dharma is always fully on and available; it never lessens or stops". The dharma is this way because reality is always present and never ceases and the dharma teaching is nothing other than an expression of that reality. One English translation gives this epithet as "it is always timely", which gives the impression that dharma teachings have a knack of coming on time, and the like. Dharma is connected with that magical quality of auspicious coincidence, it is true, but it is not the meaning of this epithet. This epithet is saying that the Buddha's dharma is always in effect, that there is never a break in the continuity of its being effective.

Gampopa continually pointed out to his great yogin disciples such as the first Karmapa, Dusum Khyenpa, in his replies to their questions, that one of the qualities of Mahāmudrā is that it is "on at all times". What he was talking about and what is being said here are the same.

Whereas the preceding three epithets showed that the dharma is free of faults, the next three show that it possesses good qualities.

It brings one in. The dharma, which represents the final blissful state in which samsara with all of its problems has been left behind, serves to take hold of the mindstream and bring it in closer and closer to that state. Finally, it brings the mind right into the state of final ease and bliss. This epithet comes from the original recollection of dharma taught by the Buddha. It consists of the single Sanskrit phrase "upanāyika" used in Hindu culture to refer to the specific situation in which a Hindu guru takes a young man, draws him right up to him, then empowers him into liberation, which the guru himself represents. Here, it means that the dharma takes you by the shoulders, guides you in from the various states of samsaric existence, and finally does the final work of bringing you into the final state of emancipation. Tāranātha and Mipham each give a useful analysis and there is an extensive explanation of the translation issues involved on page 39.

This is meaningful to see. This epithet comes from the original recollection of dharma taught by the Buddha. It is the Sanskrit phrase "ehipaśhyikaḥ" literally meaning "Come here and look at this!" but conveying the sense "This is really something worthwhile looking at, so come and have a look!" The literal translation into Tibetan also comes as "Come here and look at this!" but the further sense contained in the Sanskrit disappears. Therefore, Tibetan translations usually do not use a literal translation; instead, they give the implied meaning using the words, "This is meaningful to see".

Tāranātha and Mipham both explain this point. They say that ehipashyikaḥ is implicative in meaning so, for Tibetans, it is better to translate it by bringing out the implication. However, for English, I suspect that it might be best to revert to the original wording in this case and say, "This is to be seen!" which captures the original meaning properly in English. This is something to consider in future.

There are several ways to explain why we should go and have a look at this. Tāranātha and Mipham each give their own explanation. Essentially speaking, the Buddha's dharma is worth looking at because it is the one thing that holds the promise of total release from samsara—it is an awesome thing to behold when you realize the fullness of what it is.

It is known to experts through personal self-knowing. This dharma is extremely profound, one whose reality cannot be directly known by the ordinary, rational mind of people in the samsaric world. No matter how clever that sort of rational mind might be, it will never be able to see the reality that the words of the dharma point at. That reality can only be seen by those who have become spiritually superior—the noble ones—because they are the ones who have become expert at seeing reality in direct perception through personal self-knowing.

"Personal self-knowing" normally needs a lot of explanation but, basically, it means that kind of mind which is not looking outwards at phenomena but looking inwards at its own nature. The dualistic, rational mind of ordinary sentient beings only looks out at phenomena which seem to be over there away from itself. Personal self-knowing does not look outwards like that but looks inwards and knows itself. In doing so, it sees all phenomena individually and just exactly as they are, without dualising and making them into something concretely separate from itself. This personal self-knowing is wisdom. Specifically, it is the aspect of wisdom that a practitioner uses on the path to see emptiness directly and thus exit samsara. Therefore it is something that the practitioner has for himself. Self-knowing is a personal matter; it is something that each person individually has and uses to see reality for himself.

The next good quality explained is that the Buddha's dharma in all its forms is an utterly trustworthy teaching that leads to enlightenment. Again, there is a summary followed by a longer exposition.

The dharma spoken by the bhagavat was well taught for taming. This epithet is the most difficult of all the epithets in the *Sutra* to translate into English because of two problems with the Tibetan wording. First, the wordings of the epithet differ between editions of the *Sutra*. Second, there is an ambiguity in one of the words that cannot be resolved. These will also be problems when translating into other languages.

A lesser problem is that Mipham's edition of the *Sutra* has the verb at the end of the phrase as བརྟེན་པ་ "brten pa", which is the past of the verb རྟེན་པ་ "rten pa". It literally means "becomes a reliance", though in context means "serves as", which results in "The dharma spoken by the bhagavat serves well for taming". Every other edition of the *Sutra* I have seen has the verb as སྟོན་པ་ "ston pa", the present tense of the verb "to show" or "to teach", which results in "The dharma spoken by the bhagavat was well taught for taming".

The best way to resolve this problem would be to look at the original recollection and see what it says. However, this epithet is not in the original recollections; it is one of the extensions made

by Great Vehicle followers, as discussed in chapter one. Therefore, there is no way to determine absolutely which of the two
readings it should be. Nevertheless, the circumstantial evidence
points very strongly to Mipham's edition being one that was deliberately changed over the intended reading: firstly, the extended
recollection of dharma translated from Sanskrit into Tibetan and
incorporated into the *Translated Treatises* has the reading བསྟན་པ་
"bstan pa", the past tense of སྟོན་པ་ "ston pa". Secondly, all of the
many editions of the *Sutra* that I was able to find other than the
one in Mipham's commentary also have the reading "ston pa".

Why would someone change the wording? To understand the
possibility of change, one has to understand that, in Tibetan Buddhist tradition, whenever a text was copied or a new edition was to
be made, the original text was usually "corrected" beforehand.
Learned and not-so-learned people would do the work, often
changing the text in the process. Then, to understand the probability of change, one has to look at the epithets that follow this one
in which the issue of reliance is raised. If the wording of this
epithet as seen here is changed to the reading seen in Mipham's
commentary, a very interesting thread of meaning is established in
the section of recollections headed by this epithet. After years of
experience with Tibetans correcting Tibetan texts, I can see immediately that this would be a tempting change for someone doing
the work of correction. The conclusion is that there is a good
probability that a learned person would make this change.

Indeed, we find that Mipham, having given his general explanation
of the meaning of this epithet, goes on to note that other editions
have the reading "ston pa" and not the reading of "brten pa" found
in his edition. Thus, Mipham is aware of the difference and does
not reject the reading of his text as a mistake. He continues by
pointing out that there was a Tibetan stream of oral explanation
of the *Sutra* in which the reading "brten pa" was connected with
the later epithet in this section concerning reliability and reliance.

My conclusion is that a learned person in Tibet, a person un-known to us, saw a way to explain this section of the *Sutra* in a way that was more consistent with what he thought was the original intent of the recollections and made this change.

The second problem is actually an unsurmountable problem when translating into English, at least. The problem is that the Tibetan term འདུལ་བ་ " 'dul ba"—which is behind what is translated above as "taming"—is the same word as "Vinaya", the name of the section of the Buddha's discourses that deals with the code of discipline of personal emancipation. This ambiguity leads to a second possible translation of the epithet as "The dharma spoken by the bhagavat was well taught in the Vinaya".

As mentioned above, this epithet was not included in the original recollection, so the only way to resolve this second problem is to see how the epithet is explained by Tibetan oral tradition. Read-ing Mipham's commentary, we find that he explains it according to the meaning taming. However, he notes that there is a stream of explanation in which it is taken to mean Vinaya. He ends by saying that more research has to be done to try to determine the correct reading for and explanation of this epithet.

I followed Mipham's suggestion and researched the matter exten-sively. Turning first to the oral instructions I had already received on the text, I saw that Khenchen Padma Tshewang explained it as taming and the vidyadhara Chogyam Trungpa explained it as Vinaya. Their teachings are important because they were amongst the very top people of their generation, and received their training in Tibet before the calamity in 1959. This proved Mipham's claim that both streams of explanation did exist. Having heard the vidyadhara Chogyam Trungpa's explanation, I understood that the explanation of the term as Vinaya was a far-reaching explanation that set the whole tone of all three recollections as a one vehicle teaching with strong emphasis on the disciplines of personal emancipation.

Next, I went to a number of senior khenpos and asked for their explanation. They were unanimous in explaining it as taming and not one had heard the explanation in which it becomes Vinaya. From this, I understood that one of the effects of the Great Vehicle extensions to the original recollections was to include the understanding that Buddha taught dharma in four turnings of the wheel (the last being tantra) and to make a point that it was done as a particularly skilful way of presenting the teachings for taming all levels of beings. It seems that the alternative way of explaining it using "Vinaya" was not the intent of the people who produced the Great Vehicle extensions. Their intent was to emphasize a point which is an underpinning of Great Vehicle understanding of dharma, the presentation of the dharma through multiple turnings of the wheel for the sake of skilfully taming beings. The alternative explanation based on the understanding "Vinaya" removes that point from the *Sutra*. It also turns this epithet and the rest in the section it heads towards meaning that the dharma teaching that was most important for the śhrāvakas—the teaching of the Vinaya—is a complete teaching for travelling to enlightenment.

The conclusion is that both streams of explanation exist. However, the primary understanding is that the epithet says that "The dharma spoken by the bhagavat was well taught for taming". The hard-to-accept fact is that there is no way to make a translation in English to accommodate both meanings of taming and Vinaya at the one time (unless "Taming" were settled on as a translation of Vinaya but that has not happened yet).

Now, we continue to the explanation of this epithet. The explanations that correspond to this epithet being understood through both taming and Vinaya are presented.

The explanation of this epithet as "the dharma was well-taught in the Vinaya" is like this. After the Buddha passed away, his followers decided to commit all the teachings they had heard to writing. Initial discussions were held in order to settle on a system of categorizing the teachings. A three-basket system was settled on. The first basket was to consist of all the teachings that were concerned with the disciplines of personal liberation. This section was given the name Vinaya meaning "that which tames" because the teachings on discipline have the effect of taming or controlling body, speech, and mind. The Vinaya consists of all teachings concerned with the disciplines of personal emancipation and is taken up largely with teachings concerning monastic life. Some people think that this kind of teaching, because it is about rules and regulations, does not contain the profound depths of dharma. That is not the case because the teachings of the Lesser Vehicle, such as the Vinaya, were taught by the Buddha himself, and they were given from the wisdom of the Buddha that partakes of the space of ultimate reality. In other words, the full meaning of the dharma is the basis from which the Vinaya teachings came, so those teachings are teachings of the fullness of that meaning. The Vinaya does fully embody the teaching of the Buddha. Therefore, it does do the work not only of taming the mind at the lower level but also of leading to complete emancipation.

It is noteworthy that the vidyadhara Chogyam Trungpa chose the meaning with the explanation just given as the appropriate one for his large community of tantrikas. He taught them this way in order to impress on them the need for the personal discipline of the Lesser Vehicle teaching despite the crazy wisdom style teaching that he was training them in. In regard to that, it is striking that the next two epithets of dharma mentioned in the *Sutra* are "it is renunciation" and "leads to perfect enlightenment". This fits very well with the sense of dharma being the Vinaya, because the very essence of the Vinaya is renunciation and that renunciation does lead to enlightenment. The vidyadhara was pointing out to his students that the personal discipline of the Vinaya was important for tantrikas and that there is no contradiction between practising that and practising the higher tantras. In fact, a further epithet says that this dharma "is without disharmony and it has inclusion" which then means that a lay tantrika can incorporate the personal discipline into his life because the Vinaya is perfectly consistent with the ultimate dharma of the tantras. The Vinaya does embody the profound meaning of dharma and does lead to enlightenment. Most Western Buddhists who follow the Great Vehicle teaching follow a lay tantrika style of life and practice. This teaching of the vidyadhara's was given specifically for them so I have gone to some length not to lose it by passing it off as a lesser stream of explanation of this epithet but to give it the place it deserves.

When this epithet is explained according to the central idea being taming, it can be seen to follow on from the immediately preceding epithet. That epithet presents dharma as the dharma of realization. This epithet says that dharma is also the dharma of authoritative statement, the conventional dharma taught so that beings can arrive at the dharma of realization. The dharma of authoritative statement that the Buddha spoke was taught in a way that made it ideal for taming, that is, made it ideal for taming the mind so that the dharma of realization could be seen. All explanations of this epithet point out that the Buddha skilfully taught the conventional dharma by showing it in three, progressively more profound sutra turnings of the wheel, followed by a fourth step of ultimate teaching, the tantra turning of the wheel. Mipham has a nice explanation of this and Khyenrab Wangchuk, a former abbot of Dzongsar Shedra in India, gives this same sort of explanation following Mipham's commentary when he says,

> Every one of the dharmas in their provisional and
> definitive variety that were taught by the Buddha were,
> from his individual knowledge of the specific elements,

faculties, and thoughts of those to be tamed, taught as taming antidotes with whatever patience was needed, starting with coarse, then subtle, then very subtle ones, and then dharmas of ultimate meaning. All of those dharmas he taught, turning as they do into antidotes for the afflictions of the mindstreams of those to be tamed, will serve very well as causes for temporary and ultimate enlightenment. Therefore, it says, "The dharma spoken by the Buddha serves well for taming".

What is the essential quality of this conventional dharma the Buddha taught for the purpose of taming and which he also taught in the Vinaya? *It is renunciation.* And what does that do? *It causes one to go to complete enlightenment.* "Renunciation" translates a Sanskrit word that means to have turned towards and committed oneself to a process that is good and reliable. In other words, it refers to the positive step that we take after first being revolted by, and then renouncing, samsara. We do have to become revolted by samsara first; as it says in the *Short Great Vajradhara Prayer* of the Karma Kagyu, "Revulsion is the foot of meditation as is taught". That revulsion leads to renunciation, which is turning away from something. However, there is still a third step, which is that you now set off towards something that is good and worthwhile. Unfortunately, we do not have a good word for this third step in English so we always end up using the second word in the three-step process to refer to the third step. The tone of the Buddha's explanations was never the slightly negative connotation of renunciation, but the much more positive sense of being committed to that which really is worthwhile. Doing that is what causes us to arrive at the truly complete enlightenment of a buddha.

This kind of dharma, whose essential quality is renunciation and abandonment, is not contradictory to the path of enlightenment as expressed in the higher teachings of the Great Vehicle. The teachings as a whole were taught for sentient beings of varying capacities and inclinations and, though some might show the meaning of profound reality more explicitly than others, each teaching is still a teaching that comes from the Buddha and which therefore is in accord with reality. In short, there is no inconsistency within the many levels of the teaching, so *it is without disharmony*. *And* not only are all of the teachings consistent but each one contains the meaning of the others because all of them are teachings that come from reality. And not only does each one contain the meaning of the others but all of them can be summed up into just one, all-inclusive point of reality. Therefore, the dharma teaching as a whole is without disharmony yet at the same time *it has inclusion*. In other words, each dharma teaching does contain the seeds of all the others, even if some of them appear to be contradictory on the surface.

It has reliability. A person who becomes president of a country achieves a position of great power. He might think that he will depend on that position to accomplish many things, but the position is not reliable by any means—unexpected developments could end it the next day. The dharma is not like that. Firstly, as long as a practitioner does not let go of the dharma, it will always be totally reliable, without any loss of capability or sudden change in its capability to be so. Secondly, it will not change course after the practitioner has started to rely on it and veer off into being a different kind of reliance, so it always stays suitable for the purpose that it was originally relied upon. Thus, if it is taken up as a reliance, it can be depended on to be constantly supportive and always on course. Therefore, the Buddha's dharma is thoroughly reliable. More than that though, it is the dharma that was spoken by the Buddha after he himself attained full comprehension of the totality of reality, therefore it is not merely reliable but, because of being the Buddha's dharma with all that implies, *it has reliability* of a very special kind.

Someone might accept that the dharma is thoroughly reliable but proceed to think that it will not be a final solution. He would be thinking that it could be relied on but that there would never be an end to having to do so. However, that is not the case. Dharma practice is directed towards a final goal and travelling the dharma path is like taking a journey towards that goal. Once the goal has been reached, it has been reached and there is no more travelling to be done. Buddhahood is called "no more training" or "no more learning" because it is final and there is no more training to be done. It is also called "having laid down the burden" which makes the point that, once buddhahood has been attained, the burden of the activities of the path that was originally taken up is done with and put aside once and for all. At that point, it is not as though there is still some other thing to be done or more of the same still left to go. Therefore, *it does end the journey*.

This epithet reads the same in the editions of the *Sutra* used by Tāranātha and Mipham. The extended recollection found in the Derge edition of the *Translated Treatises* differs; it says, "It ends the continuity of the path" though the meaning is the same. Mipham has an especially good explanation of this epithet which makes it very clear that the wording shown above connects with the Buddha's way of teaching.

3. The Recollection of the Good Qualities of the Sangha

The sangha of the great vehicle is the beginning of the recollection of the sangha. Sangha here does not refer to the groups of ordinary practitioners who are called sangha but who are not the noble Jewel of refuge. Sangha here means the sangha of noble ones, the ones who have attained direct perception of emptiness.

The original recollection in Pali says "sāvakasangho" meaning the śrāvaka sangha of noble ones of the Lesser Vehicle. The Great Vehicle followers who made an extended version of the recollections deliberately changed that to be inclusive of both Lesser and Greater Vehicle sanghas. The Tibetan translation of the extended recollection found in the Derge *Translated Treatises* gives it as "the sangha of noble ones". The *Sutra* in all editions that I have seen has it as "the sangha of the great vehicle".

"The sangha of the great vehicle" here could refer to the sangha of the Great Vehicle as opposed to the Lesser Vehicle, and Tāranātha does explain it that way. He says that this really is a Great Vehicle sutra, not a Lesser Vehicle one. Mipham on the other hand explains that Great Vehicle has to be taken to mean the one vehicle that all Buddhists follow. His explanation fits with the explanation I heard from the vidyadhara Chogyam Trungpa who presented the idea that the *Sutra*, even though it was a Great Vehicle extension, should be understood with the "one vehicle" idea of Buddhism.

Yet another useful way to explain the words "Great Vehicle" here is that the noble ones collectively are at the point where their specific intentions in terms of continuing on to nirvana are great, meaning beyond those of ordinary beings. These beings, having had direct sight of reality, are so convinced of their path that they are described as the ones whose "intentions never falter". These noble beings, unlike the ordinary sangha, have arrived on the great vehicle, the one on which all the travellers have unswerving and great intentions for nirvana.

The recollection of the noble sangha's good qualities has two parts. The first part shows them to have special qualities because of having greatly purified their mindstreams. The second part praises them as a field of these highly developed good qualities which can be a source of benefit for others, just like a good field can give rise to good harvests.

What good qualities have the noble saṅgha developed? Four are given. Again, note that this is not a statement about good qualities that will be developed by the ordinary practitioner as he goes along. Rather, this is a statement of the good qualities that have already been developed by the noble ones, the ones who have become the saṅgha Jewel. (All Buddhist practice can be summed up into the three higher trainings of śhīla, samādhi, and prajñā, that is, of discipline, concentration, and correctly discerning mind. These three are being used as the basis for the following explanation.) Firstly, they *have entered into good* meaning that they have, through the principal training in discipline, entered a situation in which their minds are restrained. Secondly, they *have entered into insight* meaning that they have, through the principal training in concentration, developed one-pointed concentration of mind on the fact of reality. Thirdly, they *have entered into straightness* meaning that they have, through the principal training in prajñā, developed the prajñā of mind that sees the authentic. Fourthly, they *have entered into harmony* meaning that they have entered nirvana in which there is no discordance between the various aspects of the trainings just mentioned—view, discipline, aims of migrators, and so on.

Note that some editions have a misspelling in the second of the four above which makes it "they have entered into the types". The mistake takes the correct Tibetan spelling of རིག "rig" and changes it to the mistaken རིགས "rigs". This is definitely a later spelling problem because the original recollection clearly says "insight", corresponding to the spelling རིག "rig". There are many types of samādhi taught in the vehicles, so the explanation of this epithet comes out almost the same with and without the spelling mistake. It would be easier not to mention this spelling mistake, but Tāranātha's edition of the *Sutra* had this error in it and he gave his commentary on the basis of the mistaken spelling, saying that the saṅgha have engaged the "types" of samādhi. This is not wrong but does not go as far as the meaning based on the correct spelling goes, which is that the saṅgha have engaged (the particular one of the many types of samādhi of) insight into reality.

It is also possible to explain these qualities as qualities of how they engaged in the path as they went to being noble ones. In that case, the translation into English has to change to *"have engaged well, have engaged insightfully, have engaged undiverted, have engaged harmoniously"*. This explanation is based on a sequence of four mistaken ways of being involved with the path that they did not engage. Therefore, the four in this case are making a statement that the noble saṅgha travelled an unmistaken journey on an unmistaken path. Rather than engaging the path in a way in which they were not sure about the path and hence lost it, they engaged the path well, knowing what it was and where it was headed. Then, rather than engaging in the path without intelligence and hence making mistakes about it, they engaged it insightfully. Then, rather than engaging in the path by taking sidetracks here and there, they engaged it by going straight ahead, without diversion. Then, rather than engaging in the path in a way that was confused and led to going forwards sometimes and backwards at others, they engaged it in a way that was consistent, or you could say harmonious, with the path as it should be travelled. In ancient India, it was said that a person who progressed along a path without these four faults was a person who had a very pure sort of mind, and that is one of the good qualities of the noble saṅgha.

These noble beings filled with these excellent qualities become a field of excellence for others and, because of that, are worthy of veneration in general. Veneration in general was done in ancient India, and has been done since then in all Buddhist traditions, by joining the two palms at the heart. Therefore, *they are worthy of joined palms* means that they are worthy of veneration in general.

However, because they are a true refuge, because they are the saṅgha Jewel, they are also worthy of a higher level of respect again. The highest level of veneration in ancient India, and in all Buddhist traditions since then, has been to bend down and prostrate to a person. Thus, because of being a true refuge, *they are*, additionally, *worthy of prostration*.

They are a field of the glory of merit. "Field" means a basis for something to come forth. "Glory" translates an ancient Indian word that means "excellence" or "perfect collection". All together, these excellent qualities that they have developed have made them into a field from which other sentient beings can harvest a wealth of merit.

Because the beings of the noble saṅgha are freed of faults and have an abundance of good qualities, even whole universes could be offered to them and they would not become afflicted because of it. They have, through their training, been fully trained in the receipt of gifts, not merely in the usual sense of learning to be nice about receiving a gift, but also in the deeper sense of keeping a mind that is unaffected by any negative state in regard to the gift, and also in the deepest sense of maintaining the view of no-self while receiving the gift. They have been so well trained in those ways that they are thoroughly capable of receiving any kind of gift, thus *they are great ones thoroughly trained in gifts*.

Finally, there are two epithets which continue on directly from the last and which show that these beings of excellent qualities are supreme places for making gifts and offerings. The first says that *they are a place of generosity*. Because of the qualities that they have developed they are, as mentioned above, an excellent field from which all sorts of excellent harvests can come. Thus, in terms of giving gifts and making offerings, great benefits will arise from making offerings to them. In other words, they are the right kind of person to be generous with because generosity made in relation to them opens many doors as well as accumulating great merit. Therefore, they are indeed a place of generosity. And more than that, *they are* in fact *in all places even a great place for generosity* because in all places throughout all of the worlds there is no other place of generosity comparable to them. All in all, the mindstreams of worldly people are spoiled by afflictions whereas the mindstreams of these noble beings are completely liberated. Therefore, these noble beings are likened to a pure gem.

Why was the good quality of being a place of generosity mentioned instead of any of the many other good qualities possessed by the noble saṅgha? It is because this was a great theme in the Buddha's time. Mipham offers this quote from a sutra, which helps to understand:

> Those humans who are scared with fear
> Mostly take refuge in mountains, forests,
> Parks, and in large trees used as a place of offerings;
> Such refuges are not the principal one and
> Such refuges are not supreme.
> Someone who relies on such a refuge
> Will not be liberated from all suffering.
> Instead, when someone has gone to the buddha,
> The dharma, and the saṅgha for refuge, he will, through
> Suffering, the source of suffering,
> True transcendence of suffering, and
> The pleasant eightfold path of the noble ones
> Go to nirvana. With that,
> The four truths of the noble ones
> With prajñā used to produce the view
> Is his principal refuge;
> By relying on that refuge he will indeed
> Be liberated from all suffering.

It was and still is a part of many non-Buddhist traditions in India and Nepal to make daily worship of deities at the base of large, spreading trees, such as the Bodhi trees that are common in these lands. The trees were regarded as the home of the deities by the local people and the deities were supplicated each morning with offerings of various sorts in order to secure protection. Therefore, Buddha made a point of teaching the ordinary folk that this was the wrong way to seek protection and the wrong place to make offerings. He taught them that the community of spiritually advanced Buddhist practitioners—the saṅgha of noble ones—are a true refuge and taught them that the noble saṅgha is the best place for making offerings because of their excellent qualities in relation to gifts. They are the ones worthy of offerings, they are the ones capable of properly receiving all gifts, and they are a source of great merit when used as a place of offering.

IV. THE COLOPHON

A sutra translated into Tibetan usually has a colophon to indicate the translator and final editor, of the sutra. However, this is not a record of a discourse spoken by the Buddha but a compilation of the useful pieces of the Buddha's teachings, so a colophon is not expected to be present. The Tibetan edition of the *Sutra* used for the translation did not have an ending colophon, though other editions of the liturgy have one, for example, Mipham reports that his text of the *Sutra* says, "The Sutra of the Recollection of the Noble Three Jewels is complete".

Jetsun Tāranātha
Image courtesy of Jonang Foundation.

A LITTLE EXPLANATION OF THE MEANING OF *THE SUTRA OF THE RECOLLECTION OF* THE THREE JEWELS

by Jetsun Tāranātha

OM SVĀSTI

I prostrate to the Buddha, dharma, and saṅgha.

I will give a little explanation of the meaning of the *Sutra of the Recollection of the Three Jewels*.

Recollection as it is used here means to look into the way in which something has good qualities. This recollection, which is the root of positive dharmas in their entirety, is done for the purpose of arousing faith in the supreme objects[32].

The words "faith", "appreciation[33]", and "respect" often are used to refer to aspects of mind that are very different in character. However, they are sometimes used as different names for the same

---

[32] Supreme objects refers to the Three Jewels.

[33] Tib. mos pa. This is a specific state of mind which, having decided that something has desirable qualities, turns towards it and goes after it.

thing[34]. In this text, the three terms are used with basically the same meaning, each one presenting a different shade of that basic meaning.

Faith is of three types: admiring, trusting, and aspiring. The first one is that, having heard here of the good qualities of the Three Jewels, they are understood and believed to be supreme and, moreover, there is a joy of mind with it that is complete in every way, a joy that amounts to being supreme[35].

Then, trusting faith[36] is like this. There is trust that the tathāgata has such and such good qualities, trust that the explanations coming from the dharma of authoritative statement are true in meaning and correct in their wording, and trust that the dharma of realization and the saṅgha too have such and such good qualities[37].

---

[34] Faith, appreciation, and respect are mental events listed in the Abhidharma, with each being presented as distinctly different from the others. In this text the three are used to refer to the same thing, faith, with each one representing a variation on that basic meaning. These variations of meaning are now explained in the text.

[35] Admiring faith is a faith that has two aspects: a very clear idea of the object of faith and a strong joy because of it. The two add up to admiration for the object. This faith is sometimes called lucid faith because of the clarity accompanying it, but that loses the joy aspect.

[36] Trusting faith is generally considered to be the most important of the three types of faith for a practising Buddhist because it is the foundation for taking refuge from one's heart.

[37] The Buddha's dharma is transmitted in two ways: authoritative statement and realization. Authoritative statement is the teaching conveyed in words, both oral and written. The saṅgha is put with the dharma of realization here because it is their realization in direct perception of the actuality pointed to by authoritative statement that
(continued...)

There is trust that the superfactual dharma[38] is the truth of cessation and free of all faults, and that that, which is free of all faults, has all good qualities because that which does not have beneficial features is faulty[39].

Then, for aspiring faith: aspiring and wanting[40] to attain the rank of buddha and saṅgha, wanting to fully absorb the dharma of authoritative statement, wanting to manifest the dharma of the superfactual expanse, and wanting to produce the dharma of realization within the mindstream all are the actual aspiring faith. Those things that must be included with them, such as wanting to make offerings to the Jewels, wanting to broadcast their good qualities, wanting to spread the dharma of authoritative statement, and so on are put with aspiring faith[41]. To take this further, when admiring and trusting faith have been engendered ahead of such activities, those activities are of the faithful kind but, when wanting the things mentioned is joined with offerings, and so on made for

---

[37](...continued)
makes them into the noble saṅgha that can be a true refuge.

[38] The Buddha summed up all of his explanation of dharma into explanations of fictional and superfactual truths. See the glossary for these terms.

[39] The superfactual dharma, the reality that a buddha has realized and abides in, is always without flaw. That is equivalent to having all good qualities and is the one thing that can be true liberation. This point supports the fact that the final accomplishment of buddhahood, which is shortly to be discussed, is the perfect abandonment of all faults or flaws and the perfect realization of all good qualities.

[40] "Aspiring and wanting" refers to aspiring faith, which, is also called wishing or wanting faith.

[41] They are aspiring faith, too, but they are not the actual aspiring faith, they are merely bits and pieces related to it.

profit, fame, or competitive purposes, that is merely aspiration for the things mentioned, not faith in connection with them.

"Appreciation" in general means to see certain qualities in something that does have those qualities. Here, it specifically means to know that something which has good qualities and is not deceptive does have good qualities and is not deceptive[42]. For the most part it is trusting faith, though the Abhidharma also says that it is, "joy, respect, and wonder" and these do indeed accompany it. Here, "respect" means holding up the object as special, so it is mostly contained within admiring faith. Note that the Abhidharma explains a type of trusting faith, which it calls "respect for the trainings", and mentions "respectful application" in relation to it, which it explains as a "strong perseverance", but this subject does not apply here[43].

Someone who has a very complete type of faith in the Three Jewels will take up going for refuge, take on the vows of individual emancipation, and also will arouse the enlightenment mind. That person will then engage in the three principal trainings and the pāramitās. Thus, the root of all paths is faith and that in turn only

---

[42] Appreciation is a type of faith that inclines the mind toward something because it has been convinced of its usefulness. One has this faith in relation to the Three Jewels because of being sure that they have the two features of having good qualities and not being deceptive.

[43] The Abhidharma explains that a vessel is a person to whom it is suitable to give the teaching because he will respect and pursue the trainings involved. A vessel will have two kinds of application, of which "respectful application" is explained as strong perseverance. This subject of the Abhidharma is not what is being discussed here.

comes about through recollecting the Three Jewels. The recollection is initially done in relation to the Buddha.[44]

1. Sūtra of the Recollection of the Buddha

The recollection starts with the words *Thus it is: the bhagavat*[45]. The first nine phrases in this recollection are a summation, one which is common to and known to all in the Lesser and Great Vehicles. *"Thus it is: "* is to the effect "All of the good qualities to be explained are like this: " and those good qualities are then given in nine topics, topics which the *Summary* gives in these words:

> Having defeated obstructors; perfections of
> Explanation, abandonment, and wisdom;
> The cause; how he went;
> Looking at the world; taming fortunate ones;
> And that teacher having nine good qualities
> Who is the basis in whom they are present.[46]

---

[44] Having a complete faith with all the aspects just discussed becomes the starting point for both entering and progressing through all levels of the Buddha's path, so Tāranātha has just laid out both in relation to the Great Vehicle. The technique for creating that kind of faith is the recollection of the good qualities of the Three Jewels, starting with the Buddha Jewel.

[45] When the text of the *Sutra* is cited in the commentary, it is set off from the commentary by showing it in bold italics.

[46] These six lines of verse come from Asaṅga's *Summary of the Great Vehicle* (Skt. Mahāyānasaṃgraha). They show the topic headings for each of the nine epithets, which Tāranātha then uses to explain the nine epithets.

Of those, his having defeated obstructors is connected with the with *bhagavat* at the start of the recollection. This term stands for "the buddha characterized as a bhagavat, where bhagavat is one who has the quality of having defeated obstructors". The obstructors he has defeated are the four maras: the aggregates, the afflictions, the lord of death, and the son of the gods. He has the good quality of having defeated the four māras because he has abandoned the first three and has gone past being an object that could be harmed by the fourth.[47]

The Sanskrit term "bhagavan" has various meanings such as "chom ldan <> possessing the quality of having defeated", "skal ldan <> possessing the quality of being fortunate", "legs ldan <> possessing the qualities of goodness", and so on, because of which Ṛishi Kapila, Kṣhatriya Krishna[48], and others were also known as "bhagavan". Therefore, the term " 'das <> transcendent" for " 'jig rten las 'das pa <> transcendent over the world" was added to it in order to make a term that would be distinguished compared to the original term. The bodhisatva translators[49] of the past chose to highlight the specific meaning involved despite the fact that in the Indian language this term does not include the equivalent of " 'das <> transcendent" in it.

---

[47] See the explanation of bhagavat on page 33 of the chapter on translation issues and in my own commentary. For māra, see the glossary.

[48] These are the names of two other holy men of the Buddha's time whose followers referred to them as bhagavat. The first was a teacher who taught his own religious system and the second is the great holy being of the Hindu religion, Krishna.

[49] The thought behind his words "bodhisatva translators" is translators who were emanations of bodhisatvas dwelling on the bodhisatva levels and who were, therefore, especially knowledgeable and capable of making these translations from the Sanskrit language into the Tibetan language.

A perfection of explanation is connected with *tathāgata* which was translated into Tibetan with "de bzhin gshegs pa <> gone to such-ness". Perfection of explanation is connected with the fact that he himself realized suchness without mistake, then taught it, un-mistakenly and just as he had realized it, to others. "Tathā <> suchness" means the non-mistakenness of something just exactly as it is and "gata <> gone and also going" is used to indicate both that he realized it himself and that others will realize it[50].

A perfection of abandonment is connected with *arhat* which was translated into Tibetan with "dgra bcom pa <> one who has de-feated the enemy". In regard to this, "afflictions together with their latencies" can be re-stated in more ordinary terms as "that which harms the dharmas of virtue", and that can be further re-stated as "dgra <> an enemy". Then, corresponding to that, abandonment of the afflictions will be referred to as "bcom <> de-feated".[51]

A perfection of wisdom is connected with *truly complete buddha*. He has cleared off the entirety of not knowing—similar to a man clearing off the thickness of sleep, which is related with his coming to know unmistakenly the totality of the spheres of knowables. And the illumination of his intelligence has expanded, like a lotus that has bloomed, so that it spreads throughout all superficies.[52]

---

[50] "Perfection of explanation" is the topic heading corresponding to this epithet. It refers to the fact that the Buddha has realized things as they are and that, therefore, his explanations of it to others come without mistake; they are perfect in every way.

[51] See the explanation of arhat on page 36 of the chapter on translation issues and in my own commentary.

[52] See the explanation of buddha on page 30 of the chapter on trans-lation issues and in my own commentary.

COMPLETE COMMENTARY BY TĀRANĀTHA

Those two perfections of abandonment and wisdom paired together are known as "a perfection of accomplishment". Then,
those two plus the perfection of explanation make a set of three
that refer to his being a perfect teacher because of his ability to act
unmistakenly—that is, flawlessly—for the purpose of migrators.
Now this kind of teacher is found only in a buddha. Raudra,
Viṣṇu, and others like them[53] do not have this ability at all; it is
a good quality not found amongst ordinary beings.

In regard to that, Ṛṣi Vyāsa, and so on whose works focus on
disagreements between parties but which are not able to resolve
the matters involved which anyway are of no account, are people
whose intelligence has not fully spread throughout all dharmas[54].
Nandaka, and so on who were controlled by desire, and those who
are embroiled in suffering and living in evil deeds, have lost control of themselves to their own afflictions, so what capacity could
they have for protecting others[55]? The pratyekas and others like

---

[53] Raudra is one of the four great kings in the first level of the desire
realm gods and Viṣṇu is a very high level samsaric god. Tāranātha
has picked out gods who are commonly revered as saviours in Indian
culture and pointed out that, despite their great powers, they do not
have this ability that makes the Buddha a perfect teacher.

[54] Ṛṣi Vyāsa and others like him were ancient Indian holy men who
were very good with words and who wrote several works which have
become the basis for Hindu religion, such as the *Bhagavadgita*. These
compositions tell wondrous stories of amazing godly beings and their
fights for supremacy and, in doing so, pretend to examine issues of
reality. However, the authors were not connected with reality in the
way that a Buddha is. Therefore, their works are amazing compositions, but the logic in them is superficial and they contain investigations of things which, although they are set as the basis of true spiritu-
ality, do not contact reality.

[55] Nandaka was a person living at the time of the Buddha who was
(continued...)

them have realized the authentic but they do not talk about it so are not able to take on others as followers[56]. That is why the perfection of explanation is mentioned here.

The cause of his attainment of the teacher perfect in those ways is *insight*[57] which is right view *and* its *feet* which are thought, speech, action, livelihood, effort, mindfulness, and samādhi of the path of the noble ones[58]. Alternatively, higher prajñā is insight and the trainings of discipline and mind are the feet[59]. Alternatively

---

[55](...continued)
revered by his followers but who was known by the Buddha to be trapped by sensuality.

[56] Pratyekabuddhas have become arhats and left samsara by gaining direct insight into the absence of a personal self. However, they keep to themselves and do not teach others, so they cannot provide help, even though they have the realization needed to do so.

[57] Tib. rigpa. Rigpa does not have a good equivalent in English. It is not a general "awareness" as is commonly translated these days. It is a dynamic, direct type of knowing. Here, it means the direct knowledge of a buddha, which is like insight.

[58] Tāranātha does not quote the *Sutra* here. The *Sutra* says that a buddha is someone with insight and what comes at its feet, an epithet which can be explained in many ways. The usual first explanation is the one he has just laid out, that insight and its feet correspond to the fruitional states of the eightfold noble path.

[59] The usual second explanation of insight and what comes at its feet shows how the fruitional states of the three principal trainings taught by the Buddha correspond to insight and what comes at its feet.
The Buddha taught three principal trainings: śhīla, samādhi, and prajñā or discipline, concentration, and correctly discerning mind. He called them higher trainings to distinguish them from the trainings of the same names that were being propagated in one or another of the
(continued...)

again, insight is the three types of insight[60] and feet is the four perfections—discipline, conduct, reversal, and the blissful higher mind of seen dharmas[61].

Those three ways of enumerating them can be condensed into one key point of meaning. That is because right view, the higher training of prajñā, and the insight of the exhaustion of outflows[62] are contained in one thing; because the three insights of right insight, and so on and the training of discipline and the three of discipline, conduct, and reversal are all one entity; and because right samādhi and the training of mind and blissful higher mind of seen dharmas also have the same principal meaning.

The three insights mentioned above are the insights of former limits, of later limits, and of the exhaustion of outflows. A perfection of conduct is that he abides continuously in knowledge throughout all types of conduct and a perfection of reversal is that

---

[59](...continued)
many other religious systems of India at the time. Prajñā is equated with insight and the other two trainings are equated with the feet that carry the insight around.

Note that the second principal training is named concentration but is also—given that it is a training of mind per se—called mind, which is how Tāranātha refers to it here and in other places in his commentary.

[60] Three types of insight are enumerated in the Buddhist teachings. Tāranātha speaks more of them a little further on.

[61] The bliss of seen dharmas is a feature which accompanies abiding in the equilibria of the dhyānas. "Higher mind" is another way of saying mind abiding in the dhyānas. As with the things mentioned above, the items mentioned here are good qualities that can be developed on the path but now they are being talked about when they have become aspects of the fruition of a buddha.

[62] See the glossary for outflow.

the doors of his faculties are restrained; those two make for a pure discipline and concentration at the same time. The blissful higher mind of seen dharmas mentioned above means that he is a person of pure four dhyānas and, in terms of them being without out-flows, the fourth one is the main one among them. The extra-perceptions are produced from them, therefore the three insights arise from them[63]. That sort of insight is knowing what is and unmistakenly seeing in direct perception the topics of what is to be abandoned and what is to be taken up. Having that insight in conjunction with accomplishment and conduct consistent with it can be likened to going on a road that is being watched with the eyes, so they are called "feet". Alternatively, according to some-one else's explanation, "insight is the six extra-perceptions" in accordance with the meaning explained above in "and the feet are the four legs of miracles".

How he went is as follows. The Tibetan term is *bde bar gshegs pa*. The Sanskrit term "sugata" from which that is derived can be translated with: "bde bar gshegs pa <> he who has gone pleasantly to pleasantness"; "legs par gshegs pa <> he who has gone well to goodness", and "rab tu gshegs pa <> he who has gone utterly to utterness".

Of those, "bde bar gshegs pa <> gone pleasantly to pleasantness" indicates that he has, due to a pleasant path, gone to a pleasant or blissful fruition. At the time of the path, he abandoned activities that were not to be done, did not let arise what some others might find praiseworthy, did not shrink from the task and practised avoidance, and generally practised many things that were pleasing to mind. Thereby, at the time of the fruition, he had abandoned all types of unsatisfactoriness and obtained a perfection of

---

[63] ... because the three insights are three of the extra-perceptions of a buddha. Extra-perceptions are the various extra-sensory perceptions known in Buddhism. Six major types are listed in the sutras.

unoutflowed bliss. Therefore, being and not being engaged with limits of accomplishment no longer matters to him[64]; he has distinguished himself from samsaric beings with their accomplishment of the resultant suffering that comes from causal suffering. This might lead you to think, "The ones who live within the desire realm have that sort of suffering but not the ones who dwell in the dhyāna and formless places", but it is not like that and you should remember that the fruitions that result from being in those upper places definitely involve suffering.

Now for those who do not understand that, there is "legs par gshegs pa <> gone well to goodness" which is connected with the fact that he has finalized abandonment and does not relapse into samsara. As with a contagious disease where, once one has been well cured of it there will be no relapse into it again, for him all the obscurations of the afflictions, etcetera, that he has abandoned have been abandoned and are done with. Thus, what he has done is different from what the Tīrthikas who engage the equilibria accomplish.[65]

---

[64] The issue of needing to practice or attain something or not needing to do so are no longer an issue for the Buddha because he has truly gone to a completely satisfactory—which is real meaning of "su"— situation.

[65] The equilibria are states of complete absorption. The Tīrthikas or non-Buddhists of India have mastered them and proclaim mastery of them to be liberation. The Buddha learned and mastered all of them, realized that they did not constitute emancipation, and continued on his journey until he found the true emancipation of buddhahood. His accomplishment is not at all like that of the Tīrthika non-Buddhists.

You might think, "Yes, but this is the same as what the śhrāvakas and prateyakabuddhas have done, isn't it?!"[66] For this, there is "rab tu shegs pa <> gone utterly to utterness" meaning that going by realizing every single one of the entirety of the dharmas to be realized, he has realized them utterly and gone to such; it is like saying "filling every single vase, the vases are utterly filled". This quality is found only in the tathāgata—having gone this way, he has permanently entered the wisdom that unimpededly knows every one of the knowables.

The last two sections have determined the meaning of his being "abandoned and realized". Now for the third topic, which concerns his enlightened activity.

Of the nine topics, looking at the world is connected to *knower of the world*. He looks on constantly at all sentient beings and, with his great compassion and his knowledge of whether sentient beings are happy or pained, successful or in failure, and with good fortune or not and his knowledge of whether it is time to tame them or not, he knows all the methods needed to tame them. In other words, given that he knows the sufferings and their source without exception, he is the knower of the world.

His doing the deed of taming fortunate ones[67] is connected with *unsurpassed driver who tames* excellent humans meaning

---

[66] The arhats also have achieved non relapse into samsara. However, they do not have the full attainment of abandonment and realization that a buddha has.

[67] "Doing the deeds" and phrases like it are part of the conventional Great Vehicle's vocabulary. For example, a bodhisatva takes up the burden, does the deeds of his bodhisatva family line, and finally, having reached enlightenment, lays down the burden of having to do the deeds required of a bodhisatva on the way to enlightenment.

excellent *beings*. Excellent humans, that is, excellent beings, are those who have good fortune. For them, he does the deed of taming their mind streams and thereby placing them in the three enlightenments. For those who do not have the good fortune required to be tamed by actually following the path of emancipation, he does the deeds of drawing them back from the bad migrations, lessening the sufferings of those with great suffering, and placing them on the paths to the higher levels. It does not matter where someone is stationed within the higher levels or on the paths to liberation, there is never a case when someone's great level of good fortune is diminished because of him; such a thing is never possible.

Driver concerns his skill at taming beings. He is like the drivers of horses, elephants, and chariots who take a good road because they are knowledgeable about the roads that can be taken. *Unsurpassed* is an adjective modifying driver which is explained like this: "It shows that his activity is such that he can put even the most difficult-to-tame ones into the shrāvaka's enlightenment, as he did with his younger brother Nanda who had very great desire, Aṅgulimāla who had raging anger, Dasa's Son and Pāla and others who had extremely thick delusion, and Kāśhyapa of Uruvilva who had particularly great pride". The tathāgata's enlightened activity is indeed able to engage everyone, those who are vessels and those who are not vessels[68].

There is the statement which says that he is "the tamer of fortunate ones and tamer of excellent men". The statement sets out a group of people who can take advantage of his enlightened activity. It consists both of those who have the good fortune needed for liberation because they are vessels fit for it compared to those who are not and of those who are from the human world because,

---

[68] Vessel, meaning suitable vessel, was explained earlier.

among all the worlds, the human world is the one that is the principal source of buddhas. Note that this group is not a group made up of the only beings that the Buddha's enlightened activity can engage.

His being a teacher in whom such enlightened activity is present connects with **teacher of gods and men**. In fact, he is the teacher of all sentient beings within the three realms, but gods and men are mentioned here because seeing truth or seeing the attainment of fruition through training in virtue or the attainment of the noble ones' levels are things not seen by anyone other than the excellent ones among migrators. Thus, gods and men are considered to be the principal ones to be tamed and are accordingly mentioned here. Note that that explanation is given from the standpoint of the common vehicle[69] but, in fact, in the world too, if one says, "the king bowed and prostrated", even if it is not explicitly stated that the retinue also bowed and prostrated, it is understood by implication[70].

Now, to show the teacher in whom those kinds of good qualities are based, the words **buddha bhagavat** are repeated. There is no fault in this repetition; the first time was for the purpose of showing the good qualities themselves and this time it is primarily to understand the being in whom those good qualities are based.

❁   ❁   ❁

---

[69] The common vehicle here means the general teachings of Buddhism applicable to all Buddhists.

[70] The explanation of this epithet is given according to the general explanations of the Buddha's dharma. Nevertheless, even the world understands that someone who is in the ruler's seat, like a Buddha, will affect everyone about him, even if some of them are more capable of following his instructions than others.

Next, the extensive explanation is given. Its topic headings have been ascertained to be: definite situation, body's nature, what he is based on, function, methods, dwelling, detachment, how he enacted, and summary.

The two phrases *The tathāgata corresponds to a cause of merit. His roots of virtue do not go to waste* go with his having a definite situation, that is, with his being present in a steady way. In the expanse without remainder with good qualities that do not end, he perpetually shows deeds for the purpose of sentient beings. Samsaric beings' virtues come to an end because they are used up in full-ripening[71] and śhrāvaka and pratyeka's virtues also come to an end, being used up in the expanse of no-remainder[72]. Therefore these beings do not perpetually have an existence that corresponds to a cause of merit. The Buddha, previously when he was a bodhisatva, did not dedicate his generosity and the rest for the purpose of everyone's happiness, but dedicated every bit of it to the emancipation of every sentient being. Because such merit does not end for as long as its aim has not been completed and because he cultivated it in a way that made it equal in extent to the expanse of all dharmas, the fruition, in correspondence with its cause, also never ends. The *Highest Continuum* also speaks of this and what it says should be remembered:

> With infinite causes and unending sentient beings and
> Love and miracles and knowledge all to perfection,
> The Lord of Dharma has defeated the māra of death
> and,

---

[71] Full-ripening is one of the several types of karmic ripening that the Buddha taught his followers. The meaning here is that sentient beings are involved in a karmic process of becoming and because of that are constantly exhausting whatever seeds of virtue they create.

[72] No-remainder is the state of nirvana which arhats enter at their time of death.

Because of being no entity, is the perpetual guardian of
the world.

Therefore, his roots of virtue do not go to waste because there is
an uninterrupted fruition of all the roots of virtue that he made
previously.

The six phrases *He is ornamented with all patience*[73]. *His basis
is troves of merit. The excellent minor signs adorn him. The
flowers of the major marks bloom on him. Perceiving his activity, it being just right, there is harmony. Seeing him, there is no
disharmony* show features which are the nature of his body. The
teaching "he previously always acted uninterruptedly for the purpose of sentient beings" answers the question, "How did his body
act for the purpose of migrators?" This is about the form bodies
and the headings are: the root cause, the divisions of the causes,
what it is, and the perfection of its function in any given circum-
stance.

He is ornamented with all patience is an explanation of the root
cause of his body. His body size is tall and his colour and shape
are a perfection of beauty, all of which has come from patience.
Saying that he has a fruition ornamented with what are caused by
patience means that his body is ornamented with a naturally-
produced beauty. It is a fruition that comes because of having
abandoned the things that are not conducive to it, anger and
hatred, and having attended to the cause of it, patience.

His basis is troves of merit explains those causes according to their
divisions. The statement which says, "Each one even of the hair
pores of his body is produced by ten times ten times the merit pile

---

[73] This epithet in Tāranātha's edition of the *Sutra* differs slightly from
the same epithet in the editions of the *Sutra* used in this book and by
Mipham.

of all migrators ..." is pointing out that each of the parts of his body, each of the major and minor marks on it, and so on is produced through infinite amounts of the specified types of merit[74]. Here, "trove" means unfathomable amounts. An extensive understanding of the meaning can be obtained from the Unending Perseverance chapter of the *Akshyamati Nirdeśha Sūtra*.

In terms of what the body is like, **the excellent minor signs adorn him** refers to the eighty minor marks and **the flowers of the major marks bloom on him** refers to the thirty-two excellent marks; these show the perfection of the body itself. "Flowers bloom on him" has the same meaning as "ornament him" and "adorn" means that they are accessories to the major marks and therefore enhance their beauty.

Perceiving his activity, it being just right, there is harmony refers to perfection in any given situation. Whatever he does—going and staying, and so on[75]—is neither done in great style nor in an overly unassuming way, and so on. What is seen by others never becomes a basis for attributing a fault of some kind of non-beauty in him.

Seeing him, there is no disharmony refers to perfection of the functioning of his body. Anything that he does—going, staying, sleeping, begging for alms, looking, speaking, and so on—never becomes a cause for thinking, "This is afflicted", never scares

---

[74] This is part of a well-known teaching on how a buddha's body is produced by merit. The teaching mentions each part of the body and and specifies what kind and how much merit was needed to create it. A longer quotation from the teaching is cited in Mipham's commentary and will help to clarify what Tāranātha has just said.

[75] All behaviour is traditionally summed up under the four headings of coming and going, staying and moving.

others off, never causes them pain, and never produces craving or anything else of the sort. Every activity connected with his body which is seen or heard gives birth to compassion, renunciation, perseverance, correct discernment of the authentic, pacifies suffering, and so on; it only ever becomes a cause of others' virtue and brings them to admire him. **Disharmony** here refers either to the being who is viewing his body not having faith in him or having afflicted thoughts aroused because of seeing him. Furthermore, it has been said,

> Bodied beings who see you
> Think well of you, think you are a holy being.
> Merely seeing you brings total admiration;
> I prostrate to you.

The three phrases *He brings overt joy to those who long through faith. His prajñā cannot be overpowered. His strengths cannot be challenged* show what his activities done for the purpose of sentient beings depend on.

A person who comes before the teacher will come with one of two thoughts, either of faith or of outdoing him. The faithful includes a group of people who come driven by roots of virtue from the past but who have some doubts. It also includes a group of people who come with the highest level of faith; with that kind of *faith*, these people come intent on attaining the teacher's dharma. For all of the faithful, on seeing his body and hearing his speech, total admiration and *overt joy* arises in them. Those who come with the thought to outdo him also are of two types: those who want to outdo him with prajñā such as the Nirgrantha Jains who went to argue the case for true existence, and those who want to outdo him with body strengths such as Ātavika Yakṣha. These beings must first be tamed[76]. Because the tathāgata of no not-knowing and of infinite knowing has the confidence of knowledge to be able to teach dharma precisely in accord with any vessel, the tathāgata's *prajñā cannot be* outdone by that of others.

The meaning of *his strengths cannot be challenged* is that, because the tathāgata has infinite strengths of body, other beings' strengths cannot not challenge the strengths of his body. This has been taught, for example, in the *Hurling A Boulder Sutra*[77]. The Great Vehicle's way of classifying the strengths of the body of the tathāgata appears extensively in the *Sutra of Samādhi that Incorporates All Merit*.

Alternatively, there are those who have interest due to *faith*—the ones whose faculties are already tamed—and he makes them *joyful* through joy of dharma. *His prajñā* that *cannot be overpowered* makes them joyful through giving them attainment, and so on. *His strengths cannot be challenged* means that, because he has wisdom with the ten strengths, he cannot be defeated by any opponent.

The four phrases *He is a teacher to all sentient beings, a father to the bodhisatvas, a king to the noble persons, a captain to those who journey to the city of nirvana* show the functioning of his activity for the purposes of sentient beings.

The first phrase is given in relation to showing the pleasant path, or you could say cause, to all sentient beings. For example, for some beings in the bad migrations, he sends light rays from his

---

[76] The faithful are sufficiently tamed that they can be worked with immediately. The others have to be given some taming before they can hear the teaching.

[77] A significant portion of this sutra is cited in Mipham's commentary.

body that alleviate their sufferings and, having produced faith in them, places them in the good migrations. Then, for those in the happy migrations, he places them in various things such as generosity, discipline, and so on and so gradually ripens them into the three enlightenments.[78]

The remaining three phrases of this group of four are given in relation to showing the pleasant path to those sentient beings who have entered a vehicle. Among them, *a father to the bodhisatvas* is for those who belong to the Great Vehicle; they are bodhisatvas belonging to the family of the buddhas. Because they are born from the buddha's dharma[79] to begin with and then because, in terms of body, speech, mind, and activities, they come to abide as buddhas[80] or something corresponding to it, they are the sons of the buddhas. The tathāgata is their father because he is the object from whom they get their good qualities. That is how it works.

Then, *a king to the noble persons* is for those of the śrāvaka and pratyeka families. Stream-enterers, returners, non-returners, śrāvaka and pratyeka arhats, and so on are nourished by the buddha's dharma but do not make it as far as the tathāgata side of dharma[81]. Therefore, they remain like ordinary commoners and, because of that, buddha is a king for them.

---

[78] The first epithet says that he shows all sentient beings the cause of enlightenment though many do not take advantage of it. The remaining three epithets are for people who have heard the call and are doing something with the cause that he showed.

[79] Buddha's dharma here means the dharma corresponding to the path to truly complete buddhahood—the bodhisatva's dharma—as opposed to the arhat's dharma.

[80] Meaning truly complete buddhas as opposed to arhat buddhas.

[81] The tathāgata's side of dharma is the bodhisatva side.

A chief of merchants both leads all merchants along and goes along with them, so for them, he is their *captain*. The *city of nirvana* applies to the nirvana of all three vehicles. The Buddha unmistakenly guides the ones wanting to go there, with the result that he is their captain, and the city of emancipation is their final destination.

The six phrases *His wisdom is unfathomable. His knowledge-ability is inconceivable. His speech is complete purity. His melody is pleasing. One never has enough of viewing the image of his body. His body is unparalleled* show the means by which he enacts the purposes of others[82].

Of them, the enlightened activity of mind is that *his wisdom is unfathomable*. Given that he knows all of sentient beings' elements, inclinations, faculties, and karmic imprints, he is able unmistakenly to employ all methods and timings needed for the purposes of migrators.

The enlightened activity of speech is that *his knowledgeability is inconceivable*[83]. It is inconceivable based on attempting to write it out: if one started with one phrase about it then explained that with more and more other phrases, even if one were to do that for unfathomable kalpas, one would not finish the task. It is conceivable based on presentation of its meaning: if during unfathomable kalpas infinite sentient beings were at the same time to ask a completely different question, the Buddha could just one time,

---

[82] "Enacts the purposes" is more of the same type of vocabulary as "does the deeds".

[83] Tib. spobs pa. The quality of knowledgeability refers to an ability to instantly recall to mind the knowledge needed, for example, when teaching someone, and a confidence of knowledge that comes with it. This good quality is clearly explained in my own commentary.

effortlessly giving a reply in various different ways, supply an un-garbled answer to each being; there would be only one instance of his speech but it would convey infinite meanings that would come forth in different, individual replies. There would be an infinite amount of speech yet each single being to be tamed would have his wisdom limitlessly increased because of it. "Knowledgeability" relates to his teaching dharma; "inconceivable" relates to its ama-zing, wondrous presentation.

His speech is complete purity is like this: it has been made com-pletely pure because all faults of speech—lying, intonation with an unpleasant sound, functioning in ways which create unhappiness of mind and the like, styles of expression such as being too fast, and so on—have been removed in their entirety. In addition, from the perspective of good qualities, *his* speech has an intonation or *melody* that *is pleasing* to hear—according to the Lesser Vehicle his speech has five main aspects of intonation, according to the Great Vehicle it has sixty main aspects, and so on.

The enlightened activity of the body is that *one never has enough of viewing the image of his body*. This is because the beautiful appearance of each of the limbs of his body and each one of the parts of those limbs outdoes all the beauty of the three realms; one cannot get enough of looking at his body.

His body is unparalleled means that, for all those included in the three realms, the six migrators, and the four places of birth, why raise the issue of something that they could find that would be superior to the colour and shape of the bhagavat's body when there is nothing observable in their own experience that is even remotely comparable to his body?

The three phrases *He is not contaminated by the things of desire. He is very much not contaminated by the things of form. He is not mixed with the things of formlessness* show where the bhagavat abides. To take it further, they are saying "he does not abide in the three realms because he is situated in the expanse of dharmas[84], so, he acts within the three realms but in doing so is not contaminated with their faults".

In regard to that, when he is acting for the purpose of sentient beings in the desire realm, *he is not contaminated by* hankering after desirables or by harmful states of mind. When he is acting in the form and formless realms, the epithet says that *he is very much*, meaning highly, *uncontaminated by the* faults of equilibria in dhyāna—craving, views, pride, doubt, and so on—that come from being in such places.

Moreover, this way of talking means that his body and speech were involved with the desire and form realms but that he was not contaminated with the things connected with those places. It is held that *not mixed with* was taught because that way of being contaminated does not exist in the formless realm; this term is applied in accordance with the fact that in the formless realm there is only *formlessness.* This also applies to those places where there is form; that form is extremely subtle so there is no contradiction if it is explained like that.

The three phrases[85] *He is utterly completely liberated from the skandhas. He does not possess dhātus. His āyatanas are restrained* teach that when he is acting for the purposes of sentient beings,

---

[84] Skt. dharmadhātu. The meaning is that he does not abide in a particular location within the places of saṃsāra because he has released himself into the sphere of wisdom which pervades the entire expanse of phenomena.

[85] The phrase in the *Sutra* "he is completely liberated from the sufferings" comes at this point but is not mentioned in Tāranātha's commentary.

he has no attachment at all. Because the skandhas belong to those who have the character of taking birth again and again and the tathāgata has no birth, he is utterly completely-liberated from them. The dhātus were defined in relation to the birth of consciousness that grasps an object. Thus, given that he has abandoned the afflictions that depend on object and consciousness, he does not possess dhātus. The āyatanas were defined in relation to the cause of the production of visual and the other sense consciousnesses. Thus, given that he has restrained the afflictions that depend on them, his āyatanas are restrained. To sum this up, his is a body of wisdom which is transcendent over the meaning understood from the terms skandhas, dhātus, and āyatanas.

Next, the way of enacting the purpose of migrators through abandonment and wisdom is shown. The first four phrases *He has cut the knots. He is completely liberated from the torments. He is liberated from craving. He has crossed over the river*[86] teach his enactment of the purpose of sentient beings from the perspective of what his abandonment is like. If afflictions as a whole are summarized, they come to craving, which has the character of being a knot that occurs on meeting with an object and to a river which has the characteristic of torment on not meeting with an object.

The four are then connected with this teaching: "Because he has cut what are the knots, he is liberated from craving. Because he has liberated himself from torment, he has crossed over the river". In that, *knot* means a restraint that holds non-liberation in place and its having been *cut* means that the craving for an object—body, possessions, and so on—that has been met with has been cut. In that, *torment*, which is the acting always within a greater level of affliction when an object thought of is not met with, has been

---

[86] Tāranātha's version of the *Sutra* gives these epithets as shown; they differ slightly from the version of the *Sutra* used for this book.

abandoned. That is what it is saying. Thus, becoming is none other than craving that wholly incorporates the three realms, and the river of the afflictions is a current that carries mind off helplessly in its direction. Moreover, that is fourfold; there are the rivers of desire, becoming, ignorance, and views.[87]

The second four phrases *His wisdom is totally complete. He abides in the wisdom of the buddha bhagavats who arise in the past, present, and future. He does not abide in nirvana. He abides in the limit of the authentic itself* show how he enacts the purpose of sentient beings from the perspective of what his wisdom is like.

Wisdom is threefold: the wisdom of the knowledge of all superficies that knows all knowables; the wisdom of the knowledge of non-difference that views all buddhas within equality; and the wisdom of knowledge that is non-abiding because it does not abide in the extremes of samsara and nirvana even though it abides in the limit of the authentic[88]. These connect sequentially to the first three phrases as follows. From the standpoint of the first, wisdom is something that totally and completely pervades without one exception the spheres of knowables belonging to the three times. Then, the wisdom of all buddhas of the past, future, and present is the wisdom of a single buddha and that wisdom of a single buddha is also the wisdom of all the buddhas of the three times, so his knowledge is one that is not different from theirs. Next, *does not abide* means that he does not abide in the limited nirvana of lesser

---

[87] Tāranātha is presenting a very short summation of a body of teaching that the Buddha gave in the first turning of the wheel. He is writing for someone who is already familiar with that body of teaching.

[88] These three types of wisdom form the basis of the explanations of the Prajñāpāramitā. They are explained in Maitreya-Asaṅga's *Abhisamayālaṅkara, Ornament of Manifest Realizations*.

types, an expanse in which the continuity of others' purposes is severed[89].

The limit of the authentic is the limit of being in the authentic only, meaning that he abides in the dharmakāya of utter complete-purity, the suchness expanse of dharmas. It implies that he does not abide in samsara, which, combined with the last epithet, exposes the meaning of his non-abiding nirvana.

He abides on the level of looking upon all sentient beings is a phrase that sums up the meaning of all three. Of the tathāgata's three kāyas, the dharmakāya abides looking on the nature of the situation of all sentient beings, seeing at the same time its own nature, and while not wavering from either. The sambhogakāya abides looking on the mindstreams of sentient beings of the pure levels, the mahāsatvas[90], and teaching them dharma. The supreme nirmāṇakāya[91], because it functions as a liberator of the mindstreams of the śhrāvakas, and so on and of the ordinary beings who have a very pure eye of intelligence, abides on the level of a dwelling place from which it views their elements and inclinations.

In that way, this later portion of the recollection was contained within nine topics: definite situation, body's nature, what he is

---

[89] He does not abide in the arhat's nirvana, an expanse of realization in which one stays selfishly in a private peacefulness, without thoughts of the greater good.

[90] Mahāsatva, meaning great beings, is a specific term of the Great Vehicle meaning bodhisatvas on the eighth to tenth bodhisatva levels, the levels of the pure ones. It is usually said that the sambhogakāya teaches only the tenth level bodhisatvas.

[91] The supreme nirmāṇakāya is the nirmāṇakāya manifestation that appears as a buddha and turns the wheel of dharma, for example like Śhākyamuni Buddha.

based on, function, methods, dwelling, detachment, how he enacts the benefit of migrators through abandonment and wisdom, and a conclusion at which we have now arrived.

These are the true qualities of the greatness of the body of the buddha bhagavat is saying "all of the good qualities shown above are not found in others, they are the greatnesses owned by the tathāgata". It means that, even though it is possible that others might have something of this sort to some small extent, no-one else has all of this and has it complete like this.

That was an explanation of the meaning of the recollection of the Buddha. There are explanations made by both noble one Asaṅga and his brother of the first part of the recollection in nine parts and a commentary made by master Vasubhandu to the later part of the recollection. Compared to them, this explanation includes both parts and is clearer.

2. Sūtra of the Recollection of the Dharma

The holy dharma can refer to any of the three dharmas of authoritative statement, realization, and nirvana.

It *is good in the beginning* refers to the fact that at the time of hearing it, its meaning is ascertained and a trusting faith in it is produced. *Good in the middle* means that at the time of contemplating it, joy will be produced from understanding that there will be an attainment of benefits and fruitions just as they were stated in the explanations of dharma. *And good in the end* means that at the time of meditation, it has the meaning of creating the cause of the intelligent mind which unmistakenly realizes suchness.

Its meaning is excellent means that it shows without confusion the truths of fiction and superfact[92]. *Its wording is excellent* means that it has a superior quality of being easy to understand and grasp and that the expressions used for that purpose are easy to listen to and pleasant to hear.

It is not adulterated means that it has uncommon good qualities which are not like the ordinary versions found in the doctrines of the Tīrthika's and others; its versions of impermanence, formatives' suffering, lack of self, and so on are subtle presentations[93]. *It is totally complete* means that it is not a partial sort of antidote that works only against afflictions of desire, rather, it works against the afflictions of each of the three realms[94]. *It is total purity* means that it is the nature whose actuality is complete purity, the dharmadhātu, and the wisdom that observes it. *It is total purification* means that it is both the purifier of the adventitious stains and the fruition that comes from that, separation from the adventitious stains due to their abandonment.

Those three goodnesses together with excellent meaning and wordings makes a set of five that primarily shows the good qualities of the dharma of authoritative statement. The four of being not adulterated and so on, which are called "possessing the four qualities which are brahmacharya[95]", are the greatnesses of the

---

[92] For these two terms, see the glossary.

[93] The non-Buddhist and Buddhist religious teachers of India often presented their dharma using the same words as the Buddha. However, the way that the Buddha explained anything was uncommon compared to their very ordinary explanations.

[94] It is complete antidote because it solves every samsaric delusion.

[95] Ways of purity. For an explanation of this term, see my own commentary.

holy dharma of an object that is uncompounded and holy dharma of perceiver of it that is realization. These four are explained in a commentary to the *Abhisamayālaṅkara* by Vasubhandu.

The buddha has taught dharma well or, as seen in some other editions, ***buddha's dharma is well taught***. The dharma shown by the Tīrthikas is badly taught because what it considers to be a path is not a path of emancipation, and because, as someone else said, what it considers to be a path to higher levels of being is actually a path to the bad migrations, and because, as someone else again said, although it shows a path to the higher levels, it shows it with impurities and incompleteness. The ***dharma*** that the bhagavat has shown is the opposite of that, therefore, it ***is well taught***.

It is authentic teaching[96] means that the dharma, whether showing the fictional or superfactual situation, unmistakenly shows the individual characteristics involved.

It is free from sickness means that because it functions as an antidote to every obscuration of the afflictions and karmic imprints, it is without the sickness of the obscurations.

The phrase ***Its time has no interruption*** has the meanings of: the uncompounded expanse that is changeless and fearless; the wisdom of the noble ones' path that is without corruption; and what is to be abandoned having been abandoned, there is no need to abandon it yet again.

The phrase ***It brings one in*** is explained like this. From the term "upanāyika" we get "draws in close" which has the meaning that,

---

[96] The text of the *Sutra* cited here by Tāranātha agrees with the extended recollection found in the Derge edition of the *Translated Treatises* but differs from the text used for translation and from Mipham's commentary both of which say, "It is authentic sight".

through the approach of abandoning samsara which subsumes afflictions and unsatisfactoriness, one is brought or drawn into the un-outflowed expanse. One translator commented that this should be translated with "having insight"; if that were so, it would have to be "uparyayika", so his translation does not quite fit.[97]

This is meaningful to see means that someone sees the dharma then gains the excellence of the fruitions and does not return, therefore it is meaningful. Some texts in the Indian language have "ehipashyikaḥ" here which translates as "Look at this here!", nonetheless, it is better to translate this epithet according to main meaning in contained in it.

It is known to the experts through personal self-knowing. In this phrase, the term experts refers to the noble ones. Their equipoise of wisdom without involvement in conceptual thinking realizes the dharma[98] in direct perception. It is not an object of consciousness and sophistry.

The phrase *The dharma spoken by the bhagavat was well taught for taming* is explained like this. It might be that the dharma is to be known through personal self-knowing but that does not mean that it is not known in authoritative statement[99]. The word of the tathāgata corresponds in cause to the dharmakāya, therefore his expression of dharma in authoritative statement accords with how he knows that dharma with his dharmakāya. Thus, the implication contained in this epithet is that "what is known in personal self-

---

[97] See the explanation of upanāyika in the other two commentaries and on page 39 of the chapter on translation issues.

[98] Dharma here specifically means the superfactual dharma.

[99] The previous epithet means that the dharma is the dharma of realization. This epithet continues by saying that it is also the dharma of authoritative statement.

knowing is also explained in authoritative statement". The phrasing *well taught* appears in some Indian language texts as "supragedita" which would have to be translated with "well and thoroughly distinguished".

It is renunciation means that it is renunciation of samsara[100].

It causes one to go to complete enlightenment means that coming into contact with the dharma of authoritative statement causes a person to go along the path. The path that they are caused to go along is, according to the literal meaning of the words, that of the Great Vehicle[101]. However, putting that aside, the paths of the śrāvakas and pratyekabuddhas are implied because even śrāvakas who have chosen to enter no-remainder do, after a long time has passed, without doubt, enter the Great Vehicle. Thus, this epithet actually shows a single, ultimate vehicle.

The phrase *It is without disharmony* means that the dharmatā of what is to be realized also being one[102], the noble ones who are on the same level definitely do not have differing dharmas of their experience. *And it has inclusion* means that it has the good quality of the sort where one thing known allows total comprehension

---

[100] The Sanskrit and Tibetan words behind renunciation mean "turned towards what is definite". Thus, the explanation here actually means "the dharma is that which causes one to head towards that which is final, definite, and fully reliable".

[101] ... because "complete enlightenment" means the enlightenment of a truly complete buddha attained through following the path of the Great Vehicle.

[102] The previous good quality pointed out a single, ultimate vehicle that all Buddhists follow and now, in a similar way, the final realization also is a single, ultimate one. Therefore, there is no inconsistency—no disharmony—in the realizations of the followers at their various levels.

of many aspects, so the aspects are included in one; one wisdom realizes the entirety of impermanence, unsatisfactoriness, lack of self, and so on.

It has reliability means that every single one of the virtuous dharmas, the entire expanse of phenomena[103], is dependent on tathāgatagarbha; that is the ultimate dharma Jewel.

It does end the journey means that all movements of mind and mental events are wholly cut by its application. At the level of a tathāgata this is the case at all times and in the equipoise of the bodhisatva noble ones it means that everything other than the ālaya is stopped.

3. Sūtra of the Recollection of the Saṅgha

The literal meaning of *the saṅgha of the great vehicle*[104] indicates that this recollection concerns the saṅghas of non-reversing bodhisatvas[105]. With that as the standpoint, they *have entered into*

---

[103] Dharmadhātu or expanse of phenomena in general means *the region in which all dharmas*, good, bad, and otherwise, appear and *are contained*. However, from the perspective of nirvana, all dharmas are virtuous dharmas or dharmas of purity and thus the region of all dharmas from that perspective consists only of such dharmas.

[104] This is the one place where the original recollections were deliberately changed in meaning to include the Great Vehicle teaching. See my own commentary for an extensive discussion of this point.

[105] Bodhisatvas on all ten bodhisatva levels are non-reversing in that they cannot fall back into saṃsāra. The bodhisatvas of the eighth level and above are also non-reversing in that they cannot fall back to a lower level. The first meaning is the one in use here. Tāranātha is
(continued...)

good means that they are abiding in the three types of discipline[106].
They *have entered into the types* means that they have entered infinite samādhis[107]. They *have entered into straightness* means
that, not abiding in the extremes of permanence and nihilism, they
have entered into the expanse of phenomena's equality. Those
three taken as a progression are the higher trainings of discipline,
mind, and prajñā[108]. They *have entered into harmony* means that
they have entered into a path in which there is not the slightest
discordance between any of the above—view, conduct, referenced
object, and conduct done for the purpose of migrators.

They are worthy of joined palms because they see the profound
dharmatā not seen by others.

They are worthy of prostration because, as beings who have the
great compassion that would liberate sentient beings from samsara, they have totally abandoned their own purposes, and they
therefore are beings who have the great conduct of holy beings.

The phrase *They are a field of the glory of merit* means that the
saṅgha are meritorious and have glory because of it—in other

---

[105](...continued)
saying that the saṅgha Jewel refers to the noble bodhisatvas.

[106] The three disciplines constitute the pāramitā of discipline of the
Great Vehicle.

[107] The original recollection has the word vidyā which translates into
Tibetan with "rig" and English with "insight". The Tibetan term has
been mistakenly spelled in some Tibetan editions as the word "rigs <>
types". This mistake is present in Tāranātha's copy of the *Sutra* and
he has given his explanation according to it. Buddhism lists many *types*
of samādhi including the one for *insight* into reality. The former is the
mistaken understanding and the latter is the correct understanding.

[108] As before, mind here means samādhi in the three higher disciplines.

words, that they have a great accumulation of merit—and that a field such as that is an object to which respect could be paid.

They are great ones thoroughly trained in gifts. These beings who have abandoned what is bad and greatly adorned themselves with an inconceivable collection of good qualities are highly trained in benefiting infinite numbers of beings. Therefore, with their heap of merit equivalent to the third order thousand world, they could be worshipped with offerings perpetually but would never become obscured because of it, and, as well as that, the ones who make offerings to them will receive a very great level of benefit.

They are a place for generosity given that they are an outstanding field of generosity, like a field whose weeds have been removed. Seeing them causes all of the things of total affliction that are to be abandoned to be totally abandoned so, for the person making the gift, fruitions will grow infinitely[109].

They are in all cases even a great place of generosity[110] takes the meaning of the previous point even further. Because the class of what is to be abandoned, which includes being afflicted and being obscured in relation to the knowables and the equilibria[111], consists of many things, there is just no knowing the totality of the fruitions. *All cases even* means "in all situations".

There is an explanation of how all of this could be connected with the śrāvaka saṅgha in which it is explained that *entered into goodness* means "entered into arhathood", and so on.

---

[109]The dharmas of samsara are "total affliction".

[110] The edition of the *Sutra* used by Tāranātha differs slightly here from the one used for this book and the one by Mipham, hence the translation differs.

[111] ... of the absorptions ...

This *Sutra of the Recollection of the Jewels* now under consideration is indeed a Great Vehicle sutra. For a recollection of the Three Jewels that belongs to the Lesser Vehicle there is a rough explanation by noble one Asaṅga, but I find myself wondering whether it is extracted from within a larger commentary[112]. Then, there are so many differences seen between the wordings of these sutras that there is the question of how the two come to be so different, still, in the two later recollections, the ones that are consistent do suggest a commonality.

This complete explanation of the *Sutra of the Recollection of the Jewels* was given by the international Tāranātha[113].

Maṇgalam[114]. Corrected.[115]

---

[112] The commentary to which he is referring can be found in Tibetan translation in the *Tangyur* or *Translated Treatises*.

[113] Tāranātha was Tibetan but went to India to try to find the Buddha's dharma and lived there for some time because of which he gave himself this name. Its use suggests that he has a personal great knowledge of Sanskrit and is therefore able to speak directly to the meanings contained in this text.

[114] Maṇgalam is a Sanskrit word meaning "Goodness!" It is standard to use either it or something similar at the end of a composition to seal the composition with the thought "May there be goodness!"

[115] The edition used for the translation was the Dzamthing edition, which is regarded as the best edition of Tāranātha's works because it was carefully edited. This is shown by the last words in the text, which mean that the text was carefully examined for errors and that any errors found were corrected before it was committed to printing.

Ju Mipham Namgyal
Mural on the wall of Dzogchen Monastery, Tibet,
2007. Photograph by the author.

A COMPLETE COMMENTARY TO THE SUTRA OF THE RECOLLECTION OF THE NOBLE THREE JEWELS CALLED "A MELODY OF UNENDING AUSPICIOUSNESS"

by Ju Mipham Nyamgyal

NAMO GURU MAÑJUGHOṢHAYA

Bearer of the peace that rescues those in becoming,
The one who has the prajñā sword machinery that defeats
The massed armies of the four māras who create the deception
    of becoming,
The hero whose lotus feet beautify my crown,

Full moon of a conqueror of completed knowledge and love,
You are beautified by strings of constellations of the noble
    assemblies and
Radiate nectar-like good light of holy dharma that ends
    becoming's contagious disease;
May this bring auspiciousness![116]

---

[116] The verse is a praise to Mipham's guru seen as an embodiment of the Three Jewels in the form of Mañjuśhrī. Mipham's guru has the peace of enlightenment that rescues those who are living in becoming (see glossary) by lifting them up and putting them onto the path of enlightenment. His guru Mañjuśhrī, like a mechanized army, has the
(continued...)

Now[117], within this great ocean of becoming that has no end-point, migrators in their entirety, myself and all others included, look for a solution to their problems only within passion and aggression. If they were to examine closely their vivid colour paintings that range from the peak of becoming down to Unceasing Torment[118], which come forth from previously created causes and now appear variously as pleasant, unpleasant, and neutral, their paintings would completely fall apart. Then they would know that all the highs and lows, rises and falls, happinesses and unhappinesses, and so on of these paintings—which are like the bubblings of gruel being cooked—cannot be

---

[116](...continued)
weaponry—the sword of prajñā that cuts through grasping at a self—needed to defeat the massed armies of the māras. This sword cuts the root ignorance that comes out in various forms of negativity, personified as the maras, who fool sentient beings into staying within samsaric existence. Mipham places this grand hero above his crown as his refuge. His refuge is like a moon which is full and bright because of his complete development of wisdom and love and is draped with the brilliant constellations of the noble saṅgha, the beings who have followed the path and removed themselves from becoming. The light of his dharma is like nectar that truly cures the contagion of beings in samsara. Mipham prays that there will be auspiciousness from re-collecting the good qualities of the buddha, dharma, and saṅgha, which sums up the meaning of the text he is about to write.

[117] Tib. de la 'dir. The Tibetan phrase is a formal one used to indicate that the meaning of the text summed up in poetry is complete and that the main explanation in prose will now begin.

[118] Peak of becoming is a name for the top realm of the formless realms and Unceasing Torment the lowest of the hot hells. They are the highest and lowest points of samsara.

ascertained as a particular extreme but are merely momentary dances flickering in and out like lightning.[119]

Worse though, the minds of these beings exist within stupidity alone. This lack of knowledge means that these beings do not even begin to gravitate towards the merit of virtuous karma but, as a matter of habit, stay firmly within the state of non-virtue, just like swans inhabit lake areas and vultures inhabit charnel grounds. Because of that, their minds find it difficult to get happiness and, bearing an intense burden of unsatisfactoriness and being separated from the path of the noble ones, they wander in becoming without an end ever coming into sight.

Careful consideration of this situation leads an intelligent person to think, "Who or what could be relied on to give definite refuge from the failures of becoming for myself and all the other migrators who are equivalent to space and have been my mothers, and all of whom have been living long and deep in this kind of unsatisfactoriness?" That would lead to the thought, "Who in this world has knowledge of the methods that can put an end to unsatisfactoriness, has love that makes him willing to be a refuge for all migrators, and has activity for others that is capable of providing refuge for them? Who would that be?" Then, if that issue

---

[119] All experiences within samsara are the basic state of thick stupidity bubbling up and disappearing again. Sentient beings fixate on them, turning them into the solidified particulars—happy, sad, and so on—of the existences they have painted for themselves. These solidified particulars are extremes created by concept—the extremes of existence, non-existence, and so on. When their reality is understood, they turn into a dance of phenomena which are flickering in and out like flashes of lightning. The point is that if sentient beings were to look into these existences that they have created for themselves, they would find that they are a mistake, and that would lead them to consider what to do about it.

were examined using the Reasoning of the Force of the Thing[120], an intelligent person would come to this understanding: "Rather than merely accepting beings such as Brahmā, Indra, Kapila, and so on as a refuge because they are generally regarded as being capable of such, and rather than simply accepting the buddha bhagavat[121] as a refuge because he is someone convenient to cling to, I should accept someone who has the capacity to give definite refuge"[122]. Following that, the person could, through the application of the three analyses, understand that even though someone like the teacher, the king of the Śhākyas, is not with us now, the path that he taught is a true one[123]. When he has understood that,

---

[120] For Reasoning of the Force of the Thing, see the glossary.

[121] Bhagavat is an Indian term of respect for a holy man.

[122] Many people simply accept a being as a refuge because their family or culture told them to do so. This is true for beings like Brahmā and Indra who the Hindus take as a refuge and Kapila who led a religious movement at the time of the Buddha who do not have the qualities needed for a true refuge. It is equally true for the Buddha who is a true refuge. However, an intelligent person does not just blindly take on a refuge because of hearsay but carefully examines a potential source of refuge using the appropriate reasoning. The reasoning needed is called Reasoning of the Force of the Thing. With it, one ascertains who is a true refuge by examining whether the person does or does not actually possess the necessary qualities.

[123] "The teacher, king of the Śhākyas" is a name for Buddha Śhākyamuni. "Teacher" means that he was the founding teacher of Buddhism. He was from the Śhākya race and as a Buddha he was like a king among them.

Having determined that the Buddha is a true source of refuge, we are faced with the fact that he is no longer present in person. Thus, we have to apply correct reasoning, the general name for which is the three types of logical analysis (see the glossary for more), to see

(continued...)

a type of trust now arrives with the thought, "The teacher does have knowledge given that he himself manifested that knowledge using the very method of that true path. He does have the love to teach it to others. He does have the capability that is required for giving them assistance given that he has the capability to give definite refuge from the failings of becoming using that sort of method. The buddha bhagavat alone is someone who does have the three".

Furthermore, if the person thinks it through using the perfectly correct prajñā[124] that accompanies the authoritative statements that came from that very refuge, the person will then understand the following. These sufferings of becoming mentioned earlier are not causeless for, if they were, they would be the excesses of permanent existence and non-existence. They also are not acausal as with Śiva's everlasting quality, and so on because those qualities are not stated by their advocates to be the forward and reverse modes of cause and effect. All of these sufferings are mere

---

[123](...continued)
whether his teaching as it has been passed down to us can be used as a refuge or not. Through it, we understand that the dharma is a true refuge. A further development of faith arrives at this point. We now have trusting faith that Śhākyamuni Buddha does have all of the qualities of a buddha—the totality of which are commonly summed up in the three qualities of knowledge, love, and capacity—and that therefore his teaching, which comes from his own realization, is also trustworthy.

[124] Prajñā is a mind which looks at a situation then makes a correct decision about it. It is possible for prajñā to go wrong if the logic being used in conjunction with it is wrong. Therefore, a perfectly correct prajñā is one that is functioning correctly and is doing so in conjunction with a perfectly correct type of reasoning. The statements of the Buddha came out of prajñā which was always perfectly correct for the simple reason that his mind was beyond all delusion.

appearances that originate from the interdependency of causes and conditions.[125]

If they did not originate in that way, then they would be similar to the son of a barren woman, and also, if the validator of no-change were to be applied to the course of their appearance, it would follow that they would have to remain even during the path that puts an end to such sufferings[126]. In addition to that, if they did

---

[125] Now, in accordance with the Buddha taught, there is the point that the suffering underlying the search for a refuge does have a cause. First, if it were without cause, the consequence would be that all the phenomena of suffering would either be permanently existent or non-existent. Because those are extremes and not how things actually are, suffering is not without cause. Second, suffering could not come as the special type of acausality claimed by followers of Śiva and other great gods of Hinduism when certain qualities of those gods, such as their everlasting quality, are considered. Why? Because this acausality is a mere theory that has no connection with the actual fact of how things work. Third, there is causality as taught by the Buddha with his full and correct knowledge under the topic the forward and reverse modes of the twelve links of interdependent origination. Therefore, the sufferings of samsara are caused and the type of causality involved is the interdependent origination taught by the Buddha.

[126] Moreover, if suffering did not originate interdependently, the phenomena of suffering would be causeless like a son produced from a barren woman, something that no-one in the world would accept. Also, the application of valid cognition (see the glossary) in a test of whether the suffering could change or not would show that the suffering could not change because of being uncaused. This goes against observed fact; application of the Buddha's path to enlightenment does put an end to suffering. Therefore, the sufferings are caused and the cause can be ended by the Buddha's path to enlightenment. This is what we have been looking for; it means that the Buddha as a potential refuge teaches a dharma that will work as a refuge. Therefore we can

(continued...)

not originate in that way, it would also lead to the proclamation of perverted paths like harmful activity being proclaimed as the true way, and the proclamation of non-paths such as relying on five fires in order to exhaust karma as paths, none of which can be paths that oppose the causes of becoming[127].

In contrast to that, the path of this particular teacher, the Buddha, is an authentic path because his approach of teaching non-self uproots not knowing, the seed that is the root of becoming in its entirety[128]. As it says in a sutra,

> Those humans who are scared with fear
> Mostly take refuge in mountains, forests,
> Parks, and in large trees used as a place of offerings;

---

[126](...continued)
trust that taking refuge in the Buddha and his dharma will be effective.

[127] To go even further, if the phenomena of suffering were not part of that causality, then there would be various types of false dharma that would not only be proclaimed but would have to be accepted as valid. There would be paths that actually go in the wrong direction and also paths that do not have the effect of overcoming the causes of samsara being proclaimed as true paths. An example of the first would be a path that teaches harming others. An example of the second would be the Hindu yogic practice called The Five Fires which is a practice still performed in India: in the blistering heat of northern India, four fires are set burning, one each in the four directions, and the yogin sits in the middle, as the fifth fire, in the belief that this will burn out his karma. From the Buddhist perspective, there are many perverted paths and many non-paths to enlightenment found in the religious world of India. New age religions in the West are examples, usually, of one of these approaches.

[128] In contrast, the Buddha's path is neither a perverted path nor a non-path. It is a genuine path that leads where it says it will lead specifically because it addresses the root cause of all problems, the particular state of un-knowing that results from grasping at a self.

Such refuges are not the principal one and
Such refuges are not supreme.
Someone who relies on such a refuge
Will not be liberated from all suffering.
Instead, when someone has gone to the buddha,
The dharma, and the saṅgha for refuge, he will, through
Suffering, the source of suffering,
True transcendence of suffering, and
The pleasant noble eightfold path,
Go to nirvana. With that,
The four truths of the noble ones
Together with prajñā used to produce the view
Is his principal refuge;
By relying on that refuge he will indeed
Be liberated from all suffering.[129]

As it says there, it is faith that comes from trust based in the certainty that the Buddha bhagavat alone is the sole refuge of those wanting emancipation, that his teaching is the sole portal to it, and that his saṅgha is the unparalleled place of generosity and assistant for the path which establishes the cause for travelling the path. Up to here, the way to establish that cause has been shown. Once the cause has been established, it becomes necessary to bring to mind,

---

[129] This explains which refuges work and which do not. It was and still is a part of many non-Buddhist traditions in India to make daily worship of deities at the base of large, spreading trees such as the Bodhi tree commonly found across the land. The trees were regarded by the common folk as the home of deities, so the common folk worshipped there each morning with offerings of various sorts. This gave rise to a major theme of Buddhist explanation—and it is found in the *Sutra* in the section on the good qualities of the noble saṅgha—that the community of spiritually advanced Buddhist practitioners, the noble saṅgha, are the best place to make these kinds of offerings for worship, not the deities who dwell around trees and the like.

that is, to recollect, the good qualities of those places of refuge. This whole process is what the *Praises in Alternating Verse and Prose* is talking about when it says,

> Deep and endless samsara
> Is to dwell wholly inside an ocean
> Where the desires, and so on are an unstoppable
> Sea monster who eats the body,
> So, today, where will one take refuge?

> If there is something which definitely has
> All faults always absent and
> Which at all times has
> All good qualities present and
> It has a mind, then
> I take refuge in it and,
> Praising it, I esteem it, and
> The families who dwell within its teaching ...[130]

The trust that comes from recollecting the good qualities of one's places of refuge is indeed what forms the basis of every path.

---

[130] "If ... it has a mind" means that it has to be sentient, not a mindless thing. "The families who stay in its teaching" refers to the various families of beings who are fully involved with that being's teaching; for example, in Buddhism there are the arhat and bodhisatva families. The author of the praise is saying that he would first search for a suitable refuge. If it turned out that it had the specific quality of being sentient as opposed to a thing, the author would take refuge in that being, and would then respect him and those involved with his teaching. Just so, we search for a refuge first. If we find that the Buddha has the good qualities needed, we take refuge in him. Having done so, in order to preserve and develop our newfound faith, we hold him in high esteem and offer him praises, both of which start with recollecting his good qualities. Then we do the same for his dharma teaching, and for his realized followers.

Therefore, I will explain a little about the ways of recollecting the noble Three Jewels[131]. The explanation will come in four main parts: the meaning of the title; the translator's homage; the meaning of the text; and the meaning of the conclusion.

I. The Meaning of the Title

It says, *In Indian language: āryaratnatraya anusmṛtisūtra. In Tibetan language: 'phags pa dkon mchog gsum rjes su dran pa'i mdo* <> In English language: *The Sutra of the Recollection of the Noble Three Jewels.*[132]

There, *noble* and *'phags pa* stand for *ārya*; *Jewels* and *dkon mchog* stand for *ratna*; *three* and *gsum* stand for *traya*, *re-* and *rjes su* stand for *anu*; *-collection* and *dran pa* stand for *smṛti*; and *sūtra* and *mdo* stand for *sūtra*[133].

Noble indicates that something is special and in a higher position. How does that meaning come through in this context? The term

---

[131] This is a play on words; he is saying that he will explain the ways of doing that as are found in the sūtra of the same name.

[132] When the text of the *Sutra* is cited in the commentary, it is set off from the commentary by showing it in bold italics.

[133] The work of translating Indian texts into Tibetan was not perfect and the translators wrote rationales for their translations of many terms. Mipham uses these rationales to explain some of the words at the beginning of the *Sutra*. He presents the Tibetan perspective on these issues, but it needs the relevant English perspective to be clear to non-Tibetan readers. Therefore, all these rationales are treated in depth in the chapter on translation issues.

has several usages but here it specifically indicates things that are transcendent, beyond the world[134].

There is the term *Jewels*. The term "ratna" in this context leads to the term "rin po che <> jewel". This term has six connotations —"dkon pa <> rare" and the rest—which are the features of "rin po che <> jewels (and similar precious things)" so that is the language used here. The literal translation of ratna—"rin chen <> something of value"—did not show this so the translation was done according to meaning. The result was the word "dkon mchog, Jewel" in which the two terms "dkon pa <> rare" and "mchog <> supreme" are actually present and the four terms which go with them are understood to have their meaning implied.[135]

Three ascertains the number involved: the teacher, his teaching, and the ones training in it.

Good qualities are the things that will be explained in the body of the text as the particulars worthy of praise.[136]

---

[134] The term ārya has been a standard word in Indian culture for millenia. In general, it means that which is elevated, higher, superior, noble, aristocratic. When used to refer to the Three Jewels, it indicates that they are not worldly but transcendent over the world. The Buddha is noble because he has utterly transcended samsara. The Buddha's dharma is noble because it transcends all worldly types of dharma teaching. The ordinary sangha is the local Buddhist sangha whose members might be excellent and wonderful but it is not the noble sangha. The sangha of beings who have practised the path to the point where they have transcended samsara is the noble sangha.

[135] See the explanation of ratna on page 27.

[136] This line is here because the title of the *Sutra* is effectively "the recollection of the good qualities of the noble Three Jewels".

Recollection refers to recollection made with an intelligence that is operating correctly and made of the good qualities present from the outset in the refuge object. The result is that the object's good qualities are brought to mind with neither over- nor understatement.

The term *sūtra* conveys the sense that something is simply the root or heart of the matter.

2. The Translator's Homage

I prostrate to the All-Knowing One. This reference to one who has knowledge of every single thing that could be known both in its depth and its extent, un-mixed up and without obscuration[137], namely the Buddha himself, is the translator's homage that elucidates the section to which the translated work belongs[138].

3. The Meaning of the Text

This has three parts: recollection of the buddha's good qualities; recollection of the dharma's good qualities; and recollection of the sangha's good qualities.

---

[137] "Depth and extent" refers to the two types of knowledge of a Buddha. "Unmixed up" means that every single phenomenon is known distinctly, without one blurring into another. "Without obscuration" means that nothing gets in the way of the knowledge; everything is fully known.

[138] The homage here indicates that this is a text connected with the Vinaya.

I. Recollection of the Buddha's good qualities

This has three parts: the good qualities of the teacher summarized, which sets the basis for the details; the details of his good qualities, which is an extensive explanation of the causes and effects involved; and those sections concluded.

1. The good qualities of the teacher summarized, which sets the basis for the details

This goes from *Thus it is: the buddha bhagavat* down to *bhagavat*.

Thus are the epithets of the one who is universally known as *the buddha bhagavat*, a name which has the sense "the one who is the unsurpassed teacher". Amongst other good qualities, he has fully perfected the two purposes—what is done for one's own sake and what is done for others' sake. The explanation of his good qualities in this section begins with the first of those two purposes.

He has understood the actuality of dharmas, just exactly as it is, thus he is the *tathāgata*. He himself unmistakenly realized suchness then, as well as that, taught it to others in order to get them to realize it.[139]

Arhat[140]. Just as the term "enemy" is generally known to the world as a name for those who shred goodness and create disharmony, so here the root of all faults, the afflictions, are made out as an enemy. Thus, someone who has removed them together with

---

[139] For actuality, see the glossary. He has gone (gata) to suchness (tathā) then taught it to others so that they too can go to suchness.

[140] See the explanation of arhat on page 36.

their latencies[141] is given the name "one who has defeated the enemy".

Truly complete (samyaksaṃ) buddha. The term "buddha" principally means "rtogs <> realization" though it has additionally been given the two connotations "sangs <> cleared out" and "rgyas <> blossomed". The meaning contained in the latter pair of words was used to derive the Tibetan word for buddha, "sangs rgyas <> cleared out and blossomed", a word that shows the *style* of the realization. It shows that a buddha has "sangs <> cleared out" the sleep of ignorance and that his mind, having fully "rgyas <> blossomed", includes all knowables. It presents an image of a buddha, as a lotus that has freed itself from the muck of the swamp and fully blossomed.[142]

Thus, the meaning of "buddha" was taken into the Tibetan language by arriving at the two words "sangs <> cleared out" and "rgyas <> blossomed", then combining them into the final term "sangs rgyas <> cleared out and blossomed" as just shown. Then, the remaining part before "buddha" which starts with the upasargaḥ "sam" was translated into Tibetan with "yang dag par rdzogs pa <> truly complete"[143]. The term buddha alone can refer

---

[141] For latencies, see the glossary.

[142] See the explanation of buddha on page 30 and in my own commentary.

[143] The remaining part is "samyaksam". It contains "sam" which is an upasargaḥ, the name of a class of particles in Sanskrit that are joined onto another word to intensify or otherwise modify the word's meaning. The first upasargaḥ "sam" in "samyaksam" goes with the "yak" and intensifies its meaning to give the sense "really, truly". The second "sam" goes with "buddha" to give the sense of "complete" or "full" buddha, as will be explained.

either to a self-conqueror or a tenth-level being[144], therefore to distinguish between them, the Sanskrit term "saṃ" meaning "rdzogs pa <> complete" was added to "buddha". The combined term could still refer either to a bad māra appearing as a manifestation of buddha[145] or to someone who has actually finalized the wisdom of the tenth level, therefore the Sanskrit term "samyak", which is "yang dag par <> truly", was also added in order to provide the needed distinction.

To sum this up, the buddha that we are talking about here has obtained the realization, that is, the wisdom, of a buddha, to an unsurpassable degree—to the point where the wisdom has no impurity and is without any incompleteness. Therefore, this buddha is given the name in Sanskrit "samyaksaṃbuddha" which is "yang dag par rdzogs pa'i sangs rgyas <> truly complete buddha".

Thus, a *tathāgata* is someone who has merged totally with the mind that knows the suchness of all dharmas. He is called an arhat from the perspective that he has abandoned without exception what is to be abandoned and is called a truly complete buddha from the perspective that he has realized without exception what is to be realized. Note that these two epithets are differing perspectives on the one thing; after all, one thing can be described in various ways![146]

---

[144] The term buddha is used to refer to the two arhats of the Lesser Vehicle—śhrāvakabuddhas and pratyekabuddhas—and also to bodhisatvas who have traversed and finally gained mastery of all ten levels of the Great Vehicle. The latter are called "truly complete buddhas" to distinguish them from the former.

[145] It is said that the māra named Garab Wangchuk can take the form of a buddha and deceive sentient beings into taking a wrong path.

[146] He makes this point to solve the confusion of someone who might

(continued...)

This sort of buddha is now given epithets that show his different features in relation to causes and effects. First is cause.

Possessor of insight and its feet. Buddhahood involves infinite types of causal paths yet they are truly summed up within the three principal trainings[147]. At the noble ones' levels, these three correspond to the sub-divisions of the eightfold path of the noble ones and, of those, right view is referred to with *insight* and the remaining seven are called its *feet*. In this context, insight is equivalent in meaning to sight. It is for example, like a person going along a road seeing the place with his eyes and making the journey with his feet on the place seen by his eyes. Thus, at the time of training in this insight and its feet, the two will, in general, be related to vipashyanā and shamatha respectively, and, at the time of no more training[148], insight will be related to the three insights of recollection of former places, and so on and feet to the four feet of miracles, the four complete perfections, and so on. There are many other ways in which the two can be joined to other items but there is the one key point that there must always be a pairing of sight of the meaning and engagement in that meaning. If that is done, the understanding intended will be properly specified and appropriately comprehended. Note that in general it is not all right not to follow this approach with explanations of texts and that is especially the case when explaining sutras.

At the time of the path, right view, which is like an eye, and insight, which is like its sight, belong to the training of prajñā, and the remainder—right livelihood, and so on—belong to the two

---

[146](...continued)
be wondering how Buddha could be an arhat and a truly complete buddha at the same time. See my commentary for an explanation.

[147] For the three principal trainings, see the glossary.

[148] The fifth of the five paths; for the five paths, see the glossary.

other trainings. When the path has been finalized, insight has to be defined as the three insights of no more training, given that all not-knowing of former and later limits[149] has been dispelled, though the insight does not change from being prajñā.

Someone who has followed that pleasant path and obtained the pleasant or blissful fruition of unsurpassable rank is called a *sugata*[150]. You might ask, "Why is it a pleasant path?" It has been said,

> This vehicle, a great mansion immeasurable as space,
> Is a supreme vehicle that makes for an attainment of
>   manifest joy, happiness, and pleasantness.
> Through riding on it, all sentient beings cross over to
>   nirvana.

Further, a person who has gone to that pleasant fruition is defined as having gone in three ways. Through relying on strengths that cannot be challenged which accomplish the two purposes[151], and on limitless dances of prajñā-emptiness and of upāya-compassion with its prayers of aspiration, dhyānas, extra perceptions, and so on, he has "legs par gshegs pa <> gone well to goodness", "slar mi ldogs par gshegs pa <> gone irreversibly to irreversibility", and "ma lus par gshegs pa <> gone not missing anything to nothing missed", all of which add up to his having gone to a supreme fruition.

Of the three ways of going just mentioned, the first means that he has gone to a situation that is without the slightest stain either of

---

[149] Limits here means "lifetimes". Knowledge of former and later lifetimes are two of the three insights, and full knowledge of the exhaustion of outflows is the third. Tāranātha's commentary contains a good treatment of this epithet.

[150] See the explanation of sugata on page 38 and in my own commentary.

[151] ... of oneself and others ...

suffering or its source, both of which belong to the side of total affliction, samsara, so has gone to goodness or "mdzes par gshegs pa ◇ has gone beautifully to beauty" and is like a person with a beautiful form. In this way, he has distinguished himself from those in samsara because of having gone beyond the cause-and-effect-based suffering of those who live in becoming.

His having gone irreversibly means that, because he has removed the seed of views of a self, he will not relapse into samsara. This is like firewood which has been consumed cannot give rise to a flame again. It is comparable to a person who has fully recovered from a contagious disease like pox, given that someone who has been sick with pox disease and properly recovered from it cannot fall sick with that disease again in that life.

Those two ways of having gone set this path apart from the paths of outsiders[152] because their paths do not include abandonment of the seed of views of a self. Their paths lead up as far as the summit of existence but are not capable of crossing over the boundary of becoming.

His having gone not missing anything to nothing missed or it is also said "rdzogs par gshegs pa ◇ gone completely to completion", means that he has obtained the dharmas belonging to the qualities of finalized abandonment and realization without even the smallest part of them not having being obtained, like a vase that has been filled totally with liquid. This way of going distinguishes him from the śrāvakas and pratyekas who, although they have irreversibility, have an abandonment and realization which is not complete.

---

[152] Insiders are Buddhists and outsiders are followers of spiritual systems religions other than Buddhism.

This mode of going to buddhahood begins with the fact that mind's nature is luminosity but has adventitious stains on it. That leads to a path to be travelled that has a specific antidote for removing the stains—prajñā that realizes lack of self—and which also has methods to assist that prajñā. There is a force that comes from familiarization using the methods and, if the familiarization is taken through to the finish, the methods have the ability to produce a complete abandonment and realization. For this type of path, trust developed through logical establishment using Reasoning of the Force of the Thing is important, more about which can be known from the Indian texts of Dharmakīrti, and so on[153].

The epithets so far have shown the Buddha's perfection of activity done for his own sake. Now, the perfection of activity done for others' sake is treated with the phrases *knower of the world*, and the rest.

Knower of the world. The term "world" has many connotations—such as container, contents, suffering, and so on. Here it refers to all of the pervasive[154] sentient beings being looked upon and seen without obscuration by wisdom. "Knower of the world" refers to great compassion whose nature is prajñā; the prajñā sees sentient beings in the way just described and the great compassion acts as a sovereign for them, displaying itself in illusory ways in exact

---

[153] In other words, this path has two aspects to it: the direct antidote—prajñā—to the stains that cover the luminosity of mind—and the indirect antidote—methods—that, through the process of gradual familiarization, brings one to the enlightened state. This path of prajñā and method relies on inferential reasoning to establish trust in it, and the way to do that is taken up at length in the Indian texts on valid cognition, especially those of Dignāga and his main disciple Dharmakīrti.

[154] Meaning the sentient beings who pervade the entirety of samsara.

accordance with the fortunes[155] of those to be tamed. This compassion with a nature of prajñā looks at all worlds at all times, day
and night, seeing, as has been said, "Whoever is in failure, whoever is in misery, whoever is to be tamed", and, knowing all as it
does, gives thought to those to be tamed without pausing for even
a moment; all of this together is the cause of the perfection of
others' sakes.

Based in that sort of great compassion, he is an ***unsurpassed driver
who tames beings***. Given that beings are those to be tamed and
that he is the one who has the capability needed to put them onto
the path, he is the one "who tames beings". The world speaks of
anyone who has the job of steering chariots, horses, and so on as
a "driver"[156]. In accordance with that, because he is the one who
steers beings away from the dreadful abyss of becoming towards
the place of emancipation, he is called the driver who tames
beings. The way that he tames beings is not like the approach of
a king who imposes sanctions on his subjects; he does not create
suffering for beings but leads them to emancipation along the path
of abandonment of the two extremes, a path which is a source of
unending pleasantness[157] for as long as it is followed. There is no
question either that he can tame even those who are extremely difficult to tame—such as the Buddha's younger brother Nanda who
had attachment, Aṅgulimāla who had fierce anger, Kāśhyapa who
was overflowing with pride, and Lamchungwa who had very dull
faculties—because he has infinite types of method. Given that
throughout the whole of time and space there is not even one

---

[155] Fortune here means a being's karmic lot.

[156] Tib. kha lo bsgyur ba. The term here is the general term for someone who drives or steers a conveyance such as a vehicle or animal. It
does not mean the driver of a specific vehicle, such as a charioteer.

[157] "Pleasant" here refers to both path and fruition contexts as described above under sugata.

being to be tamed whom he carelessly disregards, his enlightened activity for all those to be tamed indeed extends throughout the reaches of space, therefore, he is said to be *unsurpassed* at this activity of taming.[158]

That covered how he tames beings in general. The next epithet, that he is *the teacher of gods and men*, concerns a specific point of that general activity. In general, the Capable One[159] teaches migrators as a whole, but there is the particular of who actually heard dharma from him then relied on the noble path, and who did not. Accordingly, although he acted to liberate the mind-streams of all migrators by teaching the noble ones' four truths, he is called *the teacher of gods and men* because it was primarily those two groups of beings who were tamed through hearing him in person and actually following the path.

Thus it was that he did the deed of completing abandonment and realization for himself and then, out of love, became the teacher of dharma for others. Understanding that this "peerless teacher", as he is called, has the qualities of being a teacher for himself and a teacher for others leads to the development of respect.

Is the buddha bhagavat draws a conclusion to those epithets. It shows that the Buddha who has finalized the two purposes in that

---

[158] Although "unsurpassed" is placed after and as a separate item from "driver who tames beings" in the Tibetan edition of the *Sutra*, the original recollections clearly show that "unsurpassed" is an adjective modifying "driver who tames beings". Mipham's explanation of the term shows that he understands this point.

[159] Skt. muni. Muni means one who is has the capacity to gain enlightenment and who is inspired or driven to gain it. It was a common name in ancient India for any spiritual practitioner who was making progress or who had completed his chosen path. It is sometimes translated as "sage" but that is not the meaning.

way is called "the bhagavat", thereby showing that "buddha" and "bhagavat" equally are terms which indicate the two good qualities of abandonment and realization. "Buddha" has already been explained earlier. In regard then to bhagavat, the root "bhaga" literally means "bcom <> defeat" and is further understood to mean "skal ba <> fortunate" and "legs pa <> goodness". Thus, bhagavat, which literally translates as "bcom ldan <> defeat possessing", means a person who has the good qualities that come from having defeated the four māras or, alternatively, a person who possesses the six qualities of "goodness" which are ascribed to Īṣhvara and others. However, the mere literal meaning was not made into the main consideration at the time of translation and a word was produced based on the uncommon meaning contained in the term. The word " 'das <> transcended" was simply added on to give "bcom ldan 'das <> defeat possessing transcended" causing it to be set above meaning the great god of the outsiders and others. That is how the terms bhagavat and buddha come to incorporate the meaning of higher abandonment and realization.

Some commentaries make the connection here between the bhagavat mentioned earlier as a feature of the Buddha and this mention of bhagavat which shows the person having the feature, though nothing special is achieved in doing so. The words "thus the bhagavat" at the beginning served to make the basis of the features known, so the way I have done it here works well.[160]

2. The extensive explanation

This has two parts: the way he appears in the world for others' sake; and the way he finalized abandonment and realization for his own sake.

---

[160] The explanations of bhagavat on page 33 and in my own commentary will clarify his explanation of bhagavat.

1. The way he appears in the world for others' sake

This has two parts: how he appears to others; and, having this appearance, how he acts for their sake.

1. How he appears to others

This is covered in the text going from *that tathāgata* down to *seeing him he is without disharmony*.

That tathāgata means the tathāgata of the sort just explained. The cause which is his source is that, out of great compassion for others and nothing else, he has finalized an immeasurable accumulation of merit. Thus it says that he *corresponds to a cause of merits*[161]. This is similar to what has been said in a sutra:

> The tathāgata is the image of dharmas of un-outflowed virtues.

The merit of which the tathāgata is a direct result was not spent on and exhausted in producing a result—as happens with the virtue of an ordinary beings, nor was it spent on and exhausted in arriving at being without remainder of aggregates—as happens with the roots of virtue of śrāvakas and pratyekas. Thus that merit was not, and for as long as there is space never will be, let go to waste.[162]

---

[161] "Corresponds to a cause" is a technical phrase used to indicate that an effect corresponds to a particular cause. For example, wheat corresponds to having the cause of wheat seed and not some other cause. To which cause does the tathāgata correspond? A tathāgata comes from merit, in particular. The quote just following this is saying the same thing; merit and virtue can be taken as synonymous here.

[162] This paragraph states that the Buddha did not allow the merits that were his cause to be wasted on lesser results such as samsaric happiness

(continued...)

Furthermore, at the fictional level he stays within the skill-in-means that comes from the universal dedications made for others' sakes and at the superfactual level he views via non-referencing the expanse of phenomena with equal taste. Therefore, at the authentic level, he arises from the blessings of having obtained the wisdom vajra kāya whose mode is unification of the two truths and then the form kāyas and the like of that wisdom kāya correspond to a cause of merit. That merit, moreover, given that it is never spent merely in a ripening that has a result just one time, never goes to waste.[163]

And furthermore, every one of *his roots of virtue* used in producing this vajra kāya is such that each one *does not go to waste.* As the *Avataṃsaka Sūtra* says,

> Even hearing, seeing, or offering to those conquerors
> Will develop an immeasurable pile of merit.
> When the afflicted states, all the sufferings of samsara,
>   are abandoned,

---

[162](...continued)
or the peace of the arhats.

[163] For fictional and dharmadhātu, see the glossary. Referencing is the act of dualistic mind in which it references a concept, not the actual object; wisdom is non-referencing because it does not know via concept. Skt. kāya means "body" in the sense of any coherent assemblage. It can refer to physical bodies, mental bodies, a whole state of being, a body of knowledge, and so on. The wisdom vajra kāya is the wisdom that constitutes the overall being of a buddha. Because it is permanent, never-ending, and so on, it is an indestructible kind of being or kāya and is therefore named a vajra kāya or indestructible type of being. The form kāyas—the saṃbhoga- and nirmāṇa-kāyas—include all that is given off by this indestructible wisdom being. The merits that are the cause of these form kāyas ripen in a manner that is consistent with the indestructible wisdom being, not in a samsaric way. Therefore, they ripen in a mode in which they could not go to waste.

It is not thrown out and does not end with this
compounded phenomenon[164].

As with the example of water drops joining a pool of water—an
example which he taught repeatedly and in many ways in the
sutras—the tathāgata aimed just one time at obtaining the vajra-
like body of the equality of the four times but, like being caught in
the mouth of an alligator and unable to get free, doing that was
like a drop of water put into an ocean[165].

He is fully ornamented with all patience. When his form kāya,
the primary cause of which is patience, is seen, there is nothing
unharmonious about it. That has been expressed in these words,

---

[164] Although compounded phenomena are discarded at the time of
leaving samsara, the pile of merit created in relationship to enlightenment is not discarded, even though it is a compounded phenomenon.

[165] This third of three connected paragraphs gives yet another reasoning in relation to "the merit which is a tathāgata's cause does not go to
waste". Any merit made in connection with enlightenment—for
example Śhākyamuni Buddha's arousing the mind for enlightenment
for the first time so many ages ago—irrevocably becomes part of the
pool of enlightenment merit. That merit is different from ordinary,
samsaric merit. It never finishes, even at the time of enlightenment.
This is another way that it does not go to waste.

The Buddha often used the example of a drop of water put into an
ocean to indicate that the individual merits of enlightenment never end
for as long as vast being of enlightenment exists.

The Buddha said that, three universes ago, he met the tathāgata of that
time and, for the first time, aroused the mind for enlightenment, the
drive to attain the ultimate vajrakāya of a truly complete buddha.
Despite the fact that he did it just one time, the force of it continued
on all the way through to buddhahood. Thus it was inextricably—as
in the example of the alligator—committed to enlightenment, just as
though it were a single drop of water put into an ocean.

> Through patience the form of excellence and vast
>   holiness will be obtained;
> It will be beautiful, golden in colour, and a sight to be
>   seen for migrators.

The form kāya arises from the pāramitā of patience having been completed in every way, therefore, with respect to its cause, it is "ornamented with patience". Or, given that this kāya which is unyielding like a vajra and has strengths complete in every way is not dependent on conditions, it is "ornamented with patience". In relation to this, even if countless third order worlds[166] batted him about, tossing him across immeasurable worlds, he would not react with harm to the migrators involved, and so on[167]. Also, even though he might sit for immeasurable kalpas while not receiving a single alm, his body would not be affected whatsoever by weariness, tiredness, and so on.

His basis is troves of merit. Troves conveys the sense of endless. The extent of merit connected with even a single hair pore of the tathāgata just cannot be comprehended. Thus, this epithet is to the effect, "his kāya is founded in merit that is complete in every way".

---

[166] For third order world, see the glossary. A third order world system is fully known as a "great order third order thousand-fold world system" where great order means that it is the largest cosmic structure in this system of cosmology and third order means to the power of three. It is also called a "great thousand" and also a "third thousand" world. These terms are used in various combinations throughout this commentary to refer to the same, largest cosmic structure. The Buddha did not say that one of these universes makes up saṃsāra; rather, he said that saṃsāra consists of an infinite number of them.

[167] That is, would not do any of the many things that are listed as results of a lack of patience.

Moreover, the *Hurling A Boulder Sutra* says,

> The merit of the sentient beings of this world totalled
> would not compare with even a one hundred thousandth
> portion of the merit of a wheel-wielding[168] owner of a
> single continent. Similarly, the merit of two continents
> would not stand up to even a fraction of the merit of a
> wheel-wielding owner of two continents, and so on[169].
> The merit of one hundred thousand times ten million
> wheel-wielding owners of four continents would not
> stand up to a one hundred thousandth portion of the
> merit of the gods of the four strata of the Great Kings.
> One hundred thousand times ten million of the gods of
> the Four Great Kings compared to the Four Great
> Kings, and one hundred thousand times ten million of
> the merits of the four kings compared to the gods of the
> Thirty Three, and one hundred thousand times ten
> million of the merits of the gods of the Thirty Three
> compared to Indra, and then Free From Strife and Son
> of the Gods[170] Best of Free from Strife, Joyous and Son
> of the Gods Completely Joyous, Enjoying Manifestat-
> ions and Son of the Gods Best of Enjoying Manifestat-
> ions, Controlling Others' Manifestations and Son of the
> Gods of Controlling, the Brahmā strata, Brahmā and so

---

[168] Skt. Chakravartin. The Sanskrit term is often translated as "wheel-turning king". He does not turn the wheel-like sceptre that he holds in his hand but wields it to govern. There are levels of this type of king which are distinguished according to the size of their domain.

[169] "And so on" means "and everything else with that wheel-wielder's domain".

[170] "Son of the gods" in each case is a name for the ruling god of that level. Up through "Controlling" is a listing of the increasingly higher levels of the desire realm and from Brahmā to Akaniṣṭha is a listing of the increasingly higher levels of the form realm.

on, up to Akaniṣṭha, all one hundred thousand times ten million compared to the top one of their type. And then, the merit of as many bodhisatvas in their last birth in existence as there are sands in the Ganges compared to a one hundred thousandth portion of the merit pile of a tathāgata, and that[171] in turn would not even go into examples, count, and causes[172].[173]

And it also says,

Again, the merit pile of all sentient beings multiplied by ten would produce one hair pore of the tathāgata. The pile of merit required to produce all the hair pores multiplied by one hundred would produce one minor sign and the merit required to produce all of the minor signs multiplied by one hundred would produce one of each of the major marks, except for the three of ūrṇā, crown protuberance, and dharma conch[174]. The merit required to produce all twenty-nine major marks multiplied by ten thousand would produce the ūrṇā. The merit required to produce the ūrṇā multiplied by one hundred thousand gives the crown protuberance. The merit required to produce the crown protuberance

---

[171] The merit of a tathāgata, which has now been arrived at …

[172] "Examples, count, and causes" is the standard way of enumerating something in the ancient Indian system of studies. Something that "will not go into them" means that the thing "is beyond the reach of normal comprehension".

[173] The translation matches the text of the sutra exactly. In some sutras, the text in these kinds of examples is not always grammatical, just a long listing of sorts.

[174] The ūrṇā is the small, curled hair between the eyebrows of a buddha's nirmāṇakāya. The dharma conch is the speech faculty of a buddha's nirmāṇakāya.

multiplied by one hundred thousand times ten million would produce the speech, the dharma conch.

Furthermore, while he was on the path, he perfected each of the levels of generosity, and the rest. Moreover, as much as he accomplished on any given level using the force of intelligence, miracles, and ripening, he accomplished in each and every moment of the next higher level. The ways in which he practised to develop this kāya and how it is a perfect accumulation of the profound and vast —the domains of the two truths—is shown in the sutras and in the *Prayer of Aspiration for Excellent Conduct*[175].

His kāya is based in immeasurable merits as just mentioned but more than that, it also forms a basis from which immeasurable merit will be developed. This can be known from his own statement, "From me, babies, youngsters, and golden-coloured ones of realization", and others like it. Also, it is like what was said in a sutra,

He has the major marks of hundreds of merits,
Thus a trove of merit[176] acts in this world inclusive of
    the gods[177],
So that the seeing of it, hearing of it, or even its smiling
Is something done to benefit all sentient beings.

---

[175] The well-known prayer of aspiration by Samantabhadra. Samantabhadra was one of the eight principal bodhisatva disciples of the Buddha. He is known for his ability at making aspiration prayers.

[176] It comes from merit and becomes the cause of merit.

[177] The main disciples of Buddha were humans and also gods from certain of the desire realms. "This world inclusive of the gods" means this world of ours and the worlds of those particular gods, too.

Although the form kāya is his own fruition, the eighty minor signs of copper-coloured nails, and so on make it stand out to others, so the *Sutra* says ***The excellent minor signs adorn him***. In addition, he is beautified by the thirty-two major marks, such as the design of a thousand-spoked wheel clearly marking the palms of his hands and soles of his feet, so the *Sutra* says ***the flowers of the major marks bloom on him***. The flowers of the major marks are like delightful, fully bloomed flowers on him and that feature itself is enhanced by the fresh anthers of the minor signs, and that altogether rouses overt joy in all migrators.

The kāya of perfected qualities having cause and effect like that acts out the four kinds of conduct[178] but, beginning with even the subtlest movement of a hair in a hair pore, the whole of it never alters in the least from being for the sake of sentient beings, so what anyone sees of it is always in harmony with that person's elements, faculties, and thoughts. Thus it says, ***perceiving his activity, it being just right, there is harmony***. What is being communicated here is that there is harmony between the Buddha's "activity as the object of some being's perception" and the mindstream of that being "for which it is just right"[179].

---

[178] The four kinds of conduct—going, staying, lying, standing—is the Indian way of summarizing all circumstances of human behaviour.

[179] The Tibetan wording of this epithet is difficult to understand to Mipham worked hard to make it clear. The Buddha's activity is always just right for any given being who might observe it because it always has the quality of being "tailor-made" for that particular being at that particular moment. When it does become an object of the perception of that being, that is, when the Buddha's activity is known to the mind of that being, there is only harmony—meaning perfect consistency—between the activity shown by the Buddha for that being and what is appropriate for the being's mindstream. In short, this epithet is on the side of the Buddha and how a buddha's actions are always fitting for

(continued...)

That was from the perspective of qualities that arrive in the mind of the person who is perceiving Buddha. Because of that quality, there is the additional quality that, when a person looks at the tathāgata's kāya, it is not possible that even the slightest appearance of disharmony could arise in the person's mind. Thus, from the perspective that faults have been abandoned, it says, *seeing him there is no disharmony*.[180]

2. Having this appearance, how he acts for their sake

This has two parts: the particulars of who goes before him; and the overview.

1. The particulars of who goes before him

There are two type of beings who go before the Buddha—those who go with faith and those who go wanting to oppose him.

The first consists of those persons who go to see a sight or who are compelled to go there by virtuous roots or who go to him out of trust to make offerings, and so on. When they see the tathāgata, their mental impurities are pacified and a lucid faith is born in them. That faith creates the cause for them to look on him with longing and they become so absorbed that they would not notice even if a monk were to strike them. Then a great joy, one free

---

[179](...continued)
the sentient beings who will perceive it. The next epithet is about the visual appearance of the Buddha as seen from the side of the viewer.

[180] This actually means that the Buddha's form has no faults, as is clearly stated in Tāranātha's commentary. Because there is nothing imperfect about it, when it is seen, there is no imperfection, no disharmony of form that comes to the viewer of the form.

from impurity, develops in them. Therefore, *he brings overt joy to those who long through faith*[181].

Some might come with the thought of opposing the tathāgata but, once they have arrived in front of him, they will not be able to withstand his brilliance and will pale in comparison, like constellations pale in the light of the sun. With their haughtiness removed, he can bring them into contact with the pleasantness of peace[182].

Moreover, there is no impediment at all to the knowing quality of the tathāgata's mind, so his prajñā can never be overpowered by anyone. For example, there was Devadatta with his many piles of charcoal powder each made from a different tree. And there was the important person from the Śhākyas with his piles of rice taken from each of the lay households where someone had died. The name indicating where each pile had come from had been written down and put inside each pile and the piles loaded onto elephants which were then led before the Buddha. The piles were pointed out one by one and the Buddha was asked to show his abilities by giving a prophecy, and so on for each. It was impossible for them to create grounds for a complaint against the Buddha because there was never a case where he did not know and did not see what was what[183]. Thus, *his prajñā cannot be overpowered.*

---

[181] The requirements of English cause the process presented in this epithet to be written out backwards. The wording in Tibetan shows the correct order, which is that there is faith, which leads to longing, which leads to joy. The joy that is so strong that it is obvious to others, hence it is overt joy.

[182] He can bring them into contact with the path, the pleasant path as described earlier that leads to the pleasant peace of enlightenment.

[183] Two separate stories are combined into one here, a story of Devadatta and a story of an important person of the Śhākya clan. In both
(continued...)

This is similar to what is found in the *Hurling A Boulder Sutra*,

> There is an ocean eighty thousand yojanas deep and of unfathomable width. It fills completely with liquid of black ink[184]. The king of mountains, Meru, subsides eighty thousand yojanas into the water and rises back up eighty thousand yojanas. The four faces are the four precious substances. There are four continents in the four directions and these turn into paper of birch bark. All the abodes whichever there are of sentient beings on the four continents turn into letters. All plants and grasses whichever there are above the earth turn into bamboo pens. Now, if they were to write, the ink, paper, and pens would completely run out. Unlike that, bhikṣhu Śhāriputra's prajñā would not be spent in the slightest[185]. A great third order world filled with those having prajñā like Śhāriputra would not amount to even a hundred thousandth portion of the tathāgata's prajñā, and that in turn cannot be shown through example, count, or cause ...

Just like the tathāgata's enlightened mind has prajñā without limit, the tathāgata's body strengths, and so on are higher than and

---

[183](...continued)
stories there was an attempt to discredit the Buddha by showing that his claims, as a tathāgata, to superior knowledge, and so forth, were false. In each case, the Buddha was able to live up to the claims of his buddhahood with its extraordinary qualities, so the people attempting to discredit him were not able to create a public complaint against him of being a charlatan and hence were not able to discredit him.

[184] A yojana is an Indian measure of distance. There are two definitions of it: it is either about ten or twenty kilometres in length.

[185] The śhrāvaka monk Śhāriputra, one of the two closest disciples of the Buddha, was known as the monk with the greatest prajñā.

unsurpassed by any other strength. Thus, given that nothing in the whole of time and space is able to challenge them, *his strengths cannot be challenged*. Strength here is explained in some commentaries as the ten mind strengths and in others as the strengths of body only, but the ten strengths, except for being distinguished as ten on the basis of object are, in fact, prajñā strengths. When it says "strengths", it is for body but not only body; correct ascertainment requires that the strengths of miracles, and so on also be included in that ascertainment.

The strengths of the body of the tathāgata are measureless. Nevertheless, I will explain them just enough to give an idea of them. From the *Hurling a Boulder Sutra*,

> Previously, when the bhagavat was staying in the forest of leeches, the strong men of that country went to offer him alms. Sitting on the road that runs between of Kuśha City and the river Vasumat was a great rock fifteen fathoms high and seven and a half fathoms across. The strong men thought amongst themselves, "If this rock were to be moved aside, the road would be cleared, we could make offerings to the Buddha, and we would also become famous". Therefore, they gathered together the strong men of Kuśha City who had very great strength, then brought up many hundreds of horses, oxen, camels, herd-leading elephants, and bulky elephants which they tied to the rock with rope. One person with a ramp tied it on with mixed grass and other types ropes, and hauled. One person used one hundred iron ploughs to try to extract it from its lodging. One person attempted to cut it with a battle-axe. One wanted to accomplish the task by pulverising it to dust with vajra strikers. And one person tried to destroy it with substances and mantra. However, none of them

could so much as budge it, so they gave up on it for the time being[186].

The bhagavat arrived there and, after receiving a joyful welcome, arranged himself to one side. The bhagavat said to them, "How did young men like you become tired by this?" They told him their story in detail, "We started twenty-nine days ago but could not even budge this big rock. Thus, with the thought, "How could we even think to move it to another place?", we gave up on it for the time being". The bhagavat offered, "Would you like to have that boulder moved off to another place?" They replied, "We request to the utmost that the bhagavat do so!" The bhagavat used the toe of his right foot to push it firmly and the whole thing was extracted from its lodging. He raised his left arm, then put his right palm on the boulder and, after thinking for just a moment, hurled it upwards as far as Brahmā's world so that it disappeared from sight. The sound made the strong men panic, so the bhagavat said, "Do not be afraid!" And, as it was going up, the sound of,

> Compounded things are impermanent and
> All dharmas are without self and
> Nirvana is peace.

---

[186] The leader of a herd of elephants is the strongest elephant in the herd. A bulky elephant is a type of elephant with very large body and hence strength. One person used a ramp to make it easier to haul the rock out of its lodging. The ropes used were made of mixed grasses, which is a particular type of very strong rope in use at the time, and others like that, too. A vajra striker is a kind of strong hammer, with a vajra on the head to symbolize its irresistible power. The person who used substances and mantra was a yogin of some kind; tantric practice includes the use of substances blessed with mantra that become powerful and can be used for various purposes.

came forth. The rock returned and the tathāgata rested the palms of his hands on it. Then the tathāgata blew on it, turning it completely to dust, and a rain of dust came down in all directions. Then, knowing that the strong men were unhappy that the boulder was no more, he gathered up the dust of the boulder in its entirety, returned the boulder to its former state, and went off to one side, where he sat alone.

The strong men were amazed and asked, "Where did that kind of strength come from? Did it come from the strength of the tathāgata's father and mother or from a miracle or from the strength of meditation?" The tathāgata said, "That strength arose from father and mother; the sound 'compound things are impermanent', and so on arose from the strength of miracles. Making it into dust by blowing on it and then re-assembling it and putting it in a different place was the strength of meditation". The strong men asked, "How do you have this sort of strength that arises from father and mother?" He said, "The strength of ten men is the strength of one ordinary oxen, and ten of those that of a blue oxen. Then, successively for each of herd-leader, rhinoceros, ordinary elephant, unyielding elephant, loud-trumpeting elephant, tusker elephant, blue mountain elephant, and similarly, yellow mountain, red, white, having supreme scent, having a gentle scent, having the scent of an Utpala[187], having the scent of a Kumud[188], those ones, and an elephant of lotus, and an elephant of great lotus, and one born in the snows, and Bal elephants[189] of greater and greater strength going ten times higher at a

---

[187] A type of lotus.

[188] A type of flower.

[189] A type of elephant that can run very quickly and is very strong.

time is as follows. The combined strength of ten bulky elephants is one half strength. Ten of the strengths that are one strength come from adding two of those together is half of an overwhelming strength. Two of those make one overwhelming strength. The strength of ten overwhelming ones are one strength of supreme strength. Ten supreme strengths make a branch supreme strength. Ten branch supreme strengths make half a Nārāyaṇā[190] strength. Two of those make one Nārāyaṇā strength. Three hundred and twenty Nārāyaṇā strengths are the strength that came from the tathāgata's father and mother. Each one of the places of the tathāgata's kāya is created holding a Nārāyaṇā strength".

And, it is similar to what the Showing Craft section of the *Lalita-vistara*[191] says,

> For Mt. Sumeru with its vajra rings,
> Any other mountain in the ten directions
> Strokes it with the hand and runs off hoofless, creating ruin,
> So what is so amazing about the human body without essence?[192]

---

[190] Nārāyaṇā is the name of one of the important figures in the Śhiva pantheon, though it can also be an alias for Viṣṇu or Kṛiṣhṇa. Here it is likely to mean Kṛiṣhṇa because he had prodigious strength.

[191] Chapter ten of this Great Vehicle sutra enumerates and discusses sixty-four items of arts, crafts, music, dance, and sport.

[192] Someone of superior strength, like the Buddha, cannot be matched by others, just as ordinary mountains cannot match the strength of Mt. Meru. They would stroke him to please him, then run off in abject fear, not waiting to put on their shoes, and leaving destruction in their

(continued...)

Furthermore, he has immeasurable strength of miracles. A sutra says,

> The bhagavat was dwelling at a place that had the grass Birana, at the base of a tree where there was a smooth hole like a yakṣha mud-hole. It was a time of famine and a beggarwoman was finding it difficult to obtain alms. The great Maudgalyāyana asked the Buddha, "Under the great earth there is a splendid corpse, so if a being of strength changed this great earth to leaves of a Plantain tree, it would change the situation to one without difficulty. If as many sentient beings as there are on this earth were to join left hands then right hands and make a ring continuously around the great earth, they could change it in an instant".

> The tathāgata replied, "Even if it were changed like that, most sentient beings would become desirous and stupid over the food-providing corpse. Also, the corpse might be a splendid one but it will not stay for long and will disappear", and he did not grant the request. He said, "Maudgalyāyana, even though a person with that kind of miraculous power were to clean this great order third order thousand-fold world system, doing so would not amount even to a one hundredth part of the tathāgata's miracle strength, on up to would not amount to a cause[193]".

Then, for the strength of meditation, it also says in a sutra,

---

[192](...continued)
wake. The ordinary human person with the ordinary strengths of the ordinary human body is nothing special.

[193] "On up to would not amount to a cause" is standard abbreviation for "could not be shown by example, count, or causes".

> A rain of the season of great clouds descended on the
> four continents and from it, the streams of the great
> rivers of the four continents ran down to the oceans.
> The tathāgata said of that, "From each of the drops of
> water, this whole situation—this continent's towns and
> its meadows, and so on, and its trees with their branches,
> leaves, seeds, and so on—fill in their names—is so".

In other words, he was saying that the tathāgata has the capacity
to see all of the atoms that are distributed in a single drop of water.
That gives an idea of it and then it can be fully understood from
the sutras. For example, it is said in one of them,

> The lesser number of gods and men of this kind of great
> order third order thousand-fold world system compared
> to the greater number of sentient beings seen to be
> present in one spot just the area of a chariot wheel by an
> outsider ṛishi[194] possessing the five extra-perceptions
> and free from attachment, and the lesser number of
> sentient beings seen as a whole in the great thousand-
> fold system by that one free from attachment compared
> to the greater number of sentient beings seen to be
> present in one spot just the area of a chariot wheel by
> the god's eye of a śhrāvaka arhat, and the lesser number
> of sentient beings seen as a whole in the great thousand-
> fold system by that śhrāvaka arhat compared to the
> greater number of sentient beings seen in the region just
> the area of a chariot wheel by the god's eye of a
> pratyekabuddha, and all sentient beings seen in the great
> thousand by the pratyekabuddha compared to the many

---

[194] Skt. ṛishi, Tib. drang srong. One of many words from ancient India
for someone who is a spiritual practitioner. This words emphasizes
that the person has good spiritual attainment and can lead others
properly because of it. The Buddha is often referred to as the ṛishi or
great ṛishi.

more seen in just the region of a chariot wheel by the god's eye of a bodhisatva. Using that approach, how many sentient beings are seen in the third order thousand by a bodhisatva compared to the greater and countless number of sentient beings seen abiding in the region just the area of a chariot wheel by the god's eye of a tathāgata?

Using that approach, the minds, mental events, and physical elements of the sentient beings as a whole dwelling in the universes of the ten directions is not easy even for the bodhisatvas who abide in levels of complete emancipation that are beyond concept[195] to count or comprehend during kalpas numbering the amount of sands in the Ganges but, spontaneously, the tathāgata knows in an instant and without mixup each and every one of all the minds and mental events of all of such sentient beings of the three times.

Moreover, in regard to this, the tathāgata comes from a cause of compassion. Being the nature of great compassion, the strength of his loving kindness, which follows the count and elements of sentient beings, is immeasurable. Even when he was training in this on the path, all of the completing, aspiring, and preparing[196] done then was done only because of great compassion for the sake of others. When those were finalized, the tathāgata had manifested inseparable emptiness and compassion, the wisdom of no

---

[195] The eighth through tenth levels of a bodhisatva.

[196] "Completing, aspiring, and preparing" comes from the *Prajñāpāramitā Sūtra* of the Great Vehicle. As a bodhisatva journeys to buddhahood, he has to complete the three acts of: preparing a buddha field for his activity; ripening or preparing those who will be his students; and making a full set of aspirations for his future activity. This is mentioned in other places in the commentary using similar words.

more learning—so how could the capacity of the particular strength which is his great loving kindness ever be fathomed? It could not because it spreads throughout the limits, whatever they are, of space and the limits, whatever they are, of time. This sort of talk is also found in a sutra where it says,

> The great king, the trainee in virtue, Gautama,
> possessing the strength of great loving kindness
> possesses a mind that does not become angry at any of
> all of the sentient beings. And, moreover, that loving
> kindness does not become obscured with attachment.
> And it always arises spontaneously, covers the whole
> area, pervades every one of the world systems, and
> operates according to the thoughts of each of the
> sentient beings.

And,

> He sends his loving kindness to pervade
> All times and all fields and all worlds.
> He sends his loving kindness to pervade
> The thoughts too of all migrators.
> Possessing knowledge and loving kindness,
> The peerless muni's love
> Does not not pervade some directions and
> Does indeed pervade the elements and thoughts[197].
> Thus it is that the all-knowing one does nothing faulty;
> For example, for a gem to be cleansed with water so that
> It is very pure, completely pure water is needed,
> Just so, the ṛishi's pure mind acts
> To cleanse the impurity of beings to purity.

And, from the *Lalitavistara*,

---

[197] "Elements and thoughts" is an abbreviation of elements, faculties, and thoughts of all sentient beings. These two lines mean that his love pervades all worlds and all sentient beings.

> This, a strong man seated at the foot of a supreme great
>   tree,
> Facing the māras with their armies and each regiment's
>   victory banners,
> Defeats their black band with the force of loving
>   kindness,
> And becomes buddha in the peace of unsurpassed
>   enlightenment.

It is to be understood accordingly that all the tathāgata's actions
in every context—path and fruition—are engaged in because of
great compassion.

Furthermore, the atoms belonging just to the area of such a tathāgata's body pores can show individually and without mixup or
obscuration every single one of the whole of the dharmas of both
peace and becoming contained within the ten directions and three
times. And, he can put every single one of the containers and
contents[198] that reach to the end of space into the area of a single
atom without the atom having to change to something more gross
nor the world having to change to something more subtle. And,
he has the ability to display in that atom in one moment the knowables of the three times, the entire play of all the doings in the
count of universes as many as there are. Again, these descriptions
used here to give an idea of the subject are fully taught in the
sutras.

A few men ride an iron chariot with supreme steeds whose strength exceeds the wind's across a pond eight thousand yojanas in size
filled with water and covered in lotuses. They run so fast that the
horses' hooves and the chariot's wheel rims do not come in contact
with it and the lotus leaves are not pierced by the hooves. A

---

[198] Containers are the abodes and contents are the beings living in
those abodes.

poisonous snake comes up from inside the pond. The chariot does not tip over; on this occasion the chariot circles it eight times. During the period of the first circling, Ānanda teaches the dharma teaching[199] eight times and makes the meaning understood. During the time taken for Ānanda to speak just one word, Maudgalyāyana teaches the dharma teaching eight times and makes the meaning understood. During the time taken for Maudgalyāyana to speak one word, Śhāriputra teaches dharma eight times and makes the meaning understood. During the time taken for Śhāriputra to speak one word, a pratyekabuddha teaches the dharma teaching an uncountable number of times. During the time taken for the pratyekabuddha to speak one word, a bodhisatva inconceivably, inexpressibly, teaches the dharma countless times. During the time taken for the bodhisatva to speak one word, Maudgalyāyana goes off to do miracles through eighty thousand world systems. During the time taken for Maudgalyāyana to go off on each of those miracles, the tathāgata has the capacity to show in all fields[200] without limit the total completion of all of his activities starting with his arousing of mind and going up to his nirvana[201].

Furthermore, Maudgalyāyana does miracles like that in each one of the fields individually of the ten directions and does so for seven days and nights without taking a rest, then makes an enclosing ring around those worlds as many he has journeyed to, then creates a

---

[199] Dharma teaching here means Buddha's dharma in its entirety.

[200] The various fields which are the worlds of both the enlightened and unenlightened sides.

[201] "Arousing of mind" is a standard technical term used throughout the text meaning "to arouse the enlightenment mind". Here it refers to the very first time that the Buddha aroused the enlightenment mind. "And going up to his nirvana" means all the activities of his journey to buddhahood following that, including all the deeds he showed as part of his final attainment of buddhahood.

common base, then heaps it up with mustard seeds to overflowing. In world systems more even than the seeds contained within that, the tathāgata's eye sees all of the individual showings of performing the conduct up through the twelve deeds[202] of those sentient beings who have engaged in enlightenment—and that only in regard to the ones whose name and family are concordant. He also sees the ones more even than that, the buddhas and bodhisatvas whose name and family are not concordant, but why mention that when, in the world systems of that sort, the fields in which buddhas arise and bodhisatvas perform the conduct are lesser in number, similar to the sands of an ocean or the sands in the river Ganges and the rarity of gold grains within them.[203]

Then, in those immeasurable fields which he sees pervasively and without mixup in that manner, his mind shines forth as all the appearances of body and speech done for taming in the displays of miracles for those to be tamed. And, at the same time, in the manner of a wish-fulfilling jewel, he engages perpetually and everywhere in the deeds of benefit and bliss but does so without discursive thought, spontaneously, as follows. All knowables of space and time are present with a nature empty of truth and he has manifested that as it is. The tathāgata who has manifested the dharmadhātu purified of the adventitious stains in which space and the palm of the hand, and an instant and an aeon have been equalized is the wisdom that does not falter from the non-duality of becoming and peace, the vajra kāya, beyond phenomena of atoms and instants, the inexpressible superfactual. He is this

---

[202] "Performing the conduct" refers to the activities of a bodhisatva on his journey to buddhahood. The twelve deeds are the deeds shown during the Buddha's lifetime.

[203] "Lesser" is correct; the tathāgata sees all of the buddhas—those easily seen, those not so easily seen but greater in number, and those very difficult to see and smaller in number.

inexpressible superfact yet, when evaluated with valid cognizers of the conventional[204], he is all faults exhausted and all good qualities complete; he is knowledge, love, and capacity without endpoint; he exists via a nature of being permanent, steady, peace, svastika[205]. He never wavers from that, yet all the while the inexhaustible appearances of his three secrets[206] permeate as many knowables as there are. Thus, no matter how much rational mind tries to distinguish them, like trying to measure space in fathoms, no end is found, so they have to be understood to be immeasurable. Moreover, the buddhas' illusions might be immeasurable like this, but the different dharmas are present in one buddha's nature, and one buddha himself is the inconceivable wisdom kāya that has each one of the individual appearances that are the displays done for taming that pervade all of space and time and which are divorced from the extremes of truth[207]. Because of all that, every single one of all the dharmas included in the buddha level, apparent yet empty, is never anything but the nature of equality wisdom. Thus, the qualities of even one hair pore and one light ray of the body pervade the space

---

[204] For valid cognizer, see the glossary.

[205] Buddhism and Bon both use the svastika as a sign of the primordial condition, the condition that is ultimate auspiciousness because it is permanent and unchanging. The specific qualities of a buddha's vajra kāya or indestructible being that has come about through the removal of all the stains of mind and the manifestation of the actual state of all phenomena, are described conventionally as "permanent, steady, peace, svastika" where svastika is not just a repeat of the first two qualities but is a further quality of the ultimate, auspiciousness that is this permanent, steady, unchanging state.

[206] For three secrets, see the glossary.

[207] Extremes of truth are the rational-minded extremes in which things are real.

element[208] and, based in that, the conquerors continue to speak all the way to the ultimate possible future limit but all for the purpose of generating a deep certainty about this unending state. To illustrate this, there are the examples of bodhisatva Shugchang examining the extent of the tathāgata's body and Maudgyalyāyana examining the limit of Buddha's speech, and others. It can be known through such examples.

2. The overview

This has two parts: he is the teacher of the various beings; and how he acts as teacher.

1. He is the teacher of the various beings

This has two parts: a summary; and an extensive explanation.

1. Summary

He is a teacher to all sentient beings. He enacts the appearance of the good path of benefit and ease without bias for every one of the migrator sentient beings throughout time and space. A sutra says,

> On seeing the various beings whose minds are
>   perpetually
> Obscured by the gloom of the darkness of delusion
> And who have entered samsara's gaol,
> That holy ṛishi arouses the mind.

Thus, the Great Compassionate One perpetually teaches the path.

---

[208] Space in Indian and Tibetan cosmology is seen as a fundamental constituent of existence, so it is called an element. This space is unconditioned space that is all pervasive.

2. Extensive explanation

There are three lines to this.

He is *a father to the bodhisatvas*. The bodhisatvas, the ones who have a force of determination that does not turn back from seeking unsurpassable enlightenment, the ones who hold the family line of the conquerors, the ones who have mastery over the treasury of the holy dharma and protect beings to be tamed who have been left out, are the ones suitable to be led through to the coronation method of inconceivable wisdom[209]. Accordingly, they can be thought of as "the sons of the ones who govern the retinue" and because of that are given the name "sons of the conquerors". For these beings the tathāgata first activates their family seed, then during the course of their development causes their abandonment and realization to grow, and finally, on the tenth level, bestows on them the empowerment which enacts their coronation as dharma kings[210]. Thus it is that the tathāgata from his side acts as their "father" and therefore he is called such.

For the noble persons who were the arhats, and so on, the bhagavat was like a king. He stayed together with those like the elder

---

[209] The coronation method of inconceivable wisdom is the final empowerment given to a bodhisatva at the end of his bodhisatva journey. Given by all the tathāgatas, it causes the bodhisatva to ascend to the throne of buddhahood. What we call empowerment in Buddhism is actually the coronation ceremony for a king. Thus, bodhisatvas are the ones who can be led through the trainings that will result in the final coronation into the position of buddhahood. The arhats, mentioned next, are not initially suited to that journey, though when they have become arhats, they are put onto the bodhisatva's path.

[210] Dharma king is a name used in the sutras for a buddha. It fits here with the process of the bodhisatva seen as a son who is led to the point where he is crowned as a king.

Śhāripūtra and great Maudgalyāyana, staying within his own command, the command of the bhagavat, king of dharma, no more and no less, not discarding the slightest training even at the cost of life specifically so that they could attain the fruition of their own path. Thus, he is *a king to the noble persons.*[211]

Further, the actual body with its ways of engagement in appropriate enlightened activity does the job of giving migrators a support; he gives them the support of the path, of setting them on to it, of causing making them follow it, and of making them finalize it. In that way, the tathāgata does the job altogether of making them go joyfully to the city of all three end enlightenments[212]. With that, he does the job of liberating them from samsara's ocean of suffering, therefore he is like a captain who does the work of liberating like-minded beings. Thus he is *a captain to those who journey to the city of nirvana* meaning that he is, in that way, a captain who does the work that is involved in getting those beings who are going to the city of nirvana to that city[213].

---

[211] The Buddha could have presented himself as a bodhisatva or tantric master. Instead, he maintained the appearance and ways of monastic Buddhism, following exactly the rules and customs that he himself laid down for that community. He was the king of the court of the noble ones of the Lesser Vehicle and followed the norms of that society. He said that he did so because it would result in greater benefit for more beings.

[212] The three end enlightenments means the enlightenments that are the endpoints of the three main vehicles—the śhrāvaka, pratyeka, and bodhisatva vehicles.

[213] Note that this is not the same as being a driver, as seen for example in "driver who tames beings". A driver merely steers. A captain welcomes the passengers, shows them to their places in the various classes of passage, oversees the vehicle and its passengers during the journey, solves problems on the way, and finally ensures that the passengers

(continued...)

2. How he acts as teacher

This has the three parts of: mind activity; speech activity; and body activity.

1. Mind activity

This is shown with two phrases.

His wisdom is unfathomable. From the standpoint of being the principal method for accomplishing the purposes of those to be tamed, wisdom is defined as the ten strengths, and from the standpoint of showing dharma to those to be tamed, it is defined as the four authentic insights[214]. After that, wisdom itself divided into its aspects is the five wisdoms, and then, entering the three times without impediment, it is the three wisdoms, and then summed up, it is the two wisdoms of knowledge of depth and extent, and then that summed up again is self-arising wisdom, the knowledge of all aspects incorporated in a single sphere. Taken from the perspective of the magnitude of the count of knowables included in space and time, that wisdom is immeasurable. Examples, count, syllogisms, and so on cannot ever come to a final assessment for wisdom, which means that his wisdom cannot be fathomed with rational mind. Therefore, it says *his wisdom is unfathomable*.

Because the tathāgata has attained that sort of inconceivable wisdom, even if a person tried to express it by starting with one word or one thing then continued on for unfathomable kalpas, the

---

[213](...continued)
disembark at their destination. Thus captain used here emphasizes that the Buddha does all the work entailed in leading and going together with the arhat types.

[214] The four authentic insights were mentioned in the explanation of the Buddha's good quality of "having insight and what is at its feet".

person could still not arrive at his level of knowledgeability[215].
Thus, *his knowledgeability is inconceivable*. A sutra says,

> It is like this: if all sentient beings asked
> Many ascertaining questions all at once,
> In one moment of mind it would be taken in,
> Then a single intonation of speech would give reply to
>   each one, and in each one's own language.

The tathāgata proclaimed the four non-fears in the midst of his
retinue with the roar of a lion[216]. Although this might seem to be
an explanation of the enlightened activity of speech, the cause of
speech is the enlightened activity of mind.

2. Speech activity
This also is shown with two phrases.

His speech is complete purity. This presents his speech from the
aspect of its being free from faults. There is not even an atom of
fault—such as illustrated by the eight faults of laziness, and so on
—in his speech, either as a fault ascribed to it or a fault in fact.
This speech of his with all trembling, indistinctness, and distortion
totally removed, like the moon shedding light in the dark, serves
only to develop total joy.

---

[215] Tib. spobs pa. The quality of knowledgeability refers to an ability
to instantly recall to mind the knowledge needed, for example, when
teaching someone, and a confidence of knowledge that comes with it.
This good quality is clearly explained in my own commentary.

[216] Tib. mi 'jigs pa bzhi. The Buddha proclaimed to his disciples that
he had no fear over proclaiming that he 1) had perfect realization, 2)
had perfect abandonment, 3) could making pronouncements about
which dharmas are obstacles to the path, and 4) could show the path
which leads to definite release. These are aspects of the confidence
that comes with his knowledgeability.

His melody is pleasing. His speech with its ocean of branches of intonation[217]—smooth, gentle, and so on—now brings joy and ultimately brings the fruition of benefit and ease to the mind-streams of those to be tamed. As the *Highest Continuum* says,

> In short, it is the cause of every single happiness,
> In the worlds including the gods and the levels of their
>   abodes.
> Appearing pervasively through everything of the worlds,
> It does, in its own intonation, express what is utterly
>   reliable ...

3. Body activity

The enlightened activity of the body is also shown with two epithets.

One never has enough of viewing the image of his body. No matter how each minute aspect of the limbs of his body is viewed, whether it is seen as beautiful or ugly, one cannot pull one's eyes away from his body. As with seeing something splendid that one has not seen before, the feast of delight continues on, unabated. Thus, this is saying, "Looking at his bodily form or his countenance one is not satisfied, one cannot get enough of seeing it".

His body is unparalleled. One hair pore and one subtle light ray of his body, either beautiful or ugly, will outshine anything within the riches of becoming, therefore, nothing else can parallel him, not even slightly. All together, the appearances of his body that

---

[217] The Buddha's speech is said to have sixty branches or aspects to its intonation. In fact, it has an endless array of intonations when you consider that it expresses itself exactly in accord with the current need, whatever it is, of sentient beings.

are enacted for those to be tamed and, likewise, the measure of his body in space and time, cannot be comprehended[218].

Someone who sees the tathāgata's body will have even intense suffering of body and mind cease like waking up at the end of a dream. The ways in which this happens are explained in detail in the sutras where they are embellished with stories.

2. The way he finalized abandonment and realization for his own sake

The perfection of abandonment and realization for his own sake has two parts: abandonment; and realization.

1. Abandonment

This has two parts: showing that, even though he dwelt in the places of becoming, he remained uncontaminated by the faults of becoming; and showing how his being is beyond becoming.

1. Showing that, even though he dwelt in the places of becoming, he remained uncontaminated by the faults of becoming

This is shown with three phrases. He dwelled in the desire realm where he was born from the womb, and so on and acted out the play of doing things in accord with the world, yet in dwelling there he was not in the slightest contaminated by the dharmas of desire such as hankering after the desirables of senses, and so on. Thus— and like a fresh, young lotus sitting in a swamp—*he is not contaminated by the things of desire.*

Similarly, he performed all the dhyānas and gained direct experience of them yet remained very much, meaning highly, unstained

---

[218] ... by dualistic mind.

because of not developing a taste or the like for them. Thus, *he is very much not contaminated by the things of form.*

He attained but did not develop a taste for the samādhis of the formless realm. He also did not teach dharma, and so on there. He also did not abide there. Therefore, *he is not mixed with the things of formlessness.*[219]

2. Showing how his being is beyond becoming

This has two parts: his fruition is beyond unsatisfactoriness; and he is beyond the source, the cause of unsatisfactoriness[220].

I. The fruition is beyond unsatisfactoriness

He has removed the seed of unsatisfactoriness and with that abandoned the entirety of unsatisfactoriness. Thus, there is the synopsis *he is completely liberated from the sufferings.*

Next is the extensive explanation, which concerns the way that he is liberated from the bases of suffering—the skandhas, dhātus, and āyatanas. The wording, *he is utterly completely-liberated from the skandhas* means that he is utterly liberated from the dharmins of birth and decay of the five skandhas of appropriation.[221]

---

[219] The buddha's body and speech were mixed in with or partook of the desire and form realms. He simply was not mixed in with or did not partake of the formless realm.

[220] The source is the second truth of the noble ones, the cause of suffering.

[221] For skandhas, āyatanas, and dhātus, see the glossary. "Complete liberation" does not mean completely liberated in general but is a technical term of specific meaning. The epithet here says that he does not have a partial complete liberation, which is possible, but has an utter complete liberation. For dharmins, see the glossary.

(continued...)

The dhātus have the meaning "each one holds the seed of its own type". Given that the tathāgata is divorced from the elaborations of birth and decay, *he does not possess dhātus.*[222]

His āyatanas are restrained. The outer six āyatanas are the referential condition and the inner six āyatanas are the governing condition. With the two, the consciousness goes out to the object and is ignited, hence the name āyatanas means "igniters"[223]. The tathāgata, due to having the quality that the elaborations have been utterly removed, does not have āyatanas that shift or move[224], thus they are called "restrained". Migrators, whose āyatanas are not restrained, see visual forms with the eyes which produces attachment due to a pleasing aspect of beauty, aversion due to a displeasing aspect of non-beauty, or stupidity due to the neutral

---

[221](...continued)

Skt. upadāna. Appropriation is a key link in the twelve links of interdependent origination. It is the point at which the karmic seed that will drive the development of the next birth is definitely selected and given power. It is common to refer to "the five skandhas of appropriation" to emphasis the samsaric process in relation to the skandhas.

[222] Dhātus are those parts of a samsaric being's aggregates that are the bases of more of the same, that is, of more samsara. The tathāgata does not have a samsaric style of being, therefore, he does not have dhātus which, by definition, are part of the samsaric process.

[223] The outer āyatanas are the six sense objects and the inner ones are the six sense faculties. The two together cause the ignition of samsaric consciousness, hence their name.

[224] Although one English translation of the *Sutra* says "his āyatanas are controlled", this epithet actually means that he keeps his āyatanas restrained so that they stay as wisdom āyatanas and do not shift into ignorance-based ones. It happens because the tathāgata has rid himself of dualistic mind with all of its elaborated concepts.

feeling of what lies in between, and then everything follows on from that[225].

In short, the skandhas, dhātus, and āyatanas do occur for a buddha, but all of them belong to a buddha's body which is, in every aspect, wisdom. Thus, a buddha's skandhas, dhātus, and āyatanas are beyond those of ordinary beings, so he never has skandhas and the rest like those of ordinary beings.

2. He is beyond the source, causes

His abandonment of the source[226], causes, is stated in four phrases.

In general, the Buddha taught many different names for affliction: knot, complete torment, river, enmesher, resistance, and so on. The first two epithets use some of these names to show how the afflictions function and the last two use some of them to illustrate what the afflictions actually are.

Normally, knot is a general term for affliction. Here though, it is specifically being used to refer to the primary cause of engagement in samsara, which is craving. Craving, the thing that does the work of binding beings into three-realmed samsara, is likened to a tight knot. The Buddha *has cut* that *knot* using the prajñā sword that realizes absence of self, with the result that *he is* completely *liberated from craving*. The afflictedness of views, ignorance, and so on creates suffering, so it is called all-over torment. It has the

---

[225] Migrators have elaborations and hence do not keep their āyatanas restrained. As a result, their minds work in a samsaric way, which has been very briefly outlined here: consciousness of object leads to feeling about the object, leads to affliction about the object, which plants a karmic seed, and one more cycle of samsara happens from there.

[226] ... of unsatisfactoriness, the second truth of the noble ones, which is the cause of samsaric being.

strength to carry beings off helplessly, like the current of a river. When the Buddha abandoned it, he gained *complete liberation from* all-over *torment*, therefore *he has crossed over the river*.[227]

Craving has bound beings as though they were tied with a knot and the current of afflictions' river is carrying them away with the result that they are in complete torment. Altogether, this is saying that "he is liberated from this fourfold set of causes and effects".

2. Realization
Realization has three parts: entity; qualities; and function.

1. Entity
This has two parts: vast; and profound.

1. Vast
The Buddha has every single type of wisdom—for example those presented in the twenty-one sets of un-outflowed dharmas[228]—and

---

[227] Mipham's commentary presents the four qualities of this section in a different order to the *Sutra* because he is explaining the first and third, and the second and fourth items, as cause and effect pairs.

[228] The Buddha's dharmakāya is summed up in twenty one sets of un-outflowed dharmas, dharmas that arise in connection with wisdom: the thirty-seven factors of enlightenment; the four immeasurables; the eight liberations; the nine places of absorption; the eight overpowering āyatanas; the ten transformational powers; the power to eradicate disturbing emotions in others; the knowledge of others' apirations; the six supernatural insights; the four authentic insights; the four purity of all aspects; the ten controls; the ten powers; the four non-fears; the eighteen unmixed qualities; the three non-protections; the three close applications of mindfulness; non-fortgetfulness; the true defeat of latencies; great compassion; and all-knowing.

has them without even one missing; the epithet *his wisdom is totally complete* refers to this.

2. Profound

He abides in the equality of the self-arising wisdom of expanse and wisdom inseparable. This wisdom of his is not unique to him, meaning that it is not different from, not other than, the mind of all those who go to buddhahood in the three times. Thus *he abides in the wisdom of the buddha bhagavats who arise in the past, present, and future.*

2. Qualities

The qualities of that wisdom are as follows. He does not abide in the extreme of a one-sided peace because he has realized the equality of becoming and peace and because he has great compassion free from meeting and parting[229]. That is called "a non-abiding nirvana". Thus, *he does not abide in nirvana*. Rather than abiding in a one-sided expanse of peace like that, he abides perpetually in all world systems encompassed by space and time where he is the cause of benefit and ease. At the same time, his being does not waver in the slightest from the expanse of dharmas of equality in the three times or, one could say, the limit of the authentic, therefore *he abides in the limit of the authentic itself*[230].

3. Function

Wisdom ascertained like that to be an equality of becoming and peace that does not abide in the extremes of becoming and peace is the actual buddha bhagavat's wisdom body or vajra kāya. It can

---

[229] His great compassion has been finalized and is present all the time, unlike the compassion of someone still on the path.

[230] He abides not in a samsaric extreme but in the final possibility or the limit, of being in the reality, the authentic situation.

be divided up into two or three or four, etcetera, kāyas or bodies according to specific aspects that can be distinguished in it and it is as those that he dwells imperishable, as the cause of unending benefit and bliss in all spheres both worldly and beyond worldly. The mode of this permanent and pervasive and spontaneous tathā-gata is that he *abides on the level of looking upon all sentient beings*. Thus he abides at a level on which he is looking at all sentient beings starting from the ordinary migrators and going all the way up to the mahāsatvas at the end of the line[231].

These last five phrases also exemplify the five wisdoms of dharma-dhātu, mirror, equality, individually discriminating, and all-ac-complishing wisdom.

3. Conclusion to those sections

These things that have been explained so far *are* the *true qualities of the greatness of the body of the buddha bhagavats*[232]. Here, body or kāya has the meanings "assemblage" and so on[233]. In this case, it is used to mean buddhahood itself, so it would not be good to take it to mean simply the body alone, one the three secrets[234].

---

[231] Starting with the lowest of sentient beings, there are those who have not done anything in terms of the path. Next, there are all the sentient beings who are on the path to enlightenment. At the very end of this line are sentient beings of the greatest development, the mahāsatva or great being or bodhisatvas at the top of the tenth level.

[232] Mipham's edition of the *Sutra* has buddha bhagavats in plural instead of singular as in all other editions.

[233] The word body in the Tibetan epithet is the honorific form used to translate the Sanskrit word "kāya". Here, kāya does not literally mean the body, but the "totality of being", of a buddha. See the discussion in my own commentary.

[234] For three secrets, see the glossary.

True here means "really like this, free from over- and understatement".

If we assess that sort of buddha of inconceivable wisdom-kāya using a fictional, conventional valid cognizer, we understand that its vajra nature of being permanent, definite, imperishable, and indestructible that spreads through all of time and space manifests in spontaneous existence which is a mine of unending benefit and ease[235]. And, if we assess it using a superfactual valid cognizer, because doing so goes beyond all elaborations of permanence, impermanence, and so on, we get to it in the authentic, where it itself is beyond elaboration. By doing all of that, we establish through the Reasoning of the Force of the Thing this inconceivable secret of the tathāgata, which is permanent, pervasive, and manifesting in spontaneous existence; if not, then it could not be what it purports to be. So, through application of logic in the form of Reasoning of the Force of Thing, we become people who decide to trust in the tathāgata's immeasurable qualities.[236]

The way this is explained in Glorious Nāgārjuna's *Root Middle Way Treatise* is that, if all these knowables have been ascertained to be without nature, then, even though they spread throughout immeasurable time and immeasurable regions, because they do not exist by way of self-entity, they could not, in the slightest, not be

---

[235] Spontaneous existence is like a massive lode of ore that provides all good things.

[236] The *Sutra* has just said that the qualities mentioned so far really are the qualities of a buddha. Rather than just believe it, we need to prove it for ourselves, so Mipham goes through the process of the proof. He starts with assessment using correct cognitive process at the conventional level, then moves to assessment at the ultimate level beyond elaboration. He says that this is how the matter is proved using the reasoning called Reasoning of the Force of the Thing. Each person has to do this for himself. When you do it yourself, you become one of the people who has trust in what a buddha actually is.

fitted into the confines of a single atom or moment. When you comprehend that the manifesting of all these appearances in space and time within timeless sameness[237] is the great point of inseparability amongst all the ones who have the wisdom body liberated from the four extremes[238], the buddhas, you will then obtain the specific certainty of the actual taking of refuge and, with it, an unfaltering faith in the good qualities of the never interrupted enlightened activity of the three buddha kāyas that arise as the self-appearances of the wisdom body's blessings. In that way, you produce certainty; the *Root Prajñā* says,

> An elaborator in the ones who are buddha
> And who are beyond elaboration and unending
> Elaborates, causing corruption,
> None of which sees the tathāgata.[239]
>
> That which is the tathāgata's nature
> Is these migrators' nature ...

When you gain an understanding which accords with that and other statements like it, that is the recollection of the tathāgata's dharmakāya, the king of all recollections[240].

---

[237] The timelessness and sameness of all these things comes from them being empty.

[238] ... that are the hallmark of dualistic thinking. The wisdom kāya has transcended dualistic mind with its concepts that are extremes.

[239] The English is exactly how the Tibetan reads. An elaborator will be a dualistic consciousness arising within the wisdom mind, which itself is buddha and has no elaboration to it. The elaboration of concepts which occurs corrupts the wisdom so that it no longer sees its own buddha nature. That buddha nature is none other than the nature of sentient beings' minds ...

[240] Generally speaking, the recollections of the *Sutra* are done using concept. Here, though, Mipham is saying that you take the words
(continued...)

Roots of virtue created in relation to such a buddha, starting with even the smallest things such as turning the mind toward such a buddha and making just one supplication, making one prostration, or offering one flower, or distractedly expressing his name one time, or seeing while irritated a drawing of his body on the face of a wall, are never lost. The reason is that the object in these cases is a buddha who, because of having perfected the wisdom of equality of the three times, is certain to be non-deceptive and unfailing. Therefore it does happen—just like beings who have been caught by potent hooking vidyāmantras or by a seven-headed snake and just like fish who have been caught on a hook do not need to add their own efforts in order to make the outcome happen because what is going to happen is being imposed outside of their control.

The words here are not like "mother's sweet foods". Application of reasoning to the reality of cause and effect will give rise to certainties of mind—free of a shadow of doubt—in relation to the certainties that there are to be discovered.[241]

---

[240](...continued)
about the Buddha's wisdom body and use them to move to a different kind of recollection in which you have a direct cognition of your own buddha nature. It is called "recollection of the tathāgata's dharma-kāya" and is not a conceptual recollection. You contact your own, innate nature directly with it, so he calls it the king of all recollections. This exactly is the meaning of the section Using the *Sutra*: The Real Meaning is The Magic in the third chapter of this book. That section and this section mutually support each other, so it would be very worthwhile to read that section in conjunction with this one.

[241] "Mother's sweet foods" is a Tibetan phrase meaning "sweet talk" or "nice pap to make you feel good". The talk here about wisdom beings is talk about what is actually the case. There are many things that are real and which await our discovery and development of certainty about them. By the application of correct logic, and so on, we can be sure

(continued...)

Thus the tathāgata of limitless benefits should always be turned to, day and night. It is extremely hard for the sound of the letters of the tathāgata's name to come to ear causing devotion to him. The reason for that is that a buddha's name, a source of inexhaustible, limitless merit, comes from the power of the dharmatā, interdependency, prayers of aspiration, samādhi, and inconceivable virtue, as the compounded phenomenon of a buddha's name which becomes known and evident within becoming as a basis for the development of benefit and ease. If a jewel that produces the wishes of this life, a wish-fulfilling tree, drinking the nectar of an excellent vase, and so on are hard to actually have in front of you, what could be said of this? Jewels, and so on cannot elucidate the path of emancipation whereas the tathāgata's name will definitely lead, at some point in time, to enlightenment.

In regard to that, the name which appears from the blessings of the tathāgata's inconceivable secret is not only the dispenser of perfect ease but belongs to the reality of things with its inconceivable capabilities of interdependency that are always non-deceptive. For that reason, if this is carefully examined, we find that jewels, and so on are assemblages of many physical atoms and vidyāmantras of accomplishment are strings of many moments of sound of speech and, therefore, not one of them has the slightest true existence. Nevertheless, it is undeniable that they give the one who uses them great glories[242], and similarly, if, because of the nature of emptiness, you have trust in the capability of things which is their non-deceptive interdependency, then everything you do will be meaningful.

---

[241](...continued)
about those things and come to understand them without doubt.

[242] Perfect glory connects with and is the same as the perfect ease mentioned in the first sentence of the paragraph.

Also, it says in a sutra,

> Compared to offering
> To sentient beings daily
> For as many kalpas as sands in the Ganges,
> Food and clothes of the gods,
> Offering one buddhist layman one meal
> Generates a countless amount of merit.
> A full monk who follows with faith,
> Stream-enterers who will return and not,
> Up to a pratyeka arhat are then joined to this[243].
> Some offer to pratyekas as many as atoms
> In the ten directions, daily,
> For as many kalpas as sands of the Ganges,
> Food and clothes of the gods.
> Compared to that, one who hears the sound buddha or
> Sees a drawing of buddha's form body or
> One made from clay,
> Has more merit, so what need to mention
> Seeing the body, joining the palms,
> Expressing even one word of praise, or
> Making an offering?
> For someone who apprehends the name buddha,
> When there is trust, devotion, and no rejection,
> The virtue of offering the ten fields filled
> With precious things to the buddhas daily
> For as many kalpas as the sands of the Ganges
> Cannot compare.
> Furthermore, for apprehending just the name
> Infinite advantages also were foretold
> For this life and later ones as well,
> So what need to mention reading and directing the
>   mind
> To this kind of praise of the conqueror …

---

[243] The same thing is then done for each of these three.

That gives an idea of it and it can then be known more extensively from the sutras.

2. Recollection of the dharma

This has two parts: a synopsis; and an extensive explanation.

1. Synopsis

This goes from *the holy dharma ...* up to *... is thoroughly purifying*.

Generally, the term dharma, which is produced from the root "ḍudha" meaning "holder of a fish"[244], has the ten usages of "knowable", and the rest[245]. For each usage, a specific connotation of "holding" is understood: a dharma which is a knowable is so because it holds its own characteristic; dharma which is the ten virtues, and so on is so because it holds one back from the bad migrations; dharma which is the path is so because it holds one back from the two extremes; and so on. The wording here in the text is *holy dharma* which is understood like this: within dharmas that are knowables, the holy or best or outstanding ones are the two dharmas of causal path and fruition—which is cessation, nirvana and, together with the two, that which corresponds to their cause, the dharma of authoritative statement. In short, the

---

[244] This is what the text says, though the usual explanation is that it is from the root "dhṛ" meaning "to hold", a meaning which is clearly presented in his words that follow.

[245] Ten meanings of the Sanskrit word dharma were transmitted to Tibet.

holy dharma is "the holy dharma of authoritative statement and realization"[246].

The holy dharma like that *is good in the beginning* because, at the beginning, when you hear it, trusting faith is born. It is *good* or fine *in the middle* because, in the middle, you taste the meaning through thinking about it and then, having become certain that it is a path of definite happiness, a special joy is born in you. *And* it is *good at the end* because, at the end when you meditate on it, authentic wisdom arises causing your definite reversal from existence. It is those three, as stated. Alternatively, this could be done in relation to what is being expressed there—the three principal trainings, taught as śhīla, samādhi, and prajñā. Done that way, "good in the beginning, middle, and end" is explained in relation to those three, a presentation which accords with the stages of the path, and the principal stages of practice in particular.

Its meaning is excellent. The holy dharma unmistakenly teaches the characteristics of the two truths, fictional and superfactual. Thus, it does not deal with subjects of passing benefit, either those of no meaning such as found in treatises that examine a crow's beak[247] or those of lesser meaning such as ones that consider the count of leaves on trees or the count of micro-organisms in the body. Rather, it gets to the meaning that has the capacity to re-

---

[246] The holy dharma is transmitted both as the realization of the buddha and through the authoritative statements both verbal and written that aid such realization. "Authoritative statement" is usually translated as "scripture" but it includes all of the spiritually authoritative statements of the buddha and his followers, verbal and written.

[247] ... as part of an examination to see whether it has teeth or not. This study was published in Tibet and is used as an example of a study that has no value.

verse stupidity in regard to the entire domain of what can be known.

Its wording is excellent. In terms of the words produced from letters, there are none of the faults of nonsensical wording, mixed-up composition, and so on, nor of less-than-good expression in the composition built up from the words. Unlike what is found in the treatises of the outsiders, where various factions use incomprehensible wordings to express their dharma, the tathāgata's mind of compassion used wording that fitted the minds of those to be tamed. Therefore, his wordings are easy to understand, easy to memorize, clear in meaning, and pleasant to hear[248].

From the perspective of the thing itself[249], the holy dharma possesses the four qualities of brahmacharya[250]. As a result *it is not adulterated.* This dharma which teaches subtle and uncommon impermanence, formatives' suffering[251], lack of self, and so on is not mixed in with the dharmas of others, the Tīrthikas[252] and the

---

[248] These are four specific qualities that are set out in relation to the style of the Buddha's words.

[249] ... as opposed to words used to express that thing or a conceptual meaning gained through the words used to express it.

[250] Ways of purity. He explains this term at the end of the next four epithets which are these four brahmacharyas, and it is explained in my own commentary.

[251] Formative's suffering is the suffering of cyclic existence that comes from having formatives. Formatives are the factors of dualistic mind that cause the formation of future states of being. They comprise the fourth skandha which is named the skandha of formatives. Formatives are mainly the afflictions.

[252] Tīrthika is a very kind name that the Buddha came up with to mean those who are followers of other ways and religions. It literally means
(continued...)

rest, and does have an uncommon quality to it. That has been said like this,

> One that corrects every one of the enemies of the
> afflictions and
> Protects from the bad migrations of becoming,
> Because it has the qualities of correcting and protecting,
> is a treatise;
> These two are not present in the systems of others.[253]

It is totally complete. It is not like methods that take a short-term approach and so only partially alleviate suffering. It is not like medicine for a specific disease that cures only that much of the problem, for example, it is not a cure for only one of the afflictions, such as desire. Instead, *it is* a *totally complete* antidote that removes the afflictions of the three realms in their entirety. It is similar to what the holy regent said,

> He said, "What is meaningful is to stay closely involved
> with the dharma;
> Doing so abandons the afflictions from all three realms".
> What functions to show the advantages of peace

---

[252](...continued)
someone who has at least arrived at the shore of taking the true journey of dharma and is trying to do something, even if the person has not found the true dharma yet.

[253] A correct and true treatise has the two qualities of being able to correct, meaning to overcome, the afflictions and be a protection for afflicted beings from the bad migrations of the lower realms. A treatise containing the Buddha's dharma will have those qualities whereas a treatise of the outsiders will not. Thus, the buddha's dharma is a special, uncommon kind of teaching that does not have the lesser and ordinary spiritual teachings of the outsiders mixed in with it. Hence it is unadulterated by them.

Is the ṛiṣhis' speech, just another conceptualized
thing[254].

It is total purity. The nature of the expanse of knowable dharmas
is complete purity, a purity of being primordially free of stains.
The holy dharma is taught in order to express that purity. It is
taught by wisdom that views that purity which is apart from the
corruptions of elaboration[255] because it is in harmony with the
expanse of dharmas.

It is total purification. The dharmadhātu or expanse of dharmas
is pure of being a thing in itself. However, the mind possessing
adventitious stains together with their latencies does not realize it
that way. The path that leads to unmistaken cognition of the
innate disposition[256] purifies the adventitious stains until they are
purified. Thus, this statement about the holy dharma concerns its

---

[254] The holy regent is Maitreya. He quotes the Buddha as saying that
the meaningful thing to do is to practise dharma because it eliminates
all samsaric delusion. Other holy men teach dharma which shows the
advantages of nirvana yet does not have the capacity to eliminate
samsara. Theirs is just another conceptualized item, a dharmin.

[255] The nature of the whole range of dharmas—the dharmadhātu—is
complete purity, meaning that it has never been defiled by the stuff of
samsara. Sentient beings need to return to this to regain their intrinsic
enlightenment, therefore, that is what the holy dharma teaches. The
teaching of the holy dharma is given by wisdom that views that purity.
Because the wisdom is of the same thing as the purity, it also has none
of the elaborations that are the defilements of samsara. Because both
what is talked about and what gives that teaching belong to the purity
of the range of dharmas, the Buddha's teaching is total purity.

[256] Tib. gshis. Innate disposition is a term used to indicate the innate
wisdom mind. The innate disposition of all beings is wisdom.

making actuality just as it is manifest, divorced from adventitious stains, through this process of purification[257].

That sort of thing referred to as "Brahmā", meaning "the Pure One", is nirvana. The dharma which is its path or "charya" meaning "way of behaviour" is then said to possess the four qualities of "brahmacharya" or "ways of purity".

Those three goodnesses, two excellences, and four types of conduct of brahma or purity are mentioned in the *Ornament of the Sutra Section*[258], too. They are similar to what it says there:

> This repairing which is the cause of those of
> Faith and joy and intelligence is virtue.
> Having the two types of meaning, it is easy to
> comprehend, and
> Having the four qualities shows conduct of the pure.[259]

and,

> The four ways of purity—
> Others and having the uncommon,
> Completely performs abandonment of the afflictions,
> The essence pure, and the stains purified—

---

[257] In other words, the previous quality was about the primordial purity that causes the dharma to be expressed and which expresses it, whereas this quality is about the dharma being the path that does the purification needed to return to that purity situation.

[258] Asaṅga's *Mahāyānasūtrālaṅkāra*.

[259] Repairing is the amendment of broken vows. It is dharma. It brings three items in a progression that correspond to good in the beginning, and so on. The two types of meaning correspond to the two excellences and the four qualities to the four ways of purity.

Are asserted to hold the four qualities of conduct of the
pure, brahmacharya.[260]

2. Extensive explanation

This has two parts: showing that it is the supreme one to be accepted; and showing that it is a definite mental reliance.

1. Showing that it is the supreme one to be accepted

This has two parts: a synopsis; and an extensive explanation.

1. Synopsis

The bhagavat has taught dharma well. The dharma teaching
taught by the buddha bhagavat, a being of valid cognition, whose
wisdom looks at the entirety of knowables, seeing them without
obscuration, is a body of teaching free from all faults and complete
in all qualities that is only good teaching. What this really says is,
"The other teachers are tainted with absence of knowledge and
their outsider systems contain harmful things contrary to dharma
together with many faults. Therefore, theirs are not good explanations".

2. Extensive explanation

This has two parts: shown from the perspective of being free of
faults; and shown from the perspective of having good qualities.

1. Shown from the perspective of being free of faults

The meaning of the three phrases here, **it is authentic sight**, and
so on are as follows.

---

[260] This also is from *The Ornament of the Sutra Section*, a highly condensed listing of the features of the sutra Great Vehicle.

The dharma taught by the Buddha was well-taught dharma. In what ways did he teach the dharma well? Firstly, *it is authentic sight* or, as some editions say, "it is the authentic shown"[261]. The Buddha views the actuality of phenomena unmistakenly, like an eye that is actually seeing the visual forms it is looking at. He then teaches in accordance with fact, with the result that those to be tamed who use his teaching also are able to see actuality unmistakenly. Thus, the Buddha's dharma is authentic sight, which has to be understood in the final analysis to mean "is without confusion".

There are some very complicated commentaries which explain that the meaning of this epithet requires ascertainment not just through the simple use of words but through analysis of reality. However, that sort of thing does not become an aspect of recollecting the good qualities and is not connected with teaching even one word of practice for a person[262].

It is free from sickness. Sickness is a word for affliction. This unoutflowed dharma that removes afflictions together with their latencies is, in itself, free from outflow or sickness, the afflictions. It is like the sun's disk which, in itself, never goes dark. On the other hand, there are all kinds of treatises on worldly arts and crafts, and so on, but these are not the opposites of outflows or

---

[261] The edition of the *Sutra* used for Tāranātha's commentary has this other reading.

[262] Some very difficult commentaries, instead of saying that one could simply understand the words of the epithet and take them as a good quality of the dharma, insist that the authentic or reality must be gained sight of in direct perception. They proceed to go deeply into the meaning of emptiness as understood in the *Prajñāpāramitā Sūtra*, an approach that was popular in one of the Tibetan schools of Buddhism. Mipham is saying that their approach does not help to turn the phrase into a useful recollection.

afflictions and so end up being equivalent to them. This dharma is superior to all of that[263].

Its time has no interruption. You might think, "Granted that this is free from fault and has good qualities, but if it were taken as a point of mental reliance, would there be a time at which its qualities did not provide refuge?" The answer is no, there is not. Good things that are beneficial in being able to provide some protection, such as jewels, excellent vases, and so on are not beneficial continuously. However, when what has to be abandoned has been abandoned through the use of this holy dharma, there is no return to that again; because of that, the type of realization that is attained to by means of the noble path does not degenerate. Thus, this holy dharma is said to be "uninterrupted in its time" or "unending in its time".

These should also be proven trustworthy using the Reasoning of the Force of the Thing but I have not written about it here out of concern that would need to be a lengthy discussion.

2. Shown from the perspective of having good qualities

This has three phrases associated with it.

It brings one in. This holy dharma, the definite state of un-out-flowed bliss attained through the abandonment of the entirety of what is to be abandoned—all miserable things—serves to bring one's own mindstream in to itself. In other words, this phrase is saying, "Except for this cause, nothing else in the entire vault of

---

[263] Outflows are the deluded states of mind that occur when wisdom loses its footing and dribbles out the elaborations of dualistic mind. Un-outflowed dharma is dharma that comes from wisdom seeing reality as it is. Books on worldly subjects might not seem to be deluded, nevertheless, they are part of samsara and help to promote it, not overcome it.

knowables has the capability to bring you into the bliss of complete liberation".

How does it bring one in? It gradually leads a person who has entered the dharma through hearing, contemplating, and meditating in from the places of becoming then guides him into the un-outflowed expanse[264].

This epithet in Indian texts is the phrase "upanāyika". It has been translated into Tibetan with "nye bar gtod pa <> brings in close". It has also been translated with "nye bar 'dren pa <> leads in close", which is the meaning exactly of the original words.[265]

This is meaningful to see. Those who have been wandering in samsara, a great ocean of suffering, from beginningless time will continue to flounder about helplessly in the mire of difficult-to-bear suffering until they meet the holy dharma and practise it. When wise ones meet the dharma, it will be like meeting with a boat in the middle of the ocean, and they will rely on it and go, without the possibility of return, to the far shore of the great waters that are a reservoir of suffering. By doing so, they come to "see", where see means to know, the whole vault of knowables. There is nothing of greater meaning than that, and in addition, the holy dharma has in it the ultimate, supreme meaning, so it is spoken of with this phrase.

Those who understand what this is saying—that the nature of this samsara is suffering and that its only antidote is the dharma—and who then rely on the dharma to eradicate their samsaric sufferings will develop an eye of trust that is very certain about the dharma.

---

[264] ... of the wisdom of a buddha.

[265] For a clearer treatment, see the explanation of upanāyika in the other two commentaries and on page 39.

They will say, "Oh my goodness! This speech of the buddha is a great truth!" Others who are stupid might have this holy dharma in their hands but, because they view it as words only and do not see it as the instrument that actually does the work of abandoning samsara, they never actually experience its meaning.

Indian editions of the text have a phrase that does not correspond to the Tibetan wording " 'di mthong ba la don yod pa <> this is meaningful to see" of this epithet. They have the phrase "ehipaśhrīkaḥ" which translates as "ltos shig <> look at it!" which implies that a great meaning comes from doing so. Although the original wording is "Look at it!", it seems better to translate it as done in the Tibetan version.

It is known to experts through personal self-knowing shows that the dharma is extremely profound and that it is not the domain of the ordinary rational mind of philosophers or worldly types. The experts who see the factual situation are the noble ones. They see it in direct perception as an object of personal self-knowing wisdom. Note that it is only the Buddha amongst them who is the ultimate wise one and who has fully made the factual situation into the object of the self-knowing. This phrase is saying, "It could be assessed using generic facts but that would still be the domain of those experts who have rational mind that knows in very fine detail".[266]

---

[266] A fact is something known on the surface of the mind. "Factual situation" here means the fact of dharma that the words of conventional dharma point at. A "generic fact" is a technical term for the generic images used in the conceptual operation of mind. For example, "cow" as a concept is an image that applies to a general class of things called cow and it appears as a generic "fact" to mind. It is not the same as a cow seen in direct perception, something which has no generic label attached to it. Some worldly people think that the factual
(continued...)

In the phrase "personal self-knowing": personal has the meaning "not mixed in with other"; self has the meaning "the entity of those objects un-mistaken"; and knowing has the meaning "to see". When put together it goes like this. Consciousness that works by being conscious of other—like an eye consciousness registers vases, and so on—will not know this profound dharma by looking in towards itself. Rather, this profound dharma will be known only by a knower that knows itself. This is the object only of an uncommon type of rational mind[267]. Therefore, the meaning here is, "The dharma is the domain of those who have personal self-knowing wisdom[268]. Because of that, the places where you can put your hopes and which are places of unchanging trust are the non-ordinary, beyond-the-world qualities experienced through meditation".

Thus the first part of this section has taught that the holy dharma is the excellence that could be gained or taken from within the

---

[266](...continued)
dharma of reality could be known through the generic images of concept. Their approach can and does lead to very subtle understandings of the nature of phenomena but, subtle as they might be, they are still rational-minded, conceptual images which do not see superfactual reality in direct perception.

[267] Rational mind (Tib. blo) implies dualistic mind. However, an uncommon type of rational mind of no self-grasping is possible; it would be discriminating wisdom. Mipham talks in this slightly unusual way apparently because he is addressing the followers of a Tibetan school who use this term and who are very attached to the idea that their dualistic rational-minded analyses are actual insight into superfact.

[268] Dharma here means the noble dharma that you actually take refuge in and which is reality, not the conventional dharma that points at that reality. The one word dharma has ten meanings, one of which is "reality" and one of which is "a teaching".

vault of knowables. The second part presents the way that this dharma will, if taken up, be a definite reliance for mind.

2. Showing that it is a definite mental reliance

This has two parts: a synopsis; and an extensive explanation.

1. Synopsis

The dharma spoken by the bhagavat serves well for taming[269]. In relation to this, one person had the thought, "It would be hard for the Buddha's dharma to be a mental reliance given its infinite variety of presentation; he taught it to some as 'the skandhas, and so on exist', he taught to others as 'they do not exist', he taught it to some as both, to some as neither, and so on". However, that is not the case. The buddha bhagavat, a being of valid cognition, knows well the elements, faculties, and thoughts of those to be tamed. Because of that, he taught each part of the dharma patiently, as one would do the work of wiping and rubbing a precious jewel. He began by teaching the two truths coarsely, then he taught them more precisely, then with great precision, and finally in their ultimate meaning[270]. Every bit of that teaching went to taming the afflictions of the mindstreams of those to be tamed and every bit of it was presented only for arriving at the meaning of ultimate enlightenment; it is not that the meanings involved contradict one

---

[269] This epithet is difficult to translate into English. There is a full explanation on page 110.

[270] This refers to an important teaching contained in the *Sutra Requested by the King Dharaneshvara*. The Buddha himself states there that his teachings in the first three turnings of the wheel were given in a progressively profound order, suited to taming his followers. He illustrates his progressive style of teaching with the analogy of a jewel that is cleaned in three steps using exactly the right technique for each step. The fourth step of ultimate meaning mentioned in Mipham's next sentence is the fourth turning of the wheel, the teaching of tantra.

another or that sometimes he did not teach the authentic meaning. Every word of the dharma without exception applies without contradiction to the one, ultimate enlightenment, therefore these words are used to describe it.

Some texts have instead of "legs par brten pa <> serves well" the words "legs par ston pa <> well taught", though the basic meaning is the same. There is also a thread of commentary which, basing itself on the term "mental reliance", explains these words to mean "caring for the restrictions that come with the Vinaya"[271]. This

---

[271] This other thread of commentary looks at the phrase that sums up this and the next several good qualities of the dharma, which is that they are a mental reliance. Then, it looks at the wording of this epithet and sees that, in Tibetan, "taming" equally means "Vinaya". It notes that the Vinaya is a particularly good form of mental reliance because it presents dharma as a series of highly defined restrictions that, if adhere to, make it easy to get on with taming the mind. Therefore, it takes this phrase to mean "the dharma spoken by the Bhagavat is well presented in the Vinaya".

That raises the translation problem that although the Tibetan wording of this epithet can have both meanings, it is not possible to create an English translation that contains both. The translation here follows the mainstream explanation in which "taming" is the central idea of this epithet. To have Vinaya as the central meaning, the epithet would have to be translated differently, for example as shown just above. That was done in the translation of the *Sutra* originally made by the Nalanda Translation Committee and is seen within Western dharma communities because of it these days. However, it is not the mainstream understanding of this epithet.

When "Vinaya" is taken as the central idea, the explanation of the epithet has to be that the Vinaya is not merely a low level, provisional type of teaching but that it fully transmits the entire teaching of the Buddha. The third to last epithet in this recollection of dharma says just that; it points out that every single word of the bhagavat's teaching

(continued...)

raises the need for examining the translation equivalents involved and commentaries on the meaning; doing so will let us to know what is and is not the meaning intended in the text itself.

2. Extensive explanation

This consists of six phrases. The first two are: *It is renunciation. It causes one to go to complete enlightenment.* You might wonder, "How could renunciation possibly be able to validly see the whole of the holy dharma, and arrive at a final understanding of it as one, ultimate superfactual type?" Renunciation—when taken to mean the renunciation that consists of various methods of renunciation in light of all of the things to be abandoned starting at the coarse level of total affliction and going up to the level of ignorance latencies[272]—is the cause of a perfect abandonment. Furthermore, when the stains of the two obscurations have been exhausted, that perfect abandonment itself is the attainment of the ultimate of realizations, unsurpassed complete enlightenment. Thus it is saying that renunciation causes one to go to complete enlightenment.

Having this final understanding of great enlightenment as the abandonment of the entirety of what is to be abandoned and the

---

[271](...continued)
—high and low, Vinaya and otherwise—is a complete teaching of dharma in itself. In this way, even though the words of the good quality are taken literally in very different ways, they end up coming down to much the same meaning.

[272] When Mipham says "total affliction", he is referring to the general samsaric situation; it is equivalent to the obscuration of the afflictions. When he says "ignorance latencies", he is referring to the very subtle obscurations that prevent the omniscience of buddhahood and are removed on the levels of practice which are beyond saṃsāra. In the next sentence he mentions these as the two obscurations.

realization of the entirety of what is to be realized is the teaching of a single, ultimate vehicle. Following on from that, if the entirety of what is to be taught as the holy dharma is one thing, there being not the slightest contradiction over what needs to be abandoned, then everything is complete in one, non-contradictory, conducive path. Thus, although the Buddha's dharma might be immeasurable because of the thoughts of those to be tamed, *it is without* any *disharmony*[273]. *And* it is not just free of all disharmony; all of the lower level qualities are contained in the higher level ones and do not falter[274], therefore all of them are complete in one key point, and so it is also the case that *it has inclusion*. Now, the individual meanings of some of the holy dharmas are contradictory. Following on from that, if one were not included within the other, then the dharma could not be suitable as an ultimate mental reliance. However, that it is not so; dharma of any stature[275] can withstand anything and because of that the dharma is said to be "suitable as a definite mental reliance".

If because of not comprehending this key point you think, "The dharma of the śrāvakas is lesser", then the tathāgata's dharma with its profound and vast approaches will not fit with your mind and your mind will start to entertain ideas that his dharma is meaningless and to be discarded.

---

[273] Disharmony can be understood as discordance.

[274] "Do not falter" means that, although they are lesser teachings, they do not fail at some point in the face of the higher teachings. All of the teachings come from ultimate reality and include that meaning, therefore, each of them stands in its own place, always, regardless of how it might be conventionally assessed as being a lower or higher, etcetera, teaching.

[275] "Stature" here means of a certain sized vehicle, such as the Lesser Vehicle. Lesser Vehicle dharma can be and is the dharma of enlightenment and can withstand any argument against its being otherwise.

It has reliability. It does end the journey. Generally, all of the composite dharmas with outflows, whatever and wherever, are in the end not "imperishable". Thus, even though you attain the sovereignty of someone such as a wheel-wielder[276], Brahmā, Indra, or the like, it will be a situation that is without reliability. You, as the one who attains it, might want it and decide that you will not let go of it but, from its side, the position attained does not have reliability and is not suited to being taken up for that purpose. Dharma is not like that because, as long as you, the one reliant on it, do not let go of it, it cannot, anywhere or anytime, lose its ability to remain reliable or to stay on course.

The word "reliability" in the phrase here should be understood to mean that, when dharma is taken as a reliance, the support given to the one relying on it will not ever change. Then, the dharma is what the teacher spoke after he had produced direct perception of the knowables so, with that as the reason, there are the words "it has reliability". One person says that the phrase here has to be taken to mean simply "dharma is reliant on buddha" and another says that it means "dharma is reliant on the tathāgata's compassion"; understand that the meaning supplied here in some texts does not get to the actual meaning[277].

Concerning that, you might have this idea, "Such dharma is suitable to be taken as a non-deceptive mental reliance. However, in

---

[276] A wheel-wielder is a chakravartin king.

[277] The word "reliability" is intended to mean that the support dharma provides will never fail or alter. When that reliability is coupled with the fact that the dharma is something that the teacher spoke after he himself produced direct perception of the knowables, the wording becomes "it has reliability". Some texts join "reliable" with other understandings and gloss the meaning with simplistic ideas like "dharma is reliant on buddha", and so on but these fail to arrive at the actual meaning contained within the words, "it has reliability".

a world like this, where all enjoyments reaped in relation to doing good and obtaining a good result are cases of 'exhaustion in a good result', but where finalized good, about which it is said that, 'at this time there is no known activity', could not be suitable to be taken as an absolute mental reliance, and dharma too must be the same"[278]. However, it is not so. When you rely on dharma, activities done for the sake of a place of finalized good do connect you with the point of laying down the burden, the fruition of no-more-training. When that has been reached, the journeying involved in either having once again to do some other type of activity and connect with something else or having to continue on and

---

[278] This sentence is as difficult in the Tibetan as it is in the English.; the following is a paraphrase.

Yes, I accept that dharma is reliable in the sense of being non-deceptive. Similarly, this world knows, understands, and takes as an absolute reliance that good results in good and that it is not final, that each person has to keep working at it to keep producing the causes by which the good can come. This idea, for example, is found in the saying, "Good begets good". Well then, what about a final good? The prevailing thought in the world is that there is no set of activities available for creating such a thing. Thus, this world does not have a process for final good which it knows, understands, and takes as an absolute reliance. Therefore, dharma too must be the same; it might be a non-deceptive reliance but is not an absolute reliance that will solve all difficulties for once and for all. However, that train of thought is incorrect because dharma is not only non-deceptive but is also absolute in the sense just mentioned.

on is truly cut, thus *it does end the journey*[279]. The *Vyākhyāyukti*[280] says,

> Nothing higher[281] itself means that journeying is ended;
> The travel towards that utterly supreme greatness is
>   journeying.
> That here has been truly cut thus the journeying is
>   ended.

Certain commentaries have their own way of explaining how these words should be understood, such as "the movement of mind and mental events is cut" and "migrating about in samsara is cut", and so on, but those are only partial explanations that do not get to the full meaning. The last two sentences in the quotation just given state the meaning in a way that definitively distinguishes the meaning of this epithet.

Given all of that and understanding that the only thing within this vault of knowable dharmas that could be cherished as an unchanging mental reliance is dharma, and given that the good paths of happiness of the conquerors of the past, present, and future, together with their sons and disciples, and of all migrators, arise only from the appearance of dharma, we have a need—we must make prayers of aspiration for holding to the holy dharma. This point

---

[279] The word is actually "movement" not journey and it is hard to understand in Sanskrit, Tibetan, and English. However, the quotation given uses wording that makes the meaning of "movement" understandable without doubt. It seems best to use "journey" here, otherwise the *Sutra* becomes too difficult to understand without commentary and hard to read, too.

[280] One of the eight prakaraṇa of Vasubandhu.

[281] Nothing higher refers to "unsurpassed" enlightenment.

was taught in the sutras, so prayers like that can be found in an enormous number of the conquerors' sons' prayers of aspiration.

Now that you have recollected the good qualities of the dharma in that way, the next step is to take up the dharma according to your own capacity with the thought, "How joyful I am now that I have met this appearance of the precious dharma". Maitreya said this about taking up dharma,

> Copying letters, offering, giving,
> Hearing, reading, comprehending,
> Explaining, reciting,
> Contemplating it, and meditating ...

which means that you should exert yourself at making this human life meaningful by practice founded in the ten dharma activities that Maitreya mentions[282].

Then, the benefits of hearing one verse of this "holy dharma" and comprehending it, explaining it, and contemplating its meaning are immeasurable and unfathomable, and those benefits can be known extensively from the sutras.

3. The way to recollect the good qualities of the saṅgha

This has two parts: showing the good qualities of the saṅgha; and praising the ones having those good qualities as supreme places for giving.

---

[282] Tib. spyod chos bcu. Maitreya teaches that the general activities of dharma are ten-fold. Their details can be found in *The Illuminator Tibetan-English Dictionary*.

1. Showing the good qualities of the sangha

This has two parts: their mindstreams are thoroughly purified; and they are a supreme field of good qualities.

1. Their mindstreams are thoroughly purified

This goes from *The sangha of the great vehicle* up to *have entered into harmony*.

The word *sangha* here in Tibetan is "dge 'dun <> intent on virtue". The Tibetan term refers to the fact that the sangha has an intention that is unfaltering[283] because they could not be torn away from the path even by millions of billions of māras. Nonetheless, the term really refers to those persons who are noble ones.[284]

The noble ones who are in *the great vehicle*, meaning either the Buddha Vehicle that is great because it transcends the world or the Great Vehicle that has the seven greats—reference, and so on—are like this[285]. Their mindstreams have been completely restrained through the principal training of discipline that has the style of separation from all types of faulty behaviour, therefore it is said that they *have entered into good*. Through having the

---

[283] The noble sangha has the prominent feature that their resolve for enlightenment is unfaltering. However, the feature that determines them is whether they are noble ones or not.

[284] The term sangha actually means community.

[285] The Buddha Vehicle is the single vehicle that all Buddhists take to reach enlightenment. It can be divided into three vehicles—Lesser, Great, and Vajra—the great one of which teaches that it is named "great" because of having seven qualities of being great compared to the Lesser Vehicle. The original recollections mentioned only the śhrāvaka vehicle. If Great Vehicle here is understood to mean Buddha Vehicle, that will include and extend the original recollections' reference to the sangha being the sangha of the śhrāvaka vehicle.

principal training[286] of mind, they have the samādhi that goes with thoroughly ascertained fact. Therefore, it is said that they *have entered into insight*. Through not abiding in the extremes of permanence and nihilism, and so on, they have opened up the prajñā mindstream with its view of the authentic, so it is said that they *have entered into straightness*. All of them, moreover, have entered a nirvana in which there is no disharmony between view, discipline, migrators' purposes, and so on, and that is referred to with they *have entered into harmony*.

Alternatively, *have entered into good* can be seen as a statement of this group of epithets in summary. In that case, the noble saṅgha have entered an authentic path that turns away the entirety of failings[287], so "they have entered into good", which is actually saying that the outsiders do not "enter into good" given that they do not have an authentic path.

Now for the more extensive explanation of these four epithets. It says they *have entered into insight*; since *insight* here means nirvana, this epithet is about the fruition. *Straightness* means the noble one's path. As a sutra says,

What is "straightness"? It is the noble one's path …

Thus these two are taught from the perspective of path. *Harmony* means that all of those who have entered the noble one's path are in harmony in that they are irreversibly going to the city of nirvana. Thus, this epithet is taught from the perspective of the persons who have entered the state of being, who are said to be, "without disharmony".

---

[286] That is, the second of the three principal trainings, samādhi.

[287] Failings here means all states and situations that falter, go down, fail, do not work; samsara as a whole is a failed state.

Alternatively, the four can be taken to mean "the noble saṅgha have entered like this", where "like this" refers to a progression of being without the four aspects successively of being lost, mistaken, side-tracked, or reversible. Their having entered a path which is true and un-mistaken because it has been freed of the four wrong approaches of not being good in relation to the meaning, and so on results in them being referred to as "persons in this world who have a purified mindstream"[288].

2. They are a supreme field of good qualities

This goes from *They are worthy of joined palms* up to *great, thoroughly trained*. The meaning of these epithets is as follows.

Being persons whose mindstreams have realized the profound dharmatā, *they* have become *worthy of* others paying them respect with hands moved into the pose of *joined palms*. Being holy guides of migrators, *they* have become *worthy of* others paying

---

[288] Mipham's wording for the main explanation and the first alternative clearly shows that the meaning intended is that the saṅgha "have entered into a certain state", which is why the *Sutra* here was translated as "have entered into goodness ...". However, this last alternative presents a picture of progress on the path, in which case the *Sutra* would have to be translated as "They have entered well, entered insightfully, entered straight, and entered harmoniously", meaning that they have avoided four faulty ways of entering. The saṅgha have entered well because they did not have the fault of being unsure of the path and then losing it. They have entered insightfully rather than with delusion that would have caused them to take a wrong path. They have entered straight because of not following diversions leading away from a direct journey down the path. They have entered harmoniously, meaning in accord with the progression of the path, because they did not get confused and regress while they were on the path. Noble beings who have travelled this way were called, in ancient India, people with a very pure kind of mind.

them homage with *prostration*, which is a greater show of respect again. And these ones whose mindstreams are now beautiful with their supreme qualities *are fields of the glory of merit*. Here "Glory" is a general name for that which is good or has some kind of perfection and their mindstreams are filled with merit, so their glory is the glory of merit. Since all perfections of the glory of merit arise in dependence on theirs, they are referred to as "field" for such.

In addition, they are divorced from faults and possess good qualities, so, worshipping them with offerings as large even as the third order thousand-fold worlds will not cause obscuration to arise in them. Therefore, these beings who have been *thoroughly trained in* relation to *gifts* offered to them will not only have no wrong action in relation to the gifts but their great training in gifts will function to complete the energy of others' accumulations.

In short, this section is saying that, "The sangha is worthy of the reverence of joined palms, and so on; and is worthy of being relied on for refuge via prostration, and so on; and is a field of the glory of inexhaustible benefit for others; and will not become obscured due to gifts". And this is comparable to these words,

> The supreme of what could be honoured due to
> worthiness of veneration,
> Worthy of homage ...[289]

In other words, this section is saying that the beings of the sangha "are worthy of worship through offerings by others" due to the fact they have thoroughly purified their own mindstreams.

---

[289] These two lines shows the first two parts of their good qualities.

2. *Praising the ones having those good qualities as supreme places for giving*

There are two phrases in this.

They are a place for generosity. Offering to any of them has great meaning because it produces fruitions of benefit and ease that are the best, outstanding, and immeasurable; it is like a good field producing its harvest.

They are in all places even a great place for generosity. In all places and circumstances even—meaning in all worlds in their totality even—they are a great place of generosity. In other words, "there is no other place of generosity equivalent to this, the saṅgha". Worldly ones have a mind that is tainted with affliction, whereas this saṅgha is completely liberated from such, therefore it is like an utterly pure king of the most valuable of gems.

There is also a claim that the last six phrases can be connected such that a person on the path of accumulation is worthy of pro-stration, one on the path of connection is worthy of prostration, and the last four connect with for stream-enterer up to arhat of no more training[290].

In short, the path of holy dharma, when accomplished by insight into the authentic, will give rise to trust in the saṅgha and in the one who has finalized the training, the Buddha. Thus, if one exerts oneself in the ways of generating true certainty in the rea-sonings of the four-part truth of the tathāgata[291] and profound interdependent origination, it will give rise to an unfaltering faith in the Three Jewels.

---

[290] As mentioned earlier, the fifth of the five paths is the path of no more training. It is the fruition of being an arhat in this case.

[291] The four truths of the noble ones.

Having understood in that way the qualities of the precious jewel, the holy dharma, in relation both to the actual saṅgha and the one that merely bears its sign[292], one should perform as many acts of reverence and as much worship with offerings towards them as one is capable of, because doing so is a source of immeasurable merit. That is also expressed in a sutra,

> Someone who every month,
> Has made worship with one hundred thousand
>   offerings,
> Will have produced faith in the members of the saṅgha
> That could not compare with a sixteenth part of him.

That sutra illustrates it. It can be known more extensively from the sutras.

4. Conclusion, the Words that Show the Completeness of the Text

The text says, *The Sutra of the Recollection of the Noble Three Jewels is complete*. The white umbrella known as the Three Precious Jewels, which is the source of benefit and ease in its entirety in all of every single one of the worlds throughout space and time, has the nature of being indestructible throughout the limits of space and becoming. Just remembering this source of enormous amounts of auspiciousness marked with virtue restores us by repairing every single problem; the *Holy Victory Banner Sutra* says,

> If something causes fear or anxiety or makes as is said "your hairs stand on end", recollect the Buddha! If you do not do that, then recollect the dharma! If you do not

---

[292] The ordinary communities of Buddhists are called saṅgha but only bear the outer signs of being saṅgha. They do not have the inner realization that would make them the actual refuge Jewel.

do that, then recollect the saṅgha! That will release you from all fears.

When the armies of the asuras came close, Kauśhika said to the gods, "When you are afraid in war, recollect my supreme victory banner that brings total victory! If you do not do that, remember the supreme victory banner of the son of gods Aiśhanī! If you do not do that, remember the supreme victory banner of the son of gods Varuṇa. Doing so will dispel fear!"[293]

The teacher said to remember the Three Jewels for a similar reason. And then there is the point that you gain immeasurable merit from doing so; in the *Hurling A Boulder Sutra* the teacher said,

Oh! You who have a mind to put something somewhere[294]! Roots of virtue created in relation to the Buddha will never be exhausted in samsara! They will not come to an end, so even though nirvana might be unending, they will cause it to be obtained. Roots of virtue created in relation to the dharma and roots of virtue created in relation to the saṅgha will never be exhausted in samsara; they will not come to an end and they will cause nirvana to be obtained.

And,

Similarly, Jambudvīpa has a height and width of seven thousand yojanas, Videha a height and width of eight thousand, the Western continent nine thousand, and the

---

[293] Kauśhika was an important follower of the Buddha. Also known as Indra, he is chief over all the chiefs of the desire gods in the heavens of the thirty-three. The others mentioned by name are chief gods who are generals of his army.

[294] This continues the quote from this sutra presented earlier on page 194. The Buddha has now sat down to one side of the rock and is addressing the strong men who had it in mind to shift the rock.

Northern continent ten thousand yojanas, and these can
be measured by pacing them out. Yet virtuous roots
created in relation to the Three Jewels cannot be
measured. Similarly, Mt. Meru and its environs can be
measured in srang-weights[295] and the great ocean can be
measured in vase-fulls[296], but the roots of virtue created
in relation to the Three Jewels cannot be measured.

Each of those provides just an illustration. In fact, the qualities of
the Three Jewels are extremely vast—bigger even than space, are
supremely stainless, and are unsurpassable. Even the measure of
the benefits of just admiration and the like for them cannot be
grasped.

For that reason, there is nothing not included in this set of Three
Jewels, the authentic refuge. Thus, if intelligent ones remember
the qualities of the three and then accept the three as the true,
definite refuge, then at that point, those beings will have begun
the work of putting an end to becoming and will have started the
journey to definite ease.

It is like this. The mind of all the buddhas might be of one taste
but, because their individual activities of arousing the mind and
prayers of aspiration are immeasurable, the tathāgata himself could
go on explaining the qualities of just one hair pore and one light
ray from the body of one of the uncountable conquerors of the
three times for as long as there is space but still would not be
finished and still would have more to say. The benefits of hearing

---

[295] A srang weight is a Tibetan base unit of weight measure. It is
roughly equivalent to an ounce or thirty grams weight. The meaning
here is the same as saying ounce-weights or gram-weights.

[296] Vase-fulls will refer to the Indian kulika vase. The meaning here is
the same as saying bottle-fulls or jug-fulls.

or reading the holy dharma contained in a single verse are explained as immeasurable, so imagine the benefits of seeing the
entire holy dharma throughout space and time as the authentic
path.   There are immeasurable numbers of noble ones of the
saṅgha in the ten directions and three times and the roots of virtue
created by just one of them abiding in the samādhi of loving
kindness also is immeasurable. Suddenly bringing all the qualities
of the buddhas that have been mentioned above to mind, or bringing all of those of the dharma to mind, or taking interest in all
those of the saṅgha has, each one, immeasurable benefits associated with it.   But leave that aside; if even one recitation of this
Sutra out of trust in these places of refuge is the source of the
whole extent of the roots of virtue that have been explained for
Three Jewels, then the benefits that come with explaining it, and
so on are limitless! And again, leave that aside; even just being
able to listen to this *Sutra* nicely one time will bring an understanding of the great meaning that comes with the attainment of
this human body!

The Three Jewels are the supreme source of tens of millions of
    the glories of auspiciousness
And the banner of hearing them with its good explanations,
A mount for questions, takes one forward.
Then the intonations of never-ending auspiciousness
Bring the failings in all worlds to an end and as well
Show the door to the good path of interdependent origination,
A perpetual play of perfect glory,
And that auspiciousness having a warehouse of dharma opens
    the door.

The superior thought, a youthful new moon, together with
Supreme intelligence perpetually dwelling in the element of
    space

Envelops the world with the white light of benefit and ease[297].
Auspiciousness of total joy develops and
In the place known as The Auspicious Peak of Gods,
At a time when the auspiciousness of perfect teacher and retinue
    have come together,
Through the auspiciousness of many conditions marked with
    virtue,
The victory banner of the story of unwaning auspiciousness is
    hoisted.

By this goodness done here, may the excellent glorious guru
Stay long and the saṅgha flourish, and
May the finalized activities that are the glory of benefit and bliss
    of the various beings
Never wane and always flourish!

*The command of the holy guru of wondrous qualities of excellent learning
and virtue was received at my crown, in which he urged me on, with an
emphasis on auspiciousness. It was like boiling water on the body causing
pain and upset but, having turned the mind to the nectar-like moon of
the Three Jewels, the composition flowed easily and I, Mipham Nampar
Gyalwa, produced a commentarial explanation which nicely settles the
various issues of meaning. It was completed in two days, on the eighth
and ninth lunar days of the waxing moon of Ashvini[298]. May it be a
cause for the thoughts in harmony with dharma of the various types of
beings to be accomplished just as the beings wish.*

---

[297] These are the two types of enlightenment mind which, in union,
envelop the world with the moonlight of enlightenment mind.

[298] This is the ninth Tibetan lunar month according to the Mongolian
calendar system. It falls somewhere between September and November depending on the year.

GLOSSARY

Actuality, Tib. gnas lugs: A key term in both sutra and tantra and one of a pair of terms, the other being apparent reality (Tib. snang lugs). The two terms are used when determining the reality of a situation. The actuality of any given situation is how (lugs) the situation actuality sits or is present (gnas); the apparent reality is how any given situation appears to an observer. Something could appear in many different ways, depending on the circumstances at the time and on the being perceiving it but, regardless of those circumstances, it will always have its own actuality of how it really is.

Adventitious, Tib. glo bur: This term has the connotations of popping up on the surface of something and of not being part of that thing. It is frequently used in relation to the afflictions because they pop up on the surface of the mind of buddha-nature but are not part of the buddha-nature itself.

Affliction, Skt. kleśha, Tib. nyon mongs: This term is usually translated as emotion or disturbing emotion, etcetera, but the Buddha was very specific about the meaning of this word. When the Buddha referred to the emotions, meaning a movement of mind, he did not refer to them as such but called them "kleśha" in Sanskrit, meaning exactly "affliction". It is a basic part of the Buddhist teaching that emotions afflict beings, giving them problems at the time and causing more problems in the future.

Alaya, Skt. ālaya, Tib. kun gzhi: This term, if translated, is usually translated as all-base or thereabouts. It is a Sanskrit term that means a range that underlies and forms a basis for something else. In Buddhist teaching, it means a particular level of mind that sits beneath all other levels of mind. However, it is used in several different ways in the Buddhist teaching and changes to a different meaning in each case.

Becoming, Skt. bhāvanā, Tib. srid pa: Becoming refers to the style of existence that sentient beings have within samsara. Beings in samsara have a samsaric existence but, more than that, they are constantly in a state of becoming. They are constantly becoming this type of being or that type of being in this abode or that, as they are driven along without choice by the karmic process that drives samsaric existence.

Bliss: Skt. sukha, Tib. bde: The Sanskrit term and its Tibetan translation are usually translated as "bliss" but in fact refer to the whole range of possibilities of everything on the side of good as opposed to bad. Thus the term will mean pleasant, happy, good, nice, easy, comfortable, blissful and so on, depending on context.

Bodhicitta: See under enlightenment mind.

Cyclic existence: See under samsara.

Dharmadhatu, Skt. dharmadhātu, Tib. chos kyi dbyings: This is the name for the range or basic space in which all dharmas, meaning all phenomena, come into being. If a flower bed is the place where flowers grow and are found, the dharmadhātu is the dharma or phenomena bed in which all phenomena come into being and are found.

Dharmakaya, Skt. dharmakāya, Tib. chos sku: In the general teachings of Buddhism, this refers to the mind of a buddha, with "dharma" meaning reality and "kāya" meaning body.

Dharmata, Tib. chos nyid: This is a general term meaning the way that something is, and can be applied to anything at all; it is similar in meaning to "actuality" *q.v.* For example, the dharmatā of water is wetness and the dharmatā of the becoming bardo is a place where beings are in a saṃsāric, or becoming mode, prior to entering a nature bardo. It is used frequently in Tibetan Buddhism to mean "the dharmatā of reality" but that is a specific case of the much larger meaning of the term. To read texts which use this term successfully, one has to understand that the term has a general meaning and then see how that applies in context.

Dharmin, Tib. chos can: A dharmin is a dharma, meaning phenomenon, belonging to the world of samsara. It is not only a dharma, a phenomenon in general, but has become a solidified dharma, a conceptualized thing, because of the samsaric context.

Discursive thought, Skt. vikalpita, Tib. rnam rtog: This means more than just the superficial thought that is heard as a voice in the head. It includes the entirety of conceptual process that arises due to mind contacting any object of any of the senses. The Sanskrit and Tibetan literally mean "(dualistic) thought (that arises from the mind wandering among the) various (superficies perceived in the doors of the senses)".

Dhyana, Skt. dhyāna, Tib. bsam gtan: A Sanskrit term technically meaning all types of mental absorption. Mental absorptions cultivated in the human realm generally result in births in the form realms which are deep forms of concentration in themselves. The practices of mental absorption done in the human realm and the godly existences of the form realm that result from them both are named "dhyāna". The Buddha repeatedly pointed out that the dhyānas were a side-track to emancipation from cyclic existence.

Enlightenment mind, Skt. bodhicitta, Tib. byang chub sems: A key term of the Great Vehicle. It is the type of mind that is connected not with the lesser enlightenment of an arhat but the enlightenment of a truly complete buddha. As such, it is a mind which is connected with the aim of bringing all sentient beings to that same level of buddhahood. A person who has this mind has entered the Great Vehicle and is either a bodhisatva or a buddha.

It is important to understand that the term is used to refer equally to the minds of all levels of bodhisatva on the path to buddhahood and to the mind of a buddha who has completed the path. Therefore it is not "mind striving for enlightenment" as is sometimes seen but "enlightenment mind", meaning that kind of mind which is connected with the full enlightenment of a truly complete buddha and which is present in all those who belong to the Great Vehicle

Entity, Tib. ngo bo: The entity of something is just exactly what that thing is. In English we would often simply say "thing" rather than entity. However, in Buddhism, "thing" has a very specific meaning rather than the general meaning that it has in English. It has become common to translate this term as "essence". However, in most cases "entity", meaning what a thing is rather than an essence of that thing, is the correct translation for this term.

Fictional, Skt. saṃvṛti, Tib. kun rdzob: This term is paired with the term "superfactual" q.v. Until now these two terms have been translated as "relative" and "absolute" but these translations are nothing like the original terms. These terms are extremely important in the Buddhist teaching so it is very important that they be corrected, but more than that, if the actual meaning of these terms is not presented, then the teaching connected with them cannot be understood.

Fictional truth, Skt. saṃvṛtisatya, Tib. kun rdzob bden pa: See under "Fictional" for an explanation of this term.

Field, Field realm, Tib. zhing, zhing khams: This term is often translated "buddha field" though there is no "buddha" in the term. There are many different types of "fields" both in samsara and in nirvana. Thus there are fields that belong to enlightenment and ones that belong to ignorance. Moreover, just as there are "realms" of samsara—desire, form, and formless—so there are realms of nirvana—the fields dharmakāya, saṃbhogakāya, and nirmāṇakāya and these are therefore called "field realms".

Five paths, Tib. lam lnga: In the Prajñāpāramitā teachings of the Great Vehicle, the Buddha explained the entire Buddhist journey as a set of five paths called the paths of accumulation, connection, seeing, cultivation, and no more training. The first four paths are part of journeying to enlightenment; the fifth path is that one has actually arrived and has no more training to undergo. There are a set of five paths that describe the journey of the Lesser Vehicle and a set of five paths that describe the journey of the Greater Vehicle. The names are the same in each case but the details of what is accomplished at each stage are different.

Great Vehicle, Skt. mahāyāna, Tib. theg pa chen po: The Buddha's teachings as a whole can be summed up into three vehicles where a vehicle is defined as that which can carry a person to a certain destination. The first vehicle, called the Lesser Vehicle, contains the teachings designed to get an individual moving on the spiritual path through showing the unsatisfactory state of cyclic existence and an emancipation from that. However, that path is only concerned with personal emancipation and fails to take account of all of the beings that there are in existence. There used to be eighteen schools of Lesser Vehicle in India but the only one surviving nowadays is the Theravāda of south-east Asia. The Greater Vehicle is a step up from that. The Buddha explained that it was great in comparison to the Lesser Vehicle for seven reasons. The first of those is that it is concerned with attaining the truly complete enlightenment of a truly complete buddha for the sake of every sentient being where the Lesser Vehicle is concerned only with a personal liberation that is not truly complete enlightenment and which is achieved only for the sake of that practitioner. The Great Vehicle has two divisions. There is a conventional Great Vehicle in which the path is taught in a logical, conventional way. There is also an unconventional Great Vehicle in which the path is taught in an unconventional and very direct way. This latter vehicle is called the Vajra Vehicle because it takes the innermost, indestructible (vajra) fact of reality of one's own mind as the vehicle to enlightenment.

Latency, Skt. vāsāna, Tib. bag chags: The original Sanskrit has the meaning exactly of "latency". The Tibetan term translates that inexactly with "something sitting there (Tib. chags) within the environment of mind (Tib. bag)". Although it has become popular to translate this term into English with "habitual pattern", that is not its meaning. The term refers to a karmic seed that has been imprinted on the mindstream and is present there as a latency, ready and waiting to come into manifestation.

Lesser Vehicle, Skt. hīnayāna, Tib. theg pa dman pa: See under Great Vehicle.

Luminosity, Skt. prabhāsvara, Tib. 'od gsal ba: The core of mind has two aspects: an emptiness factor and a knowing factor. Luminosity is a metaphor for the fundamental knowing quality of the essence of mind. It is sometimes translated as "clear light" but that is a mistake that comes from not understanding the etymology of the word. It does not refer to a light that has the quality of clearness (something that makes no sense, actually!) but refers to the illuminative property which is the hallmark of mind. Mind knows, that is what it does. Metaphorically, it is a luminosity that illuminates its own content.

Mara, Skt. māra, Tib. bdud: A Sanskrit term closely related to the word "death". Buddha spoke of four classes of extremely negative influences that have the capacity to drag a sentient being deep into samsara. They are the "maras" or "kiss of death" of: having a samsaric set of five skandhas; of having afflictions; of death itself; and of the son of gods, which means being seduced and taken in totally by sensuality.

Mindfulness, Tib. dran pa: A particular mental event, one that has the ability to keep mind on its object. Together with alertness, it is one of the two causes of developing śhamatha. See alertness for a explanation.

Noble one, Skt. ārya, Tib. 'phags pa: In Buddhist parlance, a noble one is a being who has become spiritually advanced to the point that he has passed beyond cyclic existence. According to the Buddha, the beings in cyclic existence were ordinary, commoners, and the beings who had passed beyond it were special, the nobility.

Outflow, Skt. sāśhrava, Tib. zag pa: The Sanskrit term means a bad discharge, like pus coming out of a wound. Outflows occur when wisdom loses its footing and falls into the elaborations of dualistic mind. Therefore, anything with duality also has outflows. This is sometimes translated as "defiled" or "conditioned" but these fail to capture the meaning. The idea is that wisdom can remain self-contained in its own unique sphere but, when it loses its ability to stay within itself, it starts to have leakages into dualism that are defilements on the wisdom. See also un-outflowed.

Rational mind, Tib. blo: This is a term which specifically refers to the sort of mind that creates the situation of this and that (ratio in Latin) and hence upholds the duality of samsara.

Realization, Tib. rtogs pa: Realization has a very specific meaning which is not always well understood. It refers to correct knowledge that has been gained in such a way that the knowledge does not abate. There are two important points here. Firstly, realization is not absolute. It refers to the removal of obscurations, one at a time. Each time that a practitioner removes an obscuration, he gains a realization because of it. Therefore, there are as many levels of obscuration as there are obscurations. Maitreya, in the *Ornament of Manifest Realizations*, shows how the removal of the various obscurations that go with each of the three realms of samsaric existence produces realization.

Reasoning of the Force of the Thing, Tib. dngos stobs kyi rigs pa: This is an inferential type of reasoning. It is used to validly establish that something is so by applying the test of whether the thing in question is actually the way that is has been proposed to be. Thus, through the *force of* what *the thing* itself is, we correctly know whether the proposal is true or not. For example, it is said that "fire is hot". One way to determine whether that is true or not is to look at the qualities of fire. If we find that one of those qualities is "hot" then the statement is proved to be true.

Refuge, gzhi gnas: Skt. śharaṇaṃ, Tib. bskyab pa: The Sanskrit term means "shelter", "protection from harm". Everyone seeks a refuge from the unsatisfactoriness of life, even if it is a simple act like brushing the teeth to prevent the body from decaying un-necessarily. Buddhists, after having thought carefully about their situation and who could provide a refuge from it which would be thoroughly reliable, find that three things—buddha, dharma, and sangha—are the only things that could provide that kind of refuge. Therefore, Buddhists take refuge in those Three Jewels of Refuge as they are called. Taking refuge in the Three Jewels is clearly laid out as the one doorway to all Buddhist practice and realization.

Samsara, Skt. saṃsāra, Tib. 'khor ba: The type of existence that sentient beings have which is that they continue on from one existence to another, always within the enclosure of births that are produced by ignorance and experienced as unsatisfactory. The original Sanskrit means to be constantly going about, here and there. The Tibetan term literally means "cycling", because of which it is frequently translated into English with "cyclic existence" though that is not quite the meaning of the term.

Shamatha, Skt. śhamatha, Tib. gzhi gnas: The name of one of the two main practices of meditation used in the Buddhist system to gain insight into reality. This practice creates a foundation of one-pointedness of mind which can then be used to focus the insight of the other practice, vipaśhyanā. If the development of śhamatha is taken through to completion, the result is a mind that sits stably on its object without any effort and a body which is filled with ease. Altogether, this result of the practice is called "the creation of workability of body and mind".

Skandhas, dhatus, and ayatanas, Skt. skandha dhātu āyatana, Tib. phung po khams skyed mched: The Buddha taught them to show his disciples how samsara arises through samsaric perception. Skandhas are the "aggregates" that make up a samsaric being. Dhātus are the items within a samsaric being's makeup that are the "bases" of all samsaric perception; they are a detailed listing of the things that allow samsaric perception with all of its attendant problems. Āyatanas are the specific items within the dhātus that are the igniters of samsaric consciousness.

Sugatagarbha, Tib. bde war gshegs pa'i snying po: A Sanskrit term literally meaning "the birthplace of those who go to bliss" and used as a name for the buddha nature. The buddha nature is the potential that we all have which allows us to go to the state of enlightenment, the blissful state beyond all the unsatisfactoriness of normal existence. Sugatagarbha has the same basic meaning as tathāgatagarbha though its use indicates a more practical way of talking whereas tathagātagarbha is more theoretical. A discussion which uses the term sugatagarbha is one that is talking about the practical realities of an essence that can be or is being developed into enlightened being.

Superfactual, Skt. paramārtha, Tib. don dam: This term is paired with the term "fictional" *q.v.* Until now these two terms have been translated as "relative" and "absolute" but those translations are nothing like the original terms. These terms are extremely important in the Buddhist teaching so it is very important that their translations be corrected but, more than that, if the actual meaning of these terms is not presented, the teaching connected with them cannot be understood.

The Sanskrit term literally means "a superior or holy kind of fact" and refers to the wisdom mind possessed by those who have developed themselves spiritually to the point of having transcended samsara. That wisdom is *superior* to an ordinary, un-developed person's consciousness and the *facts* that appear on its surface are superior compared to the facts that appear on the ordinary person's consciousness. Therefore, it is superfact or the holy fact, more literally. What this wisdom knows is true for the beings who have it, therefore what the wisdom sees is superfactual truth.

Superfactual truth, Skt. paramārthasatya, Tib. don dam bden pa: See under "Superfactual" for an explanation of this term.

Superfice, superficies, Tib. rnam pa: In discussions of mind, a distinction is made between the entity of mind which is a mere knower and the superficial things that appear on its surface and which are known by it. In other words, the superficies are the various things which pass over the surface of mind but which are not mind. Superficies are all the specifics that constitute appearance—for example, the colour white within a moment of visual consciousness, the sound heard within an ear consciousness, and so on.

Tathagatagarbha, Skt. tathāgatagarbha, de bzhin gshegs pa'i snying po: See under sugatagarbha.

Third order thousandfold world system, Tib. stong gsum 'jig rten: Indian cosmology has for its smallest cosmic unit a single Mt. Meru with four continents type of world system; an analogy might be a single planetary system like our solar system. One thousand of those makes a first order thousand-fold world system; an analogy might be a galaxy. One thousand of those makes a second order thousand-fold world system; an analogy might be a region of space with many galaxies. One thousand of those makes a third order thousand-fold world system (1000 raised to the power 3); an analogy would be one whole universe like ours. The Buddha said· that there were countless numbers of third order thousand-fold world systems, each of which would be roughly equivalent to a universe like ours.

Three principal trainings, Tib. bslabs pa gsum: The three principal trainings of the Buddhist path are śhila, samādhi, and prajñā—discipline, concentration, and correct discernment.

Three secrets, Tib. gsang ba: This is usually defined as a path term which refers to the body, speech, and mind of a person who is on the way to buddhahood. When a person becomes a buddha, he has reached his full state of enlightenment in which case the three secrets are referred to as the three vajras of a tathāgata because they are unchanging at that point. This path term is used to mean the three vajras of the fruition state of buddhahood.

Three types of analysis, Tib. dpyad pa gsum: There are three types of inferential reasoning that can be used to assess anything not known with direct perception. One of them is the type of reasoning called Reasoning of the Force of the Thing. The remaining two are the reasoning that relies on the trustworthiness of others who have made statements about the thing being examined and the reasoning that relies on popular knowledge concerning the status of the thing being examined. The first one is superior to the other two. When a thing is examined with all three types of reasoning and it is discerned to be valid, it is said to be "pure" after application of the three reasonings.

Three Vehicles, theg pa gsum: The entire teachings of the Buddha can be summed up into three "vehicles". Each vehicle is a complete set of teachings that will take a person to a particular level of spiritual attainment. The first one, the Lesser Vehicle, is a set of teachings that will take a person out of cyclic existence but will not lead the person to full enlightenment. The second one, the Great Vehicle, is "great" relative to the Lesser Vehicle because it can lead a person to full enlightenment. The third vehicle, the Vajra

Vehicle, also can lead a person to full enlightenment. The difference between the Great and Vajra Vehicles is that the first are exoteric teachings that are suitable for anyone whereas the second are esoteric teachings which are not.

Un-outflowed, Skt. aśrāva, Tib. zag pa med pa: See also outflowed. Un-outflowed dharmas are ones that are connected with wisdom that has not lost its footing and leaked out into a defiled state; it is self-contained wisdom without any taint of dualistic mind and its apparatus.

Valid cognizer, valid cognition, Skt. pramāṇa, Tib. tshad ma: A valid cognizer is a mind which is knowing correctly and which can therefore be used to assess the validity of whatever is placed before it. Valid cognizers are named according to the kind of test they are employed to do. A valid cognizer of the conventional or a valid cognizer of the fictional tests within conventions, within the realm of rational, dualistic mind. A valid cognizer of the ultimate or valid cornier of superfact tests for the superfactual level, beyond dualistic mind.

Vipashyana, Skt. vipaśhyanā, Tib. lhag mthong: The Sanskrit name for one of the two main practices of meditation needed in the Buddhist system for gaining insight into reality. The other one, śhamatha, keeps the mind focussed while this one, vipaśhyanā, looks piercingly into the nature of things.

Wisdom, Skt. jñāna, Tib. ye shes: This is a fruition term that refers to the kind of mind, the kind of knower possessed by a buddha. Sentient beings do have this kind of knower but it is covered over by a very complex apparatus for knowing, dualistic mind. If they practise the path to buddhahood, they will leave behind their obscuration and return to having this kind of knower.

The original Sanskrit term has the sense of knowing in the most simple and immediate way. This sort of knowing is present at the core of every being's mind. Therefore, the Tibetans called it "the particular type of awareness which is there primordially". Because of their wording, it is often called "primordial wisdom" in English translations but that is too much. It is just wisdom in the sense of the most fundamental knowing possible.

INDEX